DONALD R. GORDON

THE NEW LITERACY

University of Toronto Press

Toronto and Buffalo

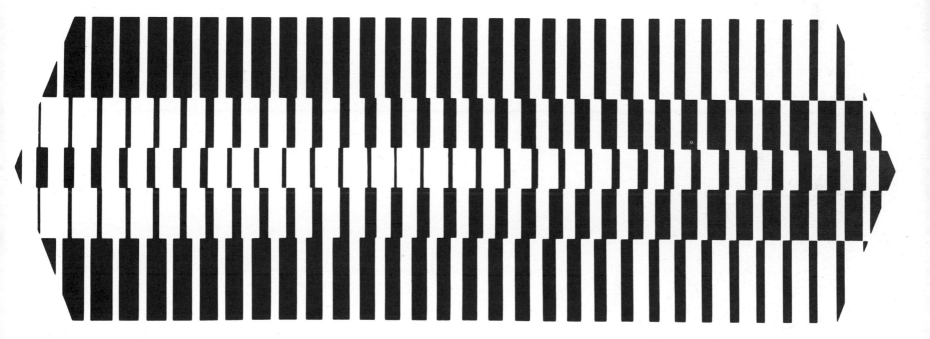

© University of Toronto Press 1971

ISBN 0-8020-1775-4 (cloth)
ISBN 0-8020-6120-6 (paper)
ISBN 0-8020-0085-1 (microfiche)
LC 71-163816

Printed in Canada

To D.J. Bruce, and Keith
in profound appreciation of
whispers and tip-toes
generously granted

CONTENTS

AN INTRODUCTION

Some people might call this a presumptuous book. It tries to deal with the inconceivable – a 'reality' defined as an infinite number of variables infinitely expressed. It ventures into subject matter well beyond any single person's demonstrable competence. It does away with many of the trappings of academic language and annotation.

All this is not entirely the consequence of bravado and sloth.

Instead, this book represents a rather earnest bid to suggest some of the characteristics and consequent requirements of fundamental change in our society. In particular, it is concerned with the central challenge we face: to deal with an information explosion in circumstances that allow for little, if any, error.

That, in turn, is why the title *The New Literacy* was selected. Our established means of dealing with data have been eclipsed. It no longer is possible for a scholar or bookworm to survey and sense his circumstances with the tools of the three R's. Radically different modes of expression have hopped forward toad-like to demand consideration. Many of their worst disfigurements have been shed in the process, so that they justifiably demand and command attention.

At the same time, it seems to be uncomfortably clear that such acknowledgement of these new modes of expression as has occurred has been both casual and quixotic. The rigorous preparation assumed as a prerequisite of the conventional literacy of reading and writing has not yet been widely applied to or accepted for the use of film, television, radio, holography, the underground, or any of the many other evolving means of human expression. As a result, we have suffered in employing these means from the misuse and under-use characteristic of illiteracy.

Here, in *The New Literacy,* it is not suggested that a new grammar be offered. That, hopefully, will be a task taken up by a new breed of dedicated grammarians.

Instead, these pages are offered as a series of explorations. First, there is a venture into the question of what a communication is. The aim here is to work out some means of description and measurement that can be shared.

Then we turn to physical human capabilities. With some shared definition of communication in mind, a measure is taken of the ability of human minds and senses to perceive, and express, communications – without assistance, augmented by technology, and with the magic of chemistry.

The cause of fuller perception and expression is carried further in the section that follows. An attempt is made to suggest how and why language in various forms is used to make contact. On the assumption that some sharing of perception and expression is both necessary and desirable, means to this end are examined.

At this point, we look to outside help. Proxy agents are surveyed to see whether they can offset some of our first-hand human failings. In particular, the mass media are examined in considerable detail – in part because they are agents that have an enormous influence on everyone's perception of the world these days, in part because they represent gross versions of the new literacy we are concerned with.

Attention next is paid to other real, potential, and imaginary inputs available to human perceivers. This is an attempt to fill in the main parts missing in the information landscape between individual perception and mass proxy perception.

And, finally, the future is explored. A fairly realistic ten-year projection of the probabilities and possibilities suggests some of the ways in which our new literacy may evolve.

Now, permit some observations and explanations. Should you actually venture into this book you may be struck by passages that are obscure, by outbreaks of tiresome simplicity, or by references that seem to require amplification. Such occurrences are not wholly the fault of an obscurantist, simple-minded, or unduly elderly writer. They are a rather important indication of the pit into which we seem to be falling. You see, even the qualified homogeneity that provided our main illusions of 'reality' as recently as the 1950s has begun to break up. In the face of wave upon wave of data, demand, and decision during the last twenty years, humans have been frag-

mented to a distressing degree. There has been the fragmentation of training and conditioning – creating a communal layer cake of age and occupational divisions that are often quite unintelligible to one another. There has been the fragmentation of experience – widening gulfs between those who have supped at vanished fountains and those who are allowed only to imagine their former existence. And, perhaps most important of all, there has been the fragmentation of pace and style – some among us treading to a measured, linear beat with finite forms while others take beats as they come, formless and unpredictable.

Given such fragmentation, it is inevitable that any venture to explore and comment upon the contemporary human condition will be viewed at a variety of levels and will be assigned a variety of meanings. And it would be argued here that, pending the acquisition of a new literacy, we are stuck with such discords.

Now some words about language and annotation. The aim, frankly, is contact. In the cause of contact, it has been assumed that familiarity is more effective than a podium, and that suggestions that you burrow through the various sources and experiences that have been consulted would only encourage indifference and fatigue. Most 'knowledge' is only opinion anyway ... so why not accept this and go on from there.

To conclude, this writer would like to express appreciation to a variety of helpers. Among the voices that muttered in his head, those of Gillis Purcell, Robert Fulford, Borden Spears, the late George Clay, and his wife were especially provocative and helpful. Among the critics, Ian Montagnes, W. D. A. McCuaig, and Sandra Sachs were the best de-foggers. Among those he would hope to impress were the fantasies of Jeanne, Yvonne, Sonia, Dian, Fadia, and Veronica. And, most of all, an imagined version of you was at the root of the whole exercise.

ON COMMUNICATION

WHAT'S GOING ON?

Does it matter?

Yes ...

because ...

... AT THIS PRECISE INSTANT ... no matter what your age, size, colour, sex, or sensibility ... *no matter what* ... YOUR VERY EXISTENCE IS BEING TOUCHED UPON ... TINKERED WITH ... EVEN SHAPED.

Well, briefly, you *can* do something about it ...

and you must.

(Which is why this book is here.)

consider this:

OPEN EVERY NIGHT TILL 10!

Fumes affect milk

aboo
estores sigh
to patient

Deaths

borrowing guara

NEWS SUMMARY

GRAIN MAR

TELEVISION

Shop at

Two-
Kill

GUMBY, POKEY
ACCESSORIES—an
sfactio

Student M

Ga

BASEBALL RECORD

LONDON (Reu

Stocks show
biggest loss
month

stillness Sun
action
demor

Oil Menaces

Beaches as
Tanker Sink

FA
S

Shooting Incident Ouch!

they

ANN LANDERS

ut May

ETIQUETTE
HOUSEHOLD
SERVICE DIRECTORY

Tying Hu
End Snoring,

POINTS FOR PAR

Model

U.S. corporate
reports

SUMMER
DANCES

Ship
Cri
Ste
raise

bdivision
jet path,
OT warns

tory for Yankees

LABOR NEWS

POGO

Garbage Men Vote
For Toronto Strike

learn!

ter Turns Pink
XWELL, N.M

That is a fragment of what is going on, in print alone ...

It represents what is, or should be, obvious.

Bluntly, survival in any form, quality, or preference that we now possess depends on *knowing*. All of us ... all the time ... must *know* as best we can ... or maybe even better than that.

knowing???

Yes, knowing.
→ Knowing what to avoid or ignore so we won't suffer pain, poisoning, or brainwashing.
→ Knowing what to seek out or espouse to gain riches for body, mind, or spirit.
→ Knowing when to act and when not to act to achieve a goal or to foster simple convenience.
→ Knowing ourselves and our myriad relationships with everyone and everything about us.

You see, the consequences of human existence nowadays have undergone drastic changes. The basic drives of life – love, lust, ambition, amiability, and so on – remain much the same, but the truly geometric increase in the numbers, forcefulness, pervasiveness, and complexity of interplay of such drives in ourselves and others makes them very much more difficult to avoid or modify. Humans in bygone days could opt out when they needed to. They could move away – physically and/or psychically.

Now they can't.

Now, for all practical purposes **all of us are involved all of the time.**

Our *actions* and *inactions* are equally significant ... and they bear upon everyone and everything.

Doubtful???

Just consider, for example:

→ A disease that could threaten the human race can be spread worldwide in about 48 hours – the time that the *Official Airline Guide* now specifies for service to all but the most remote nooks and crannies of the globe we share.

→ Ideas and evocations powerful enough to provoke widespread violence and international crisis can be disseminated worldwide in minutes. It is but a whisker from contemporary American, Soviet, Chinese, or even French rocket-rattling in the Middle East, for instance, to an actual nuclear holocaust. Some of us may survive to say, 'You had the wrong idea.'

→ An average of one vertebrate species a year is becoming extinct on this earth and, you may recall, humans are vertebrates. More than 10 per cent of all living primate species are endangered (49 species all told, as of early 1971).

→ Innovations that can drastically curtail or even eliminate whole sectors of industrial activity are probably (not possibly ... *probably*) in the works at this very instant. Japanese research on alternatives to laser beams as communications carriers, for example, may very well render laser-based industries obsolete before they even get started.

→ We are running out of space. In Canada only ten million acres of the available total of 110 million acres of arable land remain to be developed and occupied. All that remains beyond that is considered to be sub-marginal.

→ In an average urban area, the odds that you will come into contact with another person during a day are about 3,000,000 to 1, **whether you like it or not.**

10 So, there is a sharp flavour of urgency to human affairs.

We face many and fundamental questions of choice. We live with problems of inadequate performance by others – demands for excellent performance by ourselves. Such problems and demands make it more important than it has ever been that we base our choices on inputs that are accurate, complete, and timely, and that we express our choices in outputs that are also accurate, complete, and timely.

Choice now is a premium factor because the world is running out of leeway. We are faced with the nose-to-nose realities of limits on available space, resources, time, and human adaptability. Puttering about with trial and error won't work, because, increasingly, we can't afford the consequences of error. We can no longer move on like nomads from a polluted or desecrated environment because there are precious few places to move on to. We can't always let time heal, because continuing actions and interactions won't wait and won't stop. And the mystic regeneration of the human body and spirit doesn't get much of a chance in the face of pills, potions, and processes that are now perilously close to the scale of build-a-man authority able to change and enslave us.

Every one of the hundreds and thousands of options – *choices* – involved in every person's daily life has become a little more important. In the past, for example, a badly-built house might collapse and crush a family of, say, five. Now, the faulty structure may well be a high rise apartment accommodating several hundred families and, in turn, such structures themselves are but part of large planning areas in which a minor blunder can destroy or discomfit thousands.

We used to be in a world of

UNITS

such as houses.

Increasingly, we are tumbling into a world of

aggregates

such as regional planning areas.

When it all works, we gain – as with streams, ponds, rivers, and lakes linked and laced into watersheds to provide an orchestration of pure, reliable, and joyous resources.

When something doesn't work, we lose – as when northeastern North America was plunged into darkness and hysteria for 18 hours in 1965 – the result of one fault in one power station that overloaded all the power networks in a regional grid.

Furthermore, some of the aggregates we live with come close to being ultimate. The consequences of the misuse of nuclear aggregates, for example, can be catastrophic. Our familiar Freudian friend, the automobile, may be purring and clanking a total transition to '1984.' Even the sensibly popular copulative aggregate needs to be eyed cautiously as a harbinger of constantly increasing population leading to global starvation.

Choice has become a premium fact in life.

→ Choice in terms of what to pay attention to.
→ Choice in terms of what to ignore.

AND
→ Choice in terms of action or inaction.

But how?

With astrology? By discouraged default? With unquestioning obedience? By proxy – letting George do it? With gushes of hatred or love? Through divine aid? By flipping a coin?

Alas, no longer ... at least not always or by themselves.

Our choices now must be as error-free as possible. They must be based on quality inputs and must express quality output.

Which means **we need to know what is going on.**

If we opt to check the adequacy and validity of data so that we make the choices ourselves, we need to know what is going on. If we opt to hand some of the responsibility over to others – experts and the like – we still need to know what is going on so that, at least, we will have chosen people who are adequately expert *and* demonstrably aware of our upper and lower limits of real acquiescence.

However, even if we assume (i) that our concern with making choices that are correct and constructive is important and (ii) that an awareness of what is going on is central to correct and constructive making of choices, we still face a difficulty.

What <u>is</u> going on?

More to the point, what do we *mean* by 'what is going on'? (If we can figure out what we mean, perhaps we can then attempt to figure out what 'what we mean' means.) So:
→ Does 'what is going on' mean a grasp of the Mind of God?
→ Does it mean human nature?
→ Does it mean The Cosmic Order?
→ Does it mean ... Everything?

Here, we come upon one of the delights of language. It doesn't really matter what we define 'what is going on' to mean *so long as we all have roughly the same definition in mind.* We can say 'what is going on' means the Bible, or Alan Watts, or Yippeedom, or chocolate pudding – any label we like so long as the *substance* represented by that label adds up to much the same in all our perceptual aggregates.

And in defining 'what is going on' we do have some advantage. Many of the combinations of our perceptions and experiences seem to provide us with common denominators from which to start.

Since this is a book (which means *I'm* doing the talking), let us see how that works using *my* label for the meaning of 'what is going on.' Let us start with that and try to move towards parameters of a shared understanding.

In this comfortable circumstance, 'what is going on' means 'reality.' And, in turn, 'reality' means *'an infinite number of variables infinitely expressed'* ∴ or, put simply, 'everything.'

'everything?'

Everything ...

but...?...!

Exactly. So, let us go further.

12   Even in our good moments none of us can actually conceive of, let alone perceive, everything. As the chuckling waves of contemporary micro- and macro-biologists indicate virtually every day, we are constantly being informed of new entities and ingredients of our 'everything' all the time. Even classifications of chemicals are proving to be unreliable as assumptions, as evidenced by the *identification* in May 1970 of element no. 105 (many centuries after the initial labelling of what were supposed to be *all* the chemicals).

So, what *is* the 'everything' of reality?

'Everything' is what we, workably and collectively, think it is.

And, what we, workably and collectively, think 'everything' is, represents the outer range of what we can share as a definition and understanding of 'what is going on.'

Consider the aged and illustrious ocean liner, the *Queen Mary,* for example.

Should we join hands and stand about two feet away in a huge oval around and about the *Queen Mary,* we would encounter the problem and the promise of what is involved.

Individually, each one of us would be wrestling with the assorted multi-dimensional inputs of a different 'everything.'
→ For Harold, over there, 'everything' would be his perceptual, conceptual, and spiritual orchestration of about 100 square feet of black, barnacled hull.
→ For Sarah Minge, over here, 'everything' would be her perceptual, conceptual, and spiritual orchestration of a brass propeller.
→ For Admiral Blowhard (Ret'd), up there, 'everything' would be his perceptual, conceptual, and spiritual orchestration of one Captain's cabin (Ret'd), fitted and secure for sea, Sir!

And so on ...

So, as far as individuals are concerned, it appears that 'everything' cannot help but be limited to fathomable and intelligible sums and processes of data. Yet, when individual versions of 'everything' are collected and examined, it becomes clear that sums and processes of data beyond individual capacity are also present. We find it necessary to acknowledge that there are probably unfathomable and unintelligible ingredients in 'everything' quite beyond our individual comprehension.

Now, suppose we try to work on some of the shareable versions of 'everything.'

Suppose we pool our assorted orchestrations of perceptual, conceptual and spiritual *Queen Mary* inputs by
→ Sharing such data as we *can* make workably intelligible to one another,
AND
→ Sharing a scaled-down overview of the whole we are trying to perceive and understand.

Then, if there were enough of us to ensure that the summation of views was adequate, we would end up with two advantages. First, we would have pooled our data, and this would contribute to the ongoing accumulation of most of the many, many varied versions and details implicit in the totality of Queen Maryness. Second, and coincidentally, we would have scaled down the enormity and multiplicity of Queen Maryness to sizes and terms within the range of our collective capacity for comprehension. We would have a picture, mental or actual, of a large, ocean-going passenger vessel.

It wouldn't *be* the Queen Mary ... but it might be something very close to its overall substance. *And,* to the extent that pooled data and scaling effectively approximated the 'everything' of the Queen Mary, we would have common, shared, quality input upon which to base some choices.

And that, dear reader, is what is meant by 'what is going on' so far as this monologuist is concerned.

All right. Now, let us turn to some doubts that might be lingering about. The *Queen Mary* is a thing – solid, apparently finite, tangible. What about 'everything' so far as ideas, issues, emotions, and intangibles are concerned?

It's the same thing.

Tangible or intangible, object or issue, finite or infinite, 'everything' comes, in practice, to have meaning only when some process of scaling and sharing of data occurs. Meaning depends on the possibility of a common, shared input – preferably of high quality.

When we ask 'What is going on?' we are, practically speaking, asking what is our present (and potential) pool of shared and scaled data and what common, shared, and (preferably) high-quality input is being added.

That, presumptously, is the purpose of this exercise. In pages to follow, we will attempt to examine the assorted ways in which we move – individually and collectively – from the inconceivability and unintelligibility of 'everything' to assorted operational and everyday versions of it. We will seek to determine, roughly, how effective the resultant approximations are, in individual and mass experiences.

As a result, we will attempt to look at ourselves – perceptual, conceptual, and spiritual creatures of some magic and mystery. We will scan assorted enhancements of ourselves – tools and techniques that affect our perceptual, conceptual, and spiritual orchestrations. We will turn to overviews of proxy agents – print, radio, TV, film, and the like – which seek to make sense and nonsense on our behalf of 'everything.' And we will consider the assorted weights and counterweights of law and custom that can and sometimes do spice up the stew.

Finally, we'll return to this beginning again and seek to relate the need to know what is going on to the practical prospects we have of actually doing so.

Then we can all get on with our choices.

At this point you may persist – with reason – in asking what in earth is going on *here*.

Well, what we are talking about is

communication.

What we mean by communication is that process whereby the sense and substance of a happening (object, event, idea, emotion, or whatever) is wholly or approximately perceived by those associated with the happening itself (who, of course, can be human or machine, among other things) and by those outside.

What we intend to do is to examine Communication: To try to get some common understanding of how it works and doesn't work, to muse upon the assorted consequences, and to relate these workings and consequences to the individual.

That is the plan. Now to the execution.

How do we actually go about moving from the inconceivability and unintelligibility of 'everything' to assorted operational and everyday versions of it?

We do so by communication:
→ communication within ourselves involving individual efforts to perceive and formulate messages, and
→ communication with others involving collective efforts to exchange and understand messages.

These are very complicated processes. They mix aspects of the conscious and unconscious self, of fact and fancy, of many simultaneous stimuli acting and reacting upon one another, and of the many differences of kind and degree to be found from human to human in our world.

At this point, we would be wise to attempt to formulate and state some concept of the processes of communication that we can agree upon and share during subsequent explorations and evaluations.

We can begin simply – and artificially – with a basic diagram of communications processes in general. Then, as errors and omissions become apparent, we can amend (and complicate) our simple start to bring it more and more in line with reality. As a bonus, we will gain along the way some practical experience in attempting to move from one sector of inconceivable 'everything' to an operational version of it.

To start, then, what seems to be involved in communication processes in general? Let us begin with the most simple approximation.

Obviously, there has to be some kind of source, a human, a machine, a conceiver of some kind of message to be communicated. We can call that: SOURCE.

Then, there has to be a means, some kind of vehicle capable of conveying a message from Source to a destination. Such vehicles can be neural pathways, electromagnetic agitations, postmen ... all sorts of things that can connect Source to destination. We can call them: TRANSMITTERS.

Finally, we need recipients. It seems highly doubtful that a message can be confirmed to exist as a communication until some acknowledgement in the form of reception (not necessarily the intended reception) occurs. We can call this part: RECEIVERS.

This gives us a basic diagram, well-stocked with evident omissions:

(Before we tear this to pieces, note some of its advantages. As a diagrammatic description, this formulation can cover an individual communicating with him or herself, person-to-person communication, person-to-machine and machine-to-machine communication, and even mystical insights. It also reminds us that communication is essentially a *transaction* involving factors dependent upon each other for their actions and reactions.)

Now, let's quibble.

First of all, there is too much artificial independence suggested in such a diagram. Excellent or incompetent, the Source, the Transmitters, and the Receivers involved in any communication all tend to affect the message and one another. Source, for example, will be influenced in formulating its message by *anticipation* about the means of transmission available (ear trumpet, for example, or stone tablet); it may modify the message on the basis of *performance* of the Transmitters while the message is being passed (gum lodged in ear trumpet or blunting of stone chisel); it will have possible second thoughts resulting from subsequent *reactions* of the Receiver (ear trumpet removed from ear halfway through) or Transmitter (stone tablet cracking under a too-passionate blow). And the very message itself will be affected too.

Without specifying the degree of interdependence involved (clearly, this will vary widely), we can allow for it by modifying our basic diagram. We can call these influences *Feedback,* and put them into the system. Then, we have

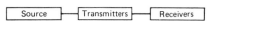

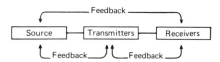

Now, what about context? No communication yet has been successfully isolated. Even in exacting and controlled scientific circumstances, we have not managed perfect vacuums, absolute soundlessness, or total freedom from resistance. In any day-to-day setting, we know very well that the background bedlam is probably going to be extensive. (Pause, for instance, and tick off the rival communications in and about you at this precise moment that are bidding to colour, cancel, or otherwise affect communications between you and this page – a runny nose communication, three debts, two courtships in mind, your own transistor radio, a car going by outside every 2.1 seconds, TV in the room next door, eight nude women or men on the wall, a trace of religious or political frenzy ... and so on.)

So, again without specifying the degree or extent of impact involved, we can improve on our system by adding context. This gives us the diagram below. (Since more than one external influence or consideration is likely to be involved, several arrows are brought to bear.)

Then there is error – human and otherwise. Some provision has to be made for the inevitable malfunctions that are bound to gum up the play and interplay of formulation, passing-on, and receipt of communications. Even the simplest communication contains many ingredients and functions. Such ingredients and functions are not likely to be error-free all the time. Each stage and influence is apt to modify them. We allow for this by modifying our diagram again. Since there is the possibility of error in *all* aspects of the communications, we acknowledge this by qualifying the simple factors *and* the modifications with broken lines. This does not mean that error always occurs ... just that it is *always a possibility to be kept in mind.*

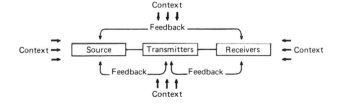

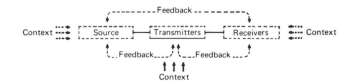

In addition to the fixed aspects of time and space covered by context or setting, some modifications of a communication are contingent upon *movement* through time and space. Movement from day towards night, for example, may be a significant consideration in the formulation, transmission, and reception of a communication. Such time movement can be a factor in the fading of the source (he always gets sleepy towards dinnertime), the energizing of the transmitter (radio waves tend to become more far reaching towards sunset), or the performance of the receiver (she starts waking up around dinnertime). Similarly, movement through space introduces such processes as seasonal and climatic variations (and our responses to them) as well as the very night and day implicit in some concepts of time. Or, to take a further concrete example, a shouted 'Hit him!' in a dark alley in downtown New York at 2 am conveys a very different kind of communication from the same shout in Maple Leaf Gardens in Toronto at 8.30 pm on a Saturday night.

The key, really, is contingency. Our sense of context or setting represents the frozen instant in time and space that we create artificially to allow us to examine and review a communication; but our acknowledgement of movement through time and space reminds us that the frozen instant of context is actually contingent upon the constant and complex whirling of the spheres.

So, another qualification should be applied to our diagram. Note that feedback and context are linked to time and space as well as our central factors. The qualities of motion and modification implicit in time and space clearly apply to all aspects of the communication transaction.

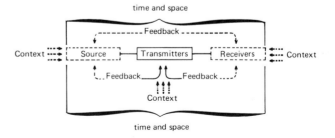

Finally, for reasons related to the purpose of the communication, the characteristics of the Source, Transmitters, and Receivers involved, and the effects of other modifying influences, there will be variations in the communication signal. Some variations will be relatively constant and deliberate – such as the contrast between a whisper or a shout, between a fuzzy generality and a chemical formula, or between a focused attention and offhand auditing. Some variations will be fluctuating and perhaps accidental – changes in the conception and relaying of a communication from instant to instant all along the pathways between conception and receipt, such as power surges which distort TV pictures. This makes for the last alteration:

That appears to take care of the main missing factors. By adding in variables and, at the same time, at least tacitly acknowledging some dilution of the perfection of an 'everything' version of communication, we have come upon a description of communication that is within the realities of day-to-day experience. Necessarily, there will be a great deal more imprecision involved. But such imprecision, in truth, is more a reminder of our human limitations than a condemnation of objective description.

We can even bid to translate our amended diagram into a form of words. This gives us a definition:

Communication is a *process* whereby the *sense and substance of a happening* (object, event, idea, motion) is *wholly or approximately perceived* (by the sensors of the happening itself or externally).

Confirmation that such a process has occurred will be provided in the form of a reconstruction or reformulation of the initial happening at the Receiver's end. The process is successful when the reconstruction is recognizable in terms of the original formulation or construction.

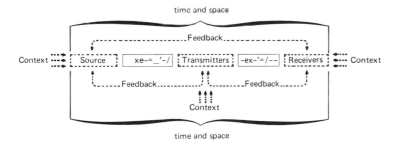

We can even bid to be specific:

This, within the limits of a printed page, represents a communication. We can seek to assess it in terms of our diagram. In our specific diagram, then ...

Source becomes Sarah Minge – mind, body, and spirit.

Transmitters become the neural pathways, the sense receptors, the air (carrying sound waves, tastes, light waves, and smells), the flesh and fabrics. They are also the vehicles for expressions of the imaginations of S. Minge (source) and of the receivers.

Receivers become Harold – mind, body, and spirit (much relieved not to be puzzling over the *Queen Mary* for a change).

Context includes the detailed fittings of a room (with bed), the physical state of Source (Sarah gets asthma when excited) and of Transmitters (the air is somewhat thick and relatively high in temperature, Sarah's blouse is very sheer) and of Receivers (Harold is terribly ticklish and somewhat preoccupied by a boil on his right elbow). It also includes consideration of the fact that Sarah is unwed and nagged about it by her mother, that the room has paper-thin walls with Harold's younger brother on the other side behind him, that both are 24, Canadian, and lonely. That will have to do as a representation ... the rest is rather private data.

Feedback becomes what Sarah i/ *anticipates* Harold and the assorted transmitters might be and do, ii/ *reacts* to in Harold and the transmitters as affairs unfold and iii/ *adjusts* to thereafter. The same kind of orchestration applies to Harold and, indeed, to the Transmitters (for instance some transmitters might be replaced – the blouse replaced by skin, the room temperature soar, and so on ...)

Time and space become 11:23 pm EDT, August 14th, 1972, the apartment of Harold and his brother Edwin, 2827 12th St., Calgary, Alberta. As such we are reminded of the drawing in of a cool foothills evening with all its nocturnal terrors.

Error includes Sarah Minge's hearing defect, Harold's astigmatism, their common conditioning to confuse physical attraction with 'love,' a mild allergy potential in Harold's wool suit, and some rather lurid feedback anticipations in Harold's imagination.

Signal Variations include a formulated 'don't' being transmitted and received as

Don't!

20 With such data, then, we can move from our general diagram to
    a specific application of it. Something like this:

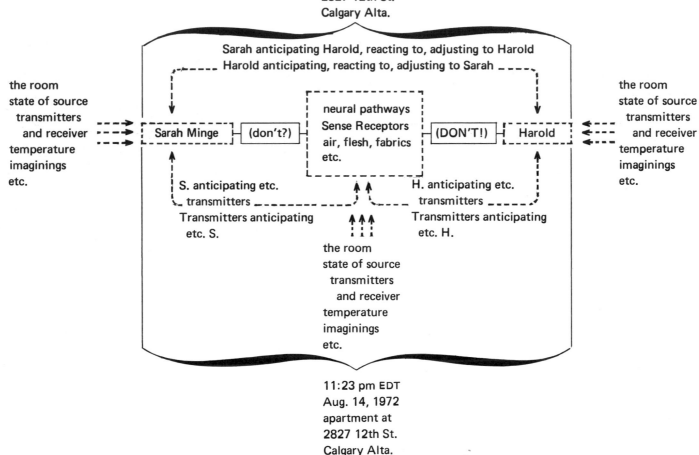

11:23 pm EDT
Aug. 14, 1972
apartment at
2827 12th St.
Calgary Alta.

Sarah anticipating Harold, reacting to, adjusting to Harold
Harold anticipating, reacting to, adjusting to Sarah

the room
state of source
    transmitters
        and receiver
temperature
imaginings
etc.

Sarah Minge   (don't?)   neural pathways
                         Sense Receptors
                         air, flesh, fabrics
                         etc.
                                          (DON'T!)   Harold

the room
state of source
    transmitters
        and receiver
temperature
imaginings
etc.

S. anticipating etc.
    transmitters
Transmitters anticipating
    etc. S.

H. anticipating etc.
    transmitters
Transmitters anticipating
    etc. H.

the room
state of source
    transmitters
        and receiver
temperature
imaginings
etc.

11:23 pm EDT
Aug. 14, 1972
apartment at
2827 12th St.
Calgary Alta.

Now, surely, it becomes quite evident that communication is a *process* – a very complex process. Even when scaled down from the boggling dimensions of 'everything,' each instant of communication is a unique orchestration of many, many influences. And the expression of, perception of, and description of any communication emerge as very tentative, tenuous, and imperfect accomplishments.

But wait a minute! Isn't this building an academic mountain out of a substantive molehill? Practically speaking, don't most of us know when we are communicating or being communicated with? Or, at the very least, can't we describe the substance of a communication in reasonably definite terms?

It's a good bet, for instance, that Sarah and Harold's instant – frozen in our analysis – was very real and apparent to both of them. Some of the finer filagrees might have been missed, but not enough to seriously affect the final result.

Well ... yes and no. That's the problem – and the missing third dimension to our exploration.

You might call it a reality scale.

We apply a reality scale relatively automatically and often unthinkingly in evaluating any communication. Faith, feel, fact, experience, and cross-reference are all combined to test the apparent communication before us. By estimating probability, and by empirical testing, we come to a workable sense of its validity – varying from communication to communication.

In other words, our outline remains the same but each item in it is tested and assessed. If it turns out that most of them ring true
→ when compared with past experience
→ when checked with others
→ as gauged by probability
→ when compared with common descriptions
OR
→ when measured beside shared faith or feel
we can be reasonably confident that what we think is a communication bears some resemblance to an actual one.

This makes for a somewhat impressionistic formulation, something like this:

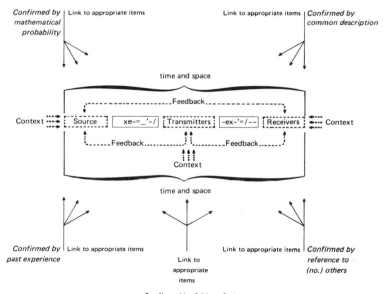

Confirmed by mathematical probability | Link to appropriate items   Link to appropriate items | Confirmed by common description

time and space

Feedback

Context → Source | xe-=_'-/ | Transmitters | -ex-'=/-- | Receivers → Context

Feedback   Feedback

Context

time and space

Confirmed by past experience | Link to appropriate items   Link to appropriate items | Confirmed by reference to (no.) others

Link to appropriate items

Confirmed by faith or feel

There will, of course, be an overlap in the confirmations involved. The existence and description of *Source,* for example, may be confirmed in terms of probability (more than 1,000 successive factors coincide with an absolute description of Sarah Minge ... this must be Sarah Minge in all probability), past experience (all such representations before have been Sarah Minge ... this is Sarah Minge), reference to others (sixteen other people and two machines also say it is Sarah Minge), faith or feel (God, fate, ideology, etc. tell me it is Sarah Minge) and common description (your choice).

There may also be contradiction, however. Since we can't be absolute and cover all variables, circumstances will be bound to occur in which one confirmation trial will disagree with another. Faith or feel, for instance, may persist in discerning and confirming Minge-like signals after Sarah has been transformed by a university education into a militant and (un-Mingeish) Women's Liberation Movement member. These aspects of faith and feel might be in direct contradiction of readings of the new university-inspired signals from Sarah on a probability curve. (I feel it's Sarah, but in all probability it can't be!)

In such bedevilment, we could go on endlessly. We can never be *absolutely* certain or foolproof, simply because the vast dimensions of 'everything' are beyond our individual and collective capacities and conceptions. So, we finally dig in and stubbornly draw a line.

About here.

And what can we say?
We can say

i/Anything that we *perceive* as a communication of reality *is* a communication of reality so far as *we* are concerned at that moment.
ii/What we perceive as a communication of reality *may* actually *be* a communication of reality on occasion.
AND
iii/Perception of a communication of reality can be improved and enhanced by consideration of additional variables and by allowance for innate perceptual abilities and disabilities; i.e., the more we know and the more we test what we know and how we know it, the more likely we are to be right.

Motion pictures can be highly instructive here. Almost everyone, nowadays, is accustomed to viewing a sequence of actions in a film as an integrated, 'real' entity. A film of Sarah and Harold as we saw them in the drawing would, in this sense, seem to be a coherent, consistent, and real description of moves up to and past a kiss.

But, in fact, such a film sequence (about a minute in duration) would literally look something like:
1/Establishing shot of Sarah and Harold in bed-sitting room.
2/Close-up of Sarah's face.
3/Reverse angle of Harold's face.
4/Cutaway shot of brother Edwin in adjoining room.
5/Long shot of apartment building, tracking down street.

① ESTABLISH SARAH & HAROLD

② C.U. SARAH

③ REVERSE C.U. HAROLD

④ CUTAWAY: EDWIN

⑤ PAN DOWN STREET

Looked at as successive frames of film, the one-minute kiss sequence we accepted as a 'real' entity doesn't exist at all. What we did was fill in gaps, by mentally moving about and supplying sets of assumptions sufficient to create a communication telling us that Sarah Minge and Harold kissed in a Calgary apartment while Harold's brother read *Popular Mechanics* in his room next door. We ignored or dismissed such things as
→ the three days that the one minute of film took to shoot
→ the fact that the 'Calgary apartment' was actually a set on a sound stage in Toronto
→ the fact that 'Sarah Minge' was actually a professional actress named Thelma Twin, that 'Harold' was played by Charles Urbane, and 'Edwin' by Chester Mince
→ the visual leaps in viewpoint – over Harold's shoulder one moment, over Sarah's another, through the wall to Edwin another, out into the street – that no human observer could achieve in one minute in reality
→ the 64 other people in and around the set.

Of course we ignored and dismissed them. They were not germane to the communication we were seeking to share in. Accordingly, we applied a quality of *visual literacy* to our consumption (adding variables, subtracting others, allowing for perceptual abilities and disabilities) so as to receive the communication of a kiss sequence.

And the key was the **knowing.**

We knew that our simple perception wasn't specifically or actually in parallel with the intended perception and so we altered and amended perception and inputs accordingly. We suspended disbelief.

On the other hand, people seeing conventional commercial film for the first time are often quite confused. The switch of perspective from Sarah's to Harold's face, for example, would strike them as introducing a third person into the scene. A zoom into a closeup would appear to be movement by the viewer rather than bringing the scene into the viewer's lap.

But we have learned to 'read' such film techniques. It is this sort of 'new literacy' with which this book is concerned.

Now we can go to work on the cataloguing and evaluation of the ingredients involved in the communications processes by which we conjure up manageable versions of 'everything' for us to live and deal with.

We start with our senses.

THE SENSE OF THE SENSES

2

26 Except for those rather vivid moments when we step on a skunk or hammer a thumb or bite into a bad egg or watch a freeway smashup, most of us tend to take our senses for granted. We concentrate on what they receive rather than on what they *are.* And, preoccupied with the messages that appear to be conveyed, we miss a remarkable orchestration of fact and fiction, commission and omission on the edge of our central cerebral core.

Both individually, and in intricate interaction, our senses provide our primary and main contact with what we take to be the world outside – our primary contact with the 'everything' of reality. They collect, balance, assign values, and determine priorities for handling data on virtually everything that we can see, touch, taste, smell, or feel. And, surprisingly, our senses carry out such tasks in a very large measure *before* any of the elements of 'brain' come to be involved.

It usually takes some deprivation of sensory capacity to make the central role of our senses clear.

Deafness, for example, casts us away in a land of whispers, until a hearing aid of some kind restores the familiar

Shortsightedness creates a fuzzy world until glasses correct the focus.

A WWW II NN TTT RR YY CCC AA RR EE SS can be meaningless until the numbness wears off.

Wid a code id da node, forget about the scent of spring lilacs.

And, consider the differences in taste

before you stop smoking

AND AFTER.

Therefore, if we are to rely upon our senses as major links to and from the 'everything' of reality about us, we need to know, quite specifically, as much as possible about
→ their capacity, and
→ their condition
at any given moment. Such knowledge will serve not only to suggest the circumstances of optimum use but also the alternative and even imaginative inputs we need to augment our senses. Then it becomes possible to scale perception to manageable size and evaluate or test the results.

Take  for a start.

The gross parameters of human sight are not unimpressive. An average person is able to see and recognize a cantaloupe at a distance of about 1,200 feet (if he has seen one before, of course). Within that range, there is a reasonably consistent capacity to discern colours, different degrees of brightness, some movement, and some depth. We get, in practice, a workable approximation of objects and actions around us for most of what exists above the microscopic and below the macroscopic. And we get this with a reasonable degree of consistency both in individual viewing and in comparative viewing between individuals.

But there are some important qualifications to this capacity that must be kept in mind.

Between any object and our mental perception of it there lie the complex mechanisms and processes of sight itself. All these relate to one another and all are subject to some error factor. As a result, the version of an object presented by sight for mental perception is a version modified by the cumulative sum of the errors introduced along the way.

With people of 'normal' vision, the effect of such errors is so great that, as nearly as can be calculated, about 20% of what is available to be seen at any instant in an object is lost or distorted in transit to the brain and/or human reflex mechanism. Of course, as we will see later, part of this 'loss' is offset by other senses and by adjustments made possible by experience and imagination. Just the same, 'sight' emerges as a somewhat flawed communication system.

The nature of the sight system and its potential for error can be seen more clearly if the process is described relatively scientifically and annotated at the same time.

The end organ involved in human sight is the eye. It lies in a socket in the upper half of the face and is moved by small muscles running from the bony walls of the eye socket to the outside of the eyeball.

Note 1: The socket may be misshapen. For example, a fractured maxilla (cheekbone) can cause a slight depression in the floor of the socket and lead to 'double vision.'

Note 2: The muscles may be out of balance as in the case of childhood squints and cross-eyed or wall-eyed conditions.

The eye is a highly specialized organ measuring, in the adult, about 24 mm in the transverse diameter and about 23.5 mm in the vertical diameter.

Note 3: Eye diameters may be out of proportion. For example, hyperthyroidism can cause exophthalmos – bulging of the eye which distorts vision: the eye is moved slightly out of its socket by the pressure of additional fluid and fat in the socket behind the eye.

The eye is a sphere made up of two chambers. The rear chamber comprises about 5/6ths of the sphere and contains the end organs of the optic nerve (the retina) which receive and react to the directed stimulations provided by objects viewed.

The front chamber is faced with a transparent wall – the cornea – through which light can pass.

Note 4: The cornea may not be fully transparent as a consequence of aging, disease, or accident (e.g., lacerations or damage from corrosive substances).

Between the two chambers, and linking them, are the iris and the lens. The iris, a membrane of circular muscle, is capable of altering the amount of light that is transmitted to the retina. It usually does this automatically.

Note 5: The iris membrane may not be fully operational. This may result from congenital faults, the effects of chemicals such as atropine and some tranquilizers, or surgery to deal with the effects of glaucoma or cataracts.

The lens, a membrane enclosing a transparent jelly, acts as a focusing device to direct the light passed through the iris to the retina in such a manner as to permit differentiation of the qualities of stimulation received.

Note 6: The lens may not be fully operational. The jelly-like material in the lens may become opaque as a result of congenital defects, aging or diseases such as diabetes (where changes in sugar and electrolyte levels result in lens damage). Cataracts are a common lens fault of such origins.

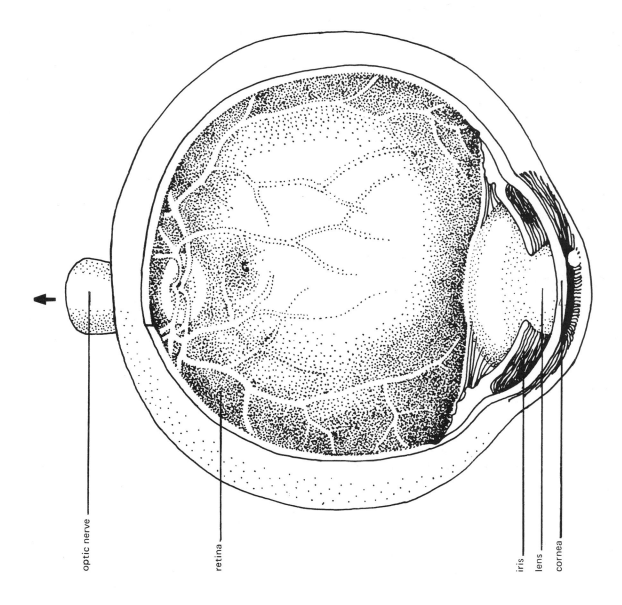

optic nerve

retina

iris

lens

cornea

The retina is made up of two types of cells which act as receptors. The most numerous, called rods, total between 100 million and 130 million. They contain a substance known as 'visual purple' or rhodosporin which disappears when exposed to light and so permits the triggering of an action current in the fibres of the optic nerve. (The underlying pigment layer of the retina acts continuously to replace this rhodosporin as it comes in contact with rod cells. In this way a continuous reaction can be maintained.)	*Note 7:* There may be too few rods as in the case of retinal detachments: this causes blind spots in vision. Or there may be too many rods, as in the case of a tumour characterized by melanoma – an excessive number of incompletely developed cells. *Note 8:* There may be an inadequate quantity or quality of 'visual purple' due, for instance, to a deficiency of vitamin A.
Rod cells, in addition to acting as containers of rhodosporin, also regulate the release of the substance by lengthening or contracting to vary contact with the pigment layer where rhodosporin is produced. Thus, reaction to relatively weak light signals is heightened and reaction to strong ones is muted.	*Note 9:* The rod cells may not lengthen or contract effectively. This can result from various retinopathies (diseases of the retina) such as those caused by diabetes or high blood pressure.
The other receptor cells, called cones, are fewer in number – usually six to seven million in all. They have a higher threshold of excitation than rod cells and also are thought to have a greater capacity to expand or contract to mute or heighten reactions to light stimuli. Cone cells also contain a colourless substance which reacts in a manner similar to that of rhodosporin and serves to facilitate the detection of shades of colour and the sharpening of the definition of focus.	*Note 10:* As with rods in Note 7, there may be too few cone cells due to retinal detachments or there may be too many as a result of a tumour. Such faults can also be congenital – as could most defects annotated here. *Note 11:* There may be an insufficient quantity or quality of the cone cell substance, again as a result of vitamin deficiency or other interferences with supply. *Note 12:* The cone cells may not lengthen or contract effectively for retinopathic reasons.
The action currents generated in the retina by the rods and cones are then passed along the many fibres of the optic nerve. Some remain within the retinal area and serve to assist in the automatic or unconscious regulation of retinal activity (primarily the production of visual purple and related substances). Others pass into the skull, mingle, and link up with various segments of the brain and with the terminals of the reflex arc area of the brain. Such terminals, at the *level of unconscious control,* serve to adjust reflexes needed to see	*Note 13:* The nerve fibres may not be capable of parallel or similar reactions to action currents for reasons, for instance, of congenital origin. *Note 14:* The terminal linkages and/or the mingling functions may be faulty as a consequence of strokes or cerebral damage due to haemorrhage or similar malfunctions. Also various drugs or chemicals can inhibit or distort such activities.

clearly – reflexes such as the position of the head, the size of the aperture of the iris, the tension of the lens, blinking, and the co-ordinated movement of both eyes in concert.

Note 15: The reflexes may be faulty as a result of various degrees of nerve paralysis affecting the muscles.

Still other optic nerve fibres carry the action current messages to the rear areas of the brain (the cortex mainly) for the conscious appreciation of sight to be registered and associated with stored memory data about other sights and associations. This permits the integration of immediate sight and memory into a pattern that can be perceived and understood in a meaningful way by the person seeing.

Note 16: The cortical functions may be faulty as a result of concussion or other accident, epileptic conditions, or other diseases or depression of the cortex due to drugs, alcohol, or other changes in the blood supply and its constituents.

Note 17: For similar reasons, 'memory' may be qualified, distorted, or blanked out so as to contribute to faulty integration.

That, with apologies to specialists, is a simplified outline. Within its limitations, however, it makes clear that the process of translating thousands of light-wave messages encompassing data of shape, colour, depth, motion, and interrelationships into nerve fibre impulses that can be received and made intelligible by the brain is a truly remarkable accomplishment. What we can see is wondrous.

At the same time, even our sketchy annotations make it equally clear that such a process is subject to many

disturbances
and
DISTORTIONS

along the way. While there is a good deal of checking and balancing built into the system, some defects are almost certain to slip by. And, since most steps in the process are dependent upon data provided primarily by the steps before them, such defects will tend to

be cumulative in their end effects. We don't have just the simple addition of defects to qualify what we 'see.' We have more of a geometric progression with the consequences of a defect at any one stage having multiple impacts at stages thereafter.

Therefore, taken by itself, sight, as we understand it to date, cannot help but be an imperfect tool for the perception of all or even part of what is going on around us. The portions of 'everything' or reality that sight will manage to serve up will probably be both incomplete and somewhat distorted.

As noted, this state of affairs is significantly improved by the fact that our other senses and elements of our brain do combine to reduce or even eliminate perceptual faults, through constant cross-checking and reference to past experience. But, before seeking consolation from this orchestral skill, let us continue and complete a catalogue of the forms and functions of individual senses.

 **Hearing** comes next, once again in a combined descriptive and annotated approach.

The end organ involved in human hearing is the ear. It lies above the jaw bone at the junction of the neck and the skull.

Note 1: The fixed location of the human ear means it is not capable of receiving sound waves of uniform quality from all directions. Further, action of the adjacent jaw (as with gum chewing) can readily distort even the existing capacity.

The outer ear consists of a dish of flexible cartilege with an aperture leading to a membrane which vibrates in response to sound waves.

Note 2: The dish of cartilage itself can be damaged by injury (such as the cauliflower ears many boxers carry from repeated blows) or disease (such as eryseplis – a strep infection) so as to wholly or partially obstruct the aperture. The aperture can also be plugged – wholly or partially – with wax or an object foreign to the body (such as a water lock from swimming).

This membrane is also the connecting link to the middle ear which houses three minute bones (the malleus, incus, and stapes) in an air chamber kept at atmospheric pressure by means of a specialized channel, the eustachian tube, opening directly into the throat.

Note 3: Acute middle ear infections may result in perforation of the membrane. Common injuries moreover include perforations from sudden air pressure changes (from diving, for instance) or very loud noises (sonic booms).

Note 4: The three small bones may be congenitally deformed, eroded by diseases such as cholesteatoma arising from chronic infections, or damaged by arthritic changes.

Note 5: The eustachian tube may be blocked by infection (the common cold for instance), by enlarged adenoids, or by congenital defects such as congenital atresia (lack of opening into the throat). When the tube is blocked, fluid tends to accumulate in the middle ear and displace the air there, distorting hearing.

The malleus is attached to the outer ear membrane and is capable of being set in motion by vibrations of the outer ear membrane. In turn, the malleus can set the incus in motion and the incus the stapes. Such vibrations are finally passed, in modified form, to a second membrane – a small oval-shaped membrane linking the areas of the middle and inner ear.

Note 6: Adhesion of the bones to each other and to the membranes they are linked with can result from scarring from middle ear infections. There can also be congenital defects.

Note 7: With aging especially, bone can slowly grow over the oval membrane, reducing and finally eliminating its functions to the point of 'deafness.'

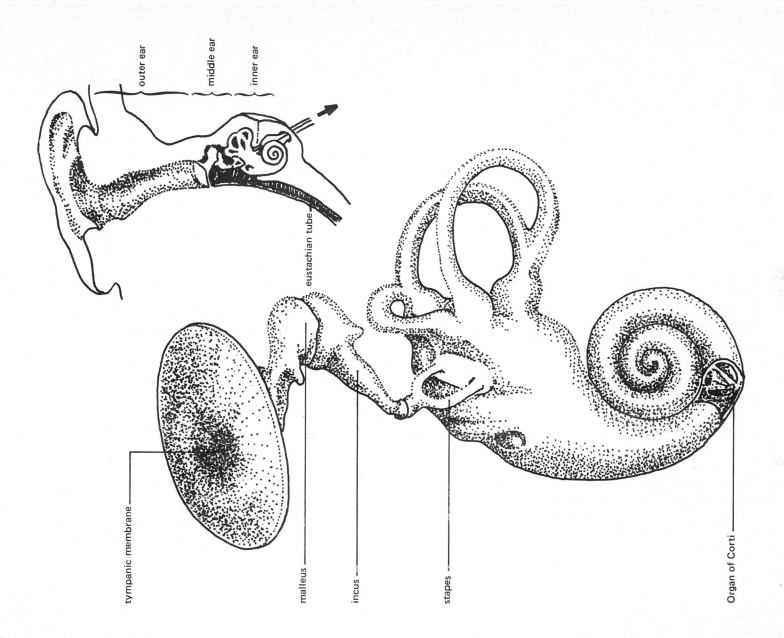

outer ear

middle ear

inner ear

eustachian tube

tympanic membrane

malleus

incus

stapes

Organ of Corti

Vibrations of the oval-shaped membrane linking middle and inner ear set up, in turn, motions and flows in the fluid contained in the inner ear – a fluid known as the endolymph fluid.

Note 8: There can be congenital defects in the inner ear chamber. In addition, diseases such as Menier's Syndrome may close off the endolymph channel through ossification.

Within the endolymph fluid there are fine hairs and cells attached to a small, spiral, membranous organ (the Organ of Corti). These hairs, stimulated by the motion and flow of endolymph, trigger action currents in the cells to which they are attached. Such currents vary in both pitch and intensity.

Note 9: There may be congenital defects and other malfunctions related to the general symptoms of so-called 'nerve deafness.' At present, however, it is not clearly established at what point such malfunctions begin in the auditory system – they may be further along the system and involve nerve fibres only.

Action currents from the cells then pass along nerve fibres to make connections with reflex arcs for unconscious adjustment related to hearing such as the positioning of the head, tension of ear membranes (partial protection against rupture caused by sudden, loud noise), or movement of eyelid or face muscles (making responses to sounds 'heard').

Note 10: There may be congenital faults in the nerve fibres.
Note 11: Reflexes may be faulty as a result of various kinds of nerve paralysis affecting the muscles involved.
Note 12: Such activities can be inhibited or distorted as a result of the presence of drugs or chemicals or, for that matter, the absence of normal substances as a result of, for instance, low blood sugar levels.

There is also an unconscious and automatic connection with the spinal cord. This allows for prompt response by the whole body to levels or kinds of sound of a threatening or unpleasant nature.

Note 13: The efficacy of this link may be diminished by congenital defects, or by the consequences of accident or illness.

Finally, action currents also pass along nerve fibre paths via two alternative routes to the mid-brain and hence to the cortex area for integration and correlation in a manner similar to that of optic nerve impulses.

Note 14: As with optic nerve currents to the cortex, the terminal linkages and/or mingling functions may be faulty as a result of strokes or other cerebral damage due to haemorrhage, concussion, or the effects of drugs, chemicals, alcohol, or altered metabolic conditions.

As with sight, hearing is an impressive accomplishment. An average person has a workably-conscious sound spectrum covering a range from 20 to 20,000 vibration cycles per second (basic high fidelity sound range) plus partly-conscious 'sensing' of higher and lower frequencies interpreted often as 'presence' or 'richness' of sound. In addition to this capacity – roughly 10 octaves – human selectivity in hearing is such that differences of as little as 1/10,000th of a second in the time of arrival of sound in one ear or the other may be detected.

But, again, our rough annotations make the magic somewhat suspect. Each stage of the process of translating external sound wave energy into human nerve fibre impulses is subject to malfunctions of various kinds, and the effect (as we have seen) tends to be cumulative. Moreover, the successive translations of the external signal cannot help but involve some loss of efficiency. With sight, the 'normal' loss in fidelity is estimated at about 20%. With sound, it is thought that 'normal' loss is slightly greater – about 22% to 25% at best.

So, hearing also is an imperfect tool for the perception of what is going on around us. Its offerings too will be incomplete and imperfect.

 turns out to be a less impressive human sense.

The end organ involved in human smelling is the nose, made up of flexible cartilage and bone. Two apertures lead to the olfactory receptors, which are set in the mucous lining of the upper, bony part of the nasal chamber.

Note 1: The cartilage and bone of the nose can be damaged by injury so as to wholly or partially obstruct the input apertures. Even relatively minor diseases (such as the common cold) can also result in the apertures being plugged. More serious diseases (such as syphillis) can destroy cartilage. Improper setting of broken noses can cause septal deviations obstructing the apertures.

Olfactory receptors in the mucous lining consist of about 600,000 specialized cells in an area about the size of 10-cent piece. They are of two types – sensory cells and supporting cells.

Note 2: The mucous lining can be incapacitated as a result of disease (again the common cold is a frequent transgressor), the effects of unduly concentrated chemicals in substances inhaled (such as cigarette smoke, ammonia fumes, or industrial air pollutants), or a short-circuiting caused by drugs or chemicals within the body. Allergies may lead as well to polyps (small growths like scars in their effects).

Note 3: The specialized cells may be subject to congenital defects. They are also somewhat more than usually vulnerable to masking by blood clots or even scarring due to the more than usually ample blood supply in the area of nasal cavity located close to the surface of the mucous lining which is apt to rupture easily.

The sensory cells are fringed with short, fine hairs (not to be confused with the longer and gross protective nasal hair) which extend into the mucous excreted by the mucous lining in the nasal chamber. Each cell is linked to about 10 to 12 hairs so as to provide a pattern of cross-linkage overall.

Note 4: There may be defects in the sensory cells and their short fine hairs as a result of temporary or long-term inflammations (again, colds, hay fever, and the like) or possible congenital faults.

Particles of an odour-causing substance, when caught in the nasal mucous, come into contact with the fine cellular hairs. Such contacts, in turn, trigger a chemical reaction in the associated sensory cells that stimulates action currents in the fibres of the olfactory nerves.

Note 5: If the mucous lining does not secrete sufficient moisture to dissolve the particles (as a result of disease or excessive dehydration) the chemical reaction cannot take place. Infections causing any 'crusting' of the nasal passage (such as chickenpox) will add to this problem.

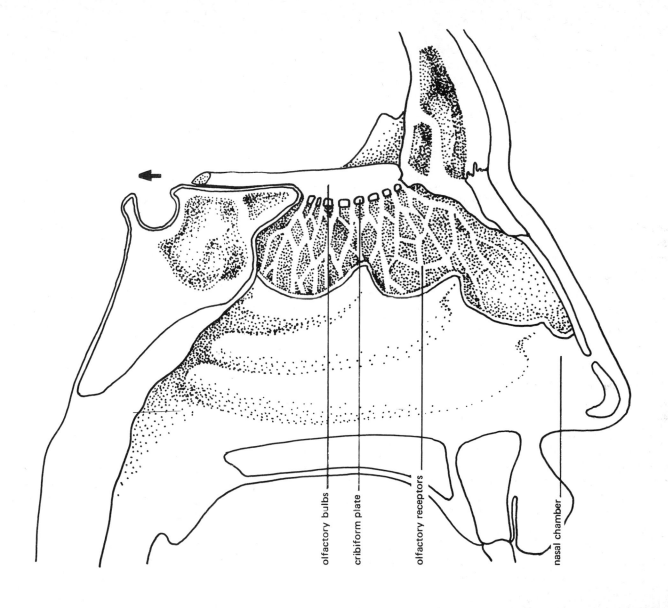

olfactory bulbs

cribiform plate

olfactory receptors

nasal chamber

Description	Annotation
Such action currents are transmitted to the olfactory bulbs at the base of the skull, just above the cribiform plate behind the bony part of the nose.	*Note 6:* Olfactory bulbs may be damaged by injury or as a consequence of surgical procedures in the area of the cribiform plate.
From the olfactory bulbs there are unconscious and automatic connections with reflex arcs linked with the salivary glands, the muscles of the eyes, head, neck, gut, and limbs, and the muscles of the pharynx and oesophagus (used in retching).	*Note 7:* Reflex arc functions may, as with the eye, be faulty due to various kinds of nerve paralysis affecting the muscles, injuries to the brain stem (from polio or neck injuries), or drug or chemical inhibitions.
There are also connections from the olfactory bulbs to the mid-brain and cortex area for integration and correlation with memory and other sensory data as with seeing and hearing.	*Note 8:* Cortical functions may be faulty as a result of concussion or other accident, diseases such as epilepsy or the effects of chemicals and drugs or other changes in the blood supply and its constituents. *Note 9:* There are also some forms of purely spontaneous activity in the cortex (the result of epilepsy-like diseases) which can result in olfactory hallucinations – usually, alas, bad smells.

As a human sense, smell is reasonably but not overwhelmingly impressive. A normal person can differentiate among about 5,000 different smells down to a threshold of stimulation of as little as roughly 400 molecules of a substance. This allows for a goodly portion of the spectrum of possible kinds and amounts of potentially pleasant and unpleasant aromas about us – at least in so far as requisite for the primary smell concerns which are facilitating the locating and selective ingestion of foods and the location and selective assessment of members of the opposite sex.

But there are inadequacies and problems. Such inadequacies as are indicated in the annotations alone suggest that human smell is both variable and vulnerable. It is very unlikely that any two persons will possess the same orchestration of smell capability.

In addition, there are vexing problems of evaluation. Unlike light and sound – which are based on standard waves that can be de-scribed with workable precision – smell is highly subjective. The same batches of molecules have triggered diametrically opposed identifications of a simple substance (described by one person as kerosene, by another as perfume) and reactions to it (retch or sensual sniff). There have even been differences of identification and evaluation by the same person at different times or in different places.

Taste

or gustation, is a sense even further down the human performance scale. For a start, about 25,000 times as many molecules of a substance are required to trigger a taste sensation of something as are required to smell it. Here are some further details:

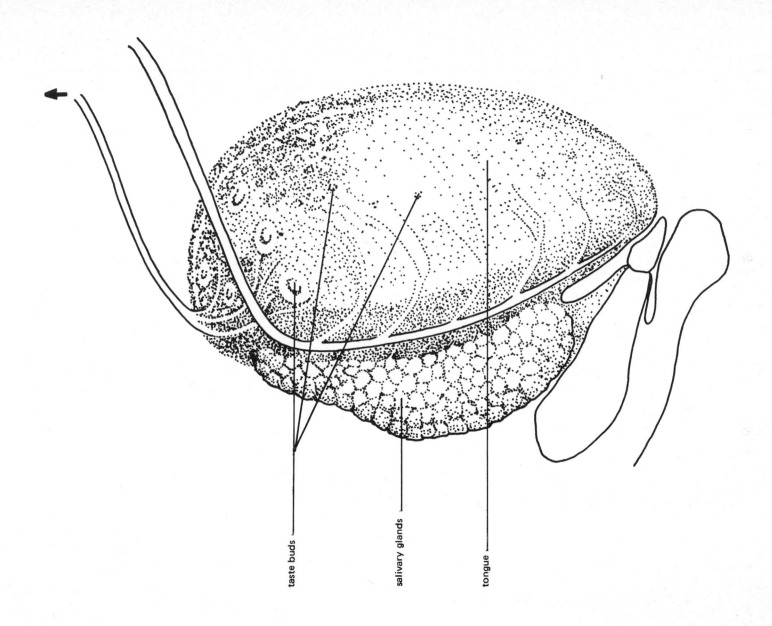

taste buds

salivary glands

tongue

The end organs involved in taste are located on the tongue, the back of the mouth, and the upper part of the throat.

Note 1: The tongue, back of the mouth, and upper part of the throat may be 'coated' as a result of smoking or various illnesses. This reduces accessibility to the end organs. Ulceration or erosion may also occur.

The end organs of taste are called taste buds – round or oval cheme-receptors about .07 mm in diameter made up of arched supporting cells with a minute opening at the top of the arch. This opening co-incides with holes in the cell below into which the fine, hair-like endings of the specialized taste cell project.

Note 2: Both supporting cells and taste cells may be faultily formed or absent as a result of congenital defects.

Molecules of the substance taken into the mouth mix with saliva. The resulting solution enters the opening at the tip of the taste bud. As the molecules brush against the hair-like endings of the taste cells, they activate nerve energy currents.

Note 3: Dryness of the mouth or of the substance ingested can reduce the efficiency of this process. Diseases of the salivary glands which reduce saliva-tion (or the wearing of dentures so positioned as to reduce salivation) can have a similar effect.

Unlike other human sense organs, taste buds house the end recep-tors of several different kinds of nerve fibre. As a result, impulses are transmitted by several different routes simultaneously. How-ever, there is some specialization in the distribution of areas of sen-sitivity. Sweet/salt sensitivity capacity is located mainly at the tip of the tongue, sour/salt sensitivity is concentrated at the sides, and bitter sensitivity tends to be mainly at the back.

Note 4: Damage to the relatively specialized areas as a result of burns, scar-ring, or other injury, or as a consequence of illness, can reduce the balance and efficiency of receptor impulses.

Note 5: Conditions arising from bacterial activity in the oral cavity (such as bad teeth) may result in the distortion or masking of the 'taste' of substances ingested.

Taste buds, because of their complex neural connections, are asso-ciated with many unconscious reflexes of the salivary glands, the gastric glands, the muscles of the face, jaw, and gut, and the mus-cles of the diaphragm and abdomen.

Note 6: The reflex links may be faulty, as in sight, as a result of various kinds of nerve paralysis or dysfunction affecting the muscles.

In addition to unconscious nerve connections, the nerve fibres linked to taste also connect with the mid-brain and cortex for iden-tification, integration with other sensory data, and association with memory links.

Note 7: Cortical functions may be faulty, as with sight, hearing, and smell.

In sum, the human sense of taste is only an approximating capacity at best. About 10,000 differentiated taste sensations are possible for an average person (assuming that he or she is a non-smoker) in relation to basic sensations of bitter, salty, sour, and sweet.

Some of the grossness of the sense of taste is offset, however, by the complex and extensive links that exist with other senses and brain components. Extensive and instantaneous cross-reference with the other senses, with memory, and with deductive ability is possible. As a result, 'tasting' has its precision enhanced and its errors reduced.

Even so, taste can be a very weak sensory reed. For reference between people, it is highly imprecise. In one experiment, for example, a statistically valid sample of people tasted a sugar called mannose: 15% reported it was tasteless, 20% claimed it was sweet, 10% said it was bitter, and 55% asserted first that it was sweet and then bitter or vice versa. Even for an individual, there are question marks. Changes in concentration (such as from a mildly to a very salty solution) can result in changed reactions (from swallowing reflexes and associated pleasurable 'taste' sensations to retching reflexes in response to unpleasant taste). Location, duration, memory, and other cerebral aberrations can result in switches of 'taste' judgment even when concentrations and other factors are constant.

So, the role of taste in our perception of the external and internal realities of 'everything' is limited. It introduces the problem of data that may be incomplete, contradictory, or downright wrong.

Touch

can be somewhat more accurate. Moreover, there now is evidence to suggest that our present capabilities can be increased and improved upon with relatively little effort.

First, the details of how our bodies report pain, temperature, and pressure:

i/PAIN

The end receptors of the human sense of pain are the tips of the endings of the peripheral nerve system located in the cells of the skin. They are distributed fairly evenly over the entire skin surface of the body.

Note 1: Receptors may be rendered less sensitive as a result of scarring, burns, skin grafts (grafted skin tends to be less responsive), corns or callouses, or of substances, such as Novocaine sprays, having the effects of a local anaesthetic.

Note 2: The transmission capacity of the peripheral nerve fibres may be affected by insufficiencies in the blood supply (as in the spasms of Reynaud's phenomenon), extremes of heat or cold that cause numbness, the effects of pressure or, again, local anaesthetic effects.

Stimulation of these nerve endings by an external source initiates an action current in the nerve fibres which is carried to the spinal cord.

Note 3: Multiple sclerosis or other de-myelinating diseases can affect these nerve fibres. Also injury, tumours, or the local effects of displaced spinal discs can affect links in the spinal cord segment involved.

At the spinal cord, the action currents are split and carried to a number of reflex arc positions governing the movement of the body and limbs, sweating, reactions of the stomach and bowel, heart rate and flushing of the skin.

Note 4: Reflex arcs to other segments of the spinal cord or to cortical areas may be faulty as a result of various kinds of nerve paralysis. As with other senses, this can be due to injury, illness, or changes in body states caused by drugs, chemicals, or the alteration of normal balances.

Contact is also made with the conscious nerve pathways (at a distance far removed from the original stimulus) and passed on to the cortex via the thalamic system. Identification, integration with other sensory data, and association with memory links occur there.

Note 5: The thalamic system is especially sensitive to infarctions (areas of tissue destruction caused by the closing off of the blood supply of an end artery) as a consequence of disease, aging, or the effects of drugs or chemicals.

Note 6: Cortical functions may be faulty as with sight, hearing, smell or taste.

ii/TEMPERATURE

The end receptors for sensing temperature and temperature changes are nerve endings covered with complex capsules capable of reacting to heat (the Bulbs of Ruffini) and cold (the Bulbs of Krause). They are located at various depths immediately beneath the outer skin layers of the human body.

Note 1: Stimulation of these bulbs may be inhibited or distorted by the same kind of skin alterations that affect pain reception: callouses, corns, scars, grafts, local anaesthetics, etc.

Note 2: There may be congenital defects in the bulbs or their associated neural connections. Also, as with pain, extremes of stimulus may cause numbness (and so no sensation); pressure may distort receptivity; local anaesthetic effects or deficiencies of blood supply may inhibit receptivity.

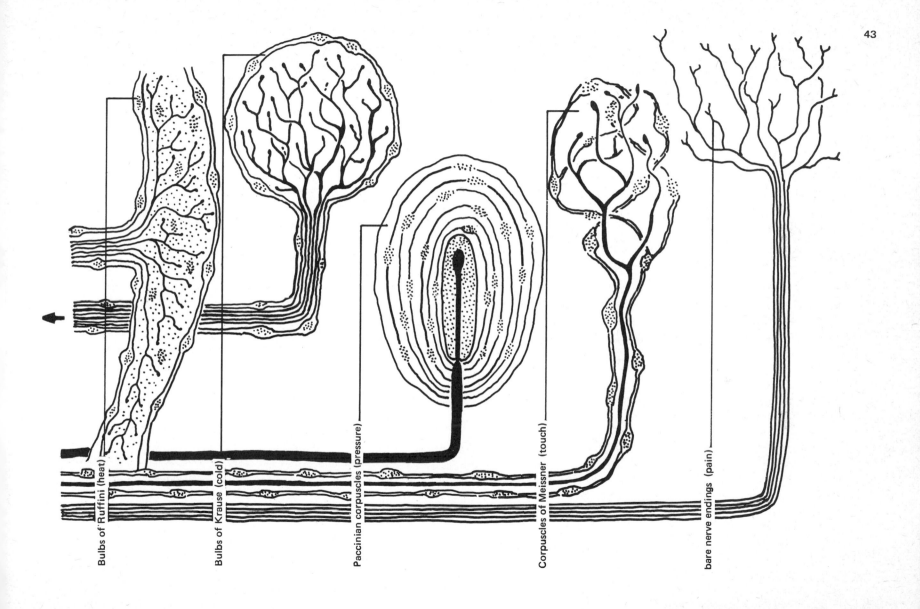

Bulbs of Ruffini (heat)

Bulbs of Krause (cold)

Paccinian corpuscles (pressure)

Corpuscles of Meissner (touch)

bare nerve endings (pain)

Reactions of these bulbs set up an action current in the attached nerve fibres. As with pain, this current is carried to a segment of the spinal cord. Extent and intensity of the effect are indicated by the location of and the number of bulbs so stimulated.

Note 3: Again, de-myelinating diseases, tumours, or spinal disc defects can affect the nerve fibres to, in, and among segments of the spinal cord.

At the spinal cord, the nerve fibre currents are split; some go to reflex arc positions, others to the conscious nerve pathways and thence, via the thalamic system, to the cortex.

Note 4: Once more, there is the possibility of faults in reflex arc links to muscles.

Note 5: As with pain references, the thalamic system may be faulty.

Note 6: Cortical functions may be faulty.

iii/PRESSURE
Five types of receptor function as end organs recording human sensations of light touch and pressure.

Distributed throughout the skin of the body are tiny, plate-shaped end expansions of nerve fibres known as Merkel's discs. Light touch or pressure on the skin in the vicinity of these discs sets off a reaction leading to an action current in the associated nerve fibres.

Note 1: Sensitivity and selectivity of these discs can be muted or distorted as with pain and temperature receptors. This may result from altered skin condition; congenital defects in the number, distribution, or reactive capacity of the discs; or 'overloading' in the sense of numbness due to extremes of temperature, pressure, or physiological alterations.

Around the follicles of human hair are nerve fibre endings called peritrichial arborizations, which react when the hair is touched to stimulate an action current.

Note 2: A great variety of infections, inflammations, infestations, and insufficiencies that can result in build-ups of dead skin and other material sufficient to mute or block the ability of either the hair or the attendant peritrichial arborizations to receive initial stimulations.

On the palm of the hand and sole of the foot, mainly, there are at the end of nerve fibres minute specialized capsules known as the Corpuscles of Meissner. Situated in tiny protruding cells, these end organs set up action currents when they are brushed or lightly pressed.

Note 3: Corns, callouses and the like, diseases such as athlete's foot, congenital defects in the endings, scars, and the consequences of blood supply alterations all can affect this sensing function markedly.

Deep within the body, around the tendons, joints, and body cavities, nerve fibre endings known as Paccinian corpuscles are enclosed in the cells of connective tissue. They react to touch or pressure by setting up action currents.

Note 4: Alterations in the state of the connective tissue may distort stimuli, as noted for skin.

The fifth type of receptor is concentrated in the external genitalia. There are thousands of tiny, capsule-like, nerve endings which, if touched or pressed, set up action currents. These are notable for their concentrated number and relatively great sensitivity.

Note 5: Congenital defects, scarring, and various diseases involving skin lesions are among the more common complications likely to mute or distort input to these sensors.

Action currents from all five types of receptors flow first to the spinal cord and link with a wide variety of reflex arcs. They will often involve the whole body, resulting in such involuntary actions as yawning, sneezing, scratching, blinking, dilation of the blood vessels, changes in pulse and breathing rates, gastro-intestinal functions. changes in movements and position, and perspiration.

Note 6: Various diseases affecting the nerve fibres, tumours, injuries to the spine and spinal cord, and the actions of drugs and chemicals and other alterations in the constituents of the human blood supply, can all affect the functioning of action currents, reflex arc links, and muscle response.

Action currents also pass into the conscious nerve pathways and thence, via the thalamic system, to the mid-brain and cortex for identification, correlation with other sensory data, and association with memory.

Note 7: As with pain and temperature, there may be faults in the thalamic system or in cortical functions.

Of all the human senses, those related to pain, temperature, and light touch and pressure appear to relate most extensively to automatic reflex-arc reactions. Virtually all action currents tend to lead to responses that are initiated before the brain consciously begins to react. For instance, when tickled we first tend to flinch – even if ever so slightly – regardless of whether or not our conscious will can then move in to counter the overt reaction. As a result, it can be suggested that these 'touch' senses are among our most useful when spontaneity and immediacy are important, since they are not as extensively subject as the other senses to conscious control and conditioning.

Some fairly impressive ranges of 'touch' perception seem possible. Sensors in the tongue, for example, are sufficiently sensitive and discriminating to identify objects as little as 1.1 mm apart as separate entities. Our fingers can function down to 3–8 mm separation and even parts of the back (our least sensitive area) can recognize as separate objects that are as little as 36–75 mm (roughly 1½–3 inches) apart.

This still doesn't represent a capacity to deal with the microscopic (including invading hordes of bacteria, for example) or the macroscopic. Furthermore, we persist in being afflicted with actual or potential breakdowns sufficient to temper both capacity and reliability of 'touch.' Once again, the broad sense is far from sufficient for our needs to relate to the inner and outer 'everything' of reality.

One other type of sensing capacity in humans deserves mention. This is the sense called

proprioception

It deals, almost entirely at the unconscious level, with the co-ordination of posture and movement.

The clearest example of proprioception is the manner in which we maintain the position of our eyes in spite of changes in the position of head and/or body. It is as if an automatic gyroscope were set to work within us. Fluid in a network of small sacs and canals in the inner ear is set in motion. The motions stimulate nerve endings and set up action currents. These in turn trigger an orchestration of varied fine muscle adjustments which maintain eye position relative to the object viewed. For example, if you focus your eyes on this

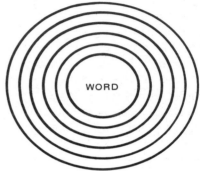

and tilt your head up and down, WORD stays in the range and focus of your vision because of reactions of proprioception set off by those inner ear fluids. You will note, too, that you didn't (and couldn't) think consciously of the adjustments required.

The sense of proprioception also comes into operation when you attempt to adjust to a sudden slip on a patch of ice, or successfully negotiate a tip-toe among some tulips. It can be regarded as balance-plus – an almost entirely automatic system that can call upon any or all of our nerve fibre and muscle set capacity to adjust rapidly to changes in bodily relationships.

Proprioception is related, in part, to the general function in humans of cross-sense co-operation. Partly because our individual senses are prey to errors and failures, many patterns of contact have evolved between senses to allow for functions of double-checking, confirmation, and amplification. Such contacts exist at every stage of the sensory process – from end organ to assorted correlations in the brain itself. They include references not only to immediate circumstances but also to aspects of memory.

With the sense of taste, for example, links with the sense of smell are very extensive – designed both to confirm and to expand upon data from the taste inputs. Such cross-sense links are so extensive, in fact, that it is ordinarily almost impossible to distinguish the parts that each sense is playing in the final cerebral perception. In the same way, sight and hearing frequently function together – as in the common situation where lip movements viewed are mixed in with sounds heard to facilitate identification and understanding of the words said. We are nearly all unconscious lip readers.

Variations within an individual and between individuals make it impossible – so far – to estimate the extent to which cross-sense cooperation helps to compensate for the basic inadequacies of our senses. About all we can deduce is that it helps.

What we end up with in general, then, is what might be called a qualified incompetence. As perceivers and processors of communications, the human body and brain operate within upper and lower limits of range, capacity, and selectivity. It has been proven many times experimentally that there exist colours, sounds, tastes, sights, touches, and scents that are ordinarily beyond human reckoning. They may even exceed – both in quantity and quality – those stimuli that we can receive. And even within our limits there are likely to be shortcomings, arising from defects in the components from moment to moment.

In short, the limitations of our constituent parts are such that we inevitably exist at a considerable distance from the goal of any *reliable* individual sensing of reality. We have made a mockery of our earlier suggestion that
→ Anything that we *perceive* as a communication of reality *is* a communication of reality so far as *we* are concerned at that moment.
Now, alas, we know better.

Furthermore, because of the inevitable and multitudinous differences from individual to individual, so far as the functions and capacities of individual parts are concerned, we are an even greater distance from any *reliable* sense of *collective* reality. We have, accordingly, also made a mockery of our other suggestion that
→ What we perceive as a communication of reality *may* actually *be* a communication of reality on occasion.
We know better about that one too.

It seems necessary to look further.

Our immediate physical and cerebral selves are neither efficient nor sufficient.

We need to find ways to extend our senses and our minds. We need widened range, capacity, and selectivity, and improved operational predictability – something to wear, or buckle on, or be tuned in to.

It is to this that we now turn.

EXTENSIONS OF THE SENSES

Most humans have wished for and mused upon extensions of their senses.

A number have done something about it.

The results overall are staggering. As a consequence of centuries of tinkering, mysticism, nibbling, injection, concocting, theorizing, and building, we now are awash with real and imaginary extensions of the senses of every conceivable shape and kind.

Contemporary fact and fiction about espionage, for example, abound with breathless descriptions of the snooping and monitoring capacity we have acquired. Telescopes, hidden microphones, wiretaps, infrared cameras, the analytic tools of forensic medicine, with a computer or two to dress up the data, taken together indicate the practical ability we have developed to project our senses to almost any finite happening in the world. (Marshall McLuhan even suggests that privacy now has become only an illusion.)

Mysteries of the human psyche and 'inner space' also are the objects of a barrage of clinical and not-so-clinical investigations: the tools are as varied as delicate probes, used by clinicians to make contact with individual brain cells, and dogmas which claim to find the answers in 'vibrations.' We grope with musings about group minds, karma, divine revelation, and astrology as valid or simply comforting ways to ease the limitations of our body envelopes.

Even the unexpected provides us with spin-off dividends. In the last decade or so, specialists in the United States have become the world's most inventive and expert authorities on artificial limbs, a grisly fallout from the Korean and Vietnam wars. The majesty of assorted space shots has provided not only really heat-proof ovenware but also a glittering assortment of gadgets including miniature radio and TV transmitters capable of extending human sensing to the edges of the universe.

Necessarily, we have to place some limits on our consideration of possible sensory extensions. Our concern is with links to the 'everything' of reality. We want to facilitate

→ more accurate perception
→ more extensive perception
→ more predictable perception
AND
→ confirmation of such gains.

This does not deny the possibilities that may lie in elegant abstraction and apparently wild theorizing. However, problems in confirming and sharing understanding of some of them (such as personal assessments of 'vibrations' or the empirical validity of astrology) seem to be too great for the evidence, time, and space we can call upon.

In this chapter, we are going to attempt to perch atop human experience to date to consider basic physical aids – gear that can be buckled, bolted, perched, inserted into, or otherwise brought into direct contact with the human body and mind to extend our senses beyond their normal capacity. In sections to follow, we will turn to possible augmentations at one remove – drugs, hypnosis, and various media that function as proxy agents on behalf of our senses.

Let us begin with sight.

What can be done to enable us to see more – and better?

Here the aim is twofold: i/to attempt to go beyond the visual spectrum of light waves and, possibly, include other parts of the electromagnetic spectrum, and, ii/to improve on the processes by which the message content reaches our sense-brain combinations, so that we will be able to see as fully and accurately as possible.

As far as is known now – although in part this is an arbitrary definition – that which can be 'seen' involves waves. These waves comprise the electromagnetic spectrum, consisting of

〜〜〜〜〜〜〜 radio waves 〜〜〜〜〜〜〜
〜〜〜〜〜〜〜 microwaves 〜〜〜〜〜〜〜
〜〜〜〜〜〜〜 infrared waves 〜〜〜〜〜〜〜
〜〜〜〜〜〜〜 visible light waves 〜〜〜〜〜〜〜
〜〜〜〜〜〜〜 ultraviolet waves 〜〜〜〜〜〜〜
〜〜〜〜〜〜〜 x-rays 〜〜〜〜〜〜〜
〜〜〜〜〜〜〜 gamma rays 〜〜〜〜〜〜〜

divided on a scale from long waves of low frequency (radio) to very short waves of high frequency. Long waves (which usually are restricted to an atmosphere) may be as much as 300 metres in diameter, measured across the full 's' of the wave. Short waves may be as little as 0.00003 angstrom units in diameter (an angstrom unit is a hundred millionth of a centimetre).

Unaided, human sight is functional within the parameters of light waves (possibly with some slight background enrichment from infrared and ultraviolet – but this overlap is neither significant enough nor certain enough to concern our explorations). This means that we start with a capability of handling waves and their messages within the range of 3,800 angstrom units and 7,600 angstrom units.

We know, from bitter experience, that direct bids to 'see' above

and below the range of light are both difficult and dangerous. Human sight can be damaged or even destroyed through exposure to these other wave stimuli. For the present, there isn't much future in approaches involving the delivery of such waves directly to our optical systems.

But we *can* translate

We can use equipment that is sensitive to the unseen movements of waves above and below the range of light and that is able to convert such waves into visual equivalents. (This is one version of the scaling to manageable proportions considered in Chapter 1.) In a mechanical sense, the waves sensed are scaled down from unseeable rapidity or scaled up from unseeable slowness.

Television provides a familiar example of this in practice. The home receiver takes electromagnetic 'picture' signals (received as invisible wave movements in the upper portion of the radio section of the spectrum) and translates these into signals that set your screen fluorescing. The fluorescence provides equivalent light waves that the eye can perceive. Similarly, the reflected radio beams bouncing back from objects in radar are made visible by being translated into glows on a cathode ray tube (a simple TV tube).

Film makes other forms of translation possible. With special chemicals, film stock can be used to register radiation above or below the wavelengths of the visual portion of the electromagnetic spectrum. Such translations into visual terms are *fixed* so that they can be viewed and reviewed at leisure. Film sensitive to infrared waves can even move back a bit in time by sensing the ordinarily invisible traces of infrared rays left after the source of visible rays has disappeared. (One source of infrared is human body heat. Some scientists claim to be able to build up fairly detailed outlines of the occupants of a room as much as twelve hours after they have left the room by photographing the lingering infrared emissions from lingering body heat.)

With special equipment, ventures into the ordinarily invisible parts of the spectrum can be spectacular. For instance, electron beams (which harness and accelerate the negative energy charges rotating about the nucleus of an atom) can be used to detect wavelengths as much as 100,000 times shorter than the 3,800 angstrom visual limit. These, in turn, can be translated into visible trackings on a fluorescent screen or photographic plate. And these can be enlarged photographically in the darkroom up to wall-size if desired. In practice, we can use various forms of detection and translation to cover about 500,000 times more of the electromagnetic spectrum than the unaided eye can see.

Equally, much can be done to extend the companion limits of visible intensity and duration. Unless the thing 'seen' produces a sufficiently strong stimulus to be registered by the human sense, and unless the stimulus lasts long enough to be recorded in some way by the human sense, it may well remain invisible. With normal sight, the threshold of unaided visual perception is calculated to be about one-twentieth of a second duration from a constant light source of about five quanta of electron energy. There is, inescapably, a reciprocal relationship here: the longer the time, the less the intensity needed for the image to trigger a perception in the eye, and vice versa. Somewhat simplified, we can take the threshold of

An electron microscope, magnifying about 3,000 times, picks up a microscopic indentation in an aluminum sheet, caused by corrosion, which could cause the end of an airplane.

normal sight for our purposes to mean, as Wyburn, Pickford, and Hirst kindly explain in their book *Human Senses and Perception* (University of Toronto Press, 1968, p. 90) that with reasonable duration of emission 'the light emitted by a standard candle would be visible at a distance of nearly a mile.'

We can improve on even this by freezing time in tiny segments (the way a camera does) or by increasing sensitivity to the wave emission source (the way some film does). It is possible to take slices of time as brief as 1/100,000th of a second (in controlled settings using strobe lights and film run very rapidly behind prisms rather than lenses) and to deal with emission sources as minute as the movement of a single electron in a single atom (provided, of course, that other emission sources are virtually eliminated).

All this becomes important when efforts to 'see' very short-wave emissions are involved. Such waves move so very quickly and can originate from such weak emission sources that they can be overlooked entirely. In much the same way, humans called the complex battleground of thousands of white blood cells and bacteria a boil for centuries until they began to understand what was going on below the surface visibility.

Well, what have we got?

Given the possibility of various kinds of controlled circumstance, it has proven to be possible to extend the sense of sight to the point where humans can theoretically 'see':
→ A universe roughly eight billion times larger (using a 500–inch telescope) than can be seen with unaided eye;
→ A single object as tiny as 0.000 000 003 8 millimetres in diameter (with an electron microscope and photographic enlargement);
→ The whole electromagnetic spectrum (with film and/or electronic sensors);
→ An emission arising from an energy source (and, clearly, there has to be energy to make waves) as small as a single electron.

Conceivably that doesn't cover 'everything,' but it is an impressive step in that direction.

However, there's a catch to all this.

Who can lug a 200–inch telescope or an electron microscope around?

Such capacities, unfortunately, are still dependent upon the mustering of massive arrays of costly, complex, and often cumbersome equipment. Such gear must be operated in highly controlled (and thus artificial) circumstances. Put directly, even NHL moguls with all their expertise and resources haven't managed to make use of 200–inch telescopes in the Montreal Forum – that's too big a sledgehammer for too small a flea.

Realistically, then, it is necessary to modify our catalogue of *possible* extensions of sight quite drastically if it is to be relevant to daily life. We must limit it to means of enhancing visual perception with equipment that is portable, reasonably convenient, and relatively inexpensive. We end up then with a much more modest list.
→ Binoculars (practically speaking, capable of increasing the range of vision up to 10 times normal).
→ Magnifying glasses (practically speaking, capable of making objects up to eight times larger – twenty times is possible but cumbersome).
→ Infrared (and possibly ultraviolet) scopes such as those used on rifle sights (practically speaking, capable of delving below (or above) the usual visual range and, on occasion, extending distance capability as well, when magnification is added in).
→ Simple devices such as thermometers to detect the presence of some invisible energy sources and so indicate the presence of waves. Also lightweight cameras to help detect some invisible waves.

The result: In workable, day-to-day terms, humans can increase their normal capacity within the visual spectrum by about eight to ten times, and can make, by translation of the invisible to the visible, some encroachments into the electromagnetic spectrum above and below light waves.

Now, what about improvements in the processes by which the message content (normal or enhanced) reaches our sense-brain combinations?

Two aspects of this question deserve attention: i/progress in standardization of human vision, to improve the chances of our all 'seeing' the same things, and ii/progress in pushing forward overall capacity of the sense of sight itself.

Of the two, standardization has been the area of most significant accomplishment to date. When really necessary, humans can now call upon processes of definition and diagnosis sufficient to arrive at much common meaning and agreement about what we see.

Such processes do not guarantee that you will see exactly what I see when we look at the same thing. But they do allow for some common denominators of description. With a spectograph, for example, it is possible to specify the exact wavelengths of colours, and to check on attempts to reproduce them. Green is no longer defined as a mixture of blue and yellow but as light emitted at a given range of frequencies. This precise knowledge can then be applied by tests to determine the extent to which individuals share perceptions of specific stimuli.

In much the same way, we can establish practical relationships between distance and apparent size, between intensity of light source and the visibility of objects, between location of an object in relation to a viewer and his ability to detect it. (The latter includes the peripheral vision prized by quarterbacks.) Then, with a general averaging standard to go by, we can compare it with individual capacities and performances.

The second aspect – improving upon the capacity of our sight – has also been marked by some progress. Most simply, we can prescribe eyeglasses to bring an individual's sight up to a fairly general standard or even to make it better than average. We may also use the proven ability of carotene (found in Vitamin A) to increase visual acuity (especially twilight vision). This was why, for example, some bomber pilots were encouraged to eat raw carrots during the latter part of the second world war. More important, a long, depressing catalogue of what to avoid has been compiled. Alcohol, tranquilizers, and many other substances affecting blood pressure and supply can have an adverse effect on vision.

Exercise can be important too. The aim is to achieve and maintain muscle balance so that the eyes can function at their best, singly *and* in tandem.

And there seems to be an important role for **practice.**

Urban dwellers develop an almost uncanny ability to pick out important survival information from the bedlam of signs flapping all about them; hunting guides become adept at spotting objects at great distances; connoisseurs become expert at bust measurements at 40 paces – all as a consequence of selective development of their visual sensory-cerebral chains.

In the case of hearing, our aims are almost exactly the same as with sight: i/to attempt to enlarge upon the aural spectrum and extend our capacity to 'hear' parts of the electromagnetic spectrum, and, ii/to improve on the processes for getting the message content to our sense-brain combinations as fully and accurately as possible.

Put simply, unaided, average human hearing capacity results from the combination of potentially audible *waves* (very roughly, 10^5–10^7 metres in frequency) and sufficient *force* (from about 6 decibels to about 140 decibels – a decibel being a sound wave pressure level based on comparison with atmospheric pressure) and sufficient *duration* (about 1/10,000th of a second) to trigger the human hearing reflexes. (The need to have a physical force to set off hearing reflexes explains why there has to be an atmosphere of some kind for human hearing to function.)

Without bogging down in the technical theories and complexities involved, we can conclude that such capacity covers only a fraction of potentially 'hearable' stimuli. Dogs respond to whistles pitched at a wavelength humans can't hear, for example. As with sight, we can also note that many sound stimuli *have to be missed* so far as direct hearing is concerned because of their potential for damaging or destroying existing hearing capabilities. Already, for example, members of electronic rock groups (and their more devoted fans) are showing evidence of damage to their hearing nerves as a result of prolonged exposure to the force and high frequency of powerful sound waves.

So, as with sight, we have to turn to translation as the main means of widening aural capacity. We turn to equipment sensitive to the movements of waves above and below the auditory range and able to convert such detections into audible equivalents. And we turn to devices able to translate sounds too weak to trigger human hearing into augmented versions that can be heard.

By means of translation it is possible, in fact, to secure sound equivalents of the whole electromagnetic spectrum. This, then, allows for an option – some people perceive better by hearing than

by seeing, for instance, and some invisible and inaudible wave phenomena can be better presented in auditory translation than visual translation. With appropriate gear, we can take our pick.

Once again, our existing sense can be augmented to the point of being microminiature or galactic.

In addition, questions of duration and intensity can be resolved. Very high speed tape recorders can be used in much the same way as high speed film to take 'slices' of sound down to the 1/100,000 of a second level (a useful facility for 'voice print' identification). Sensitive microphones and some kinds of antennae can be used to pick up sound emissions so weak that the unaided ear misses them entirely – including, at least in theory, Brownian motion (the movement of particles due to molecular agitation). Even the crackling sounds of individual brain cells at work can now be taped, amplified, and heard – not to mention the curses of huddling quarterbacks, the mysteries of bugged boardrooms and bedrooms, and the sounds of the stars in the cosmos.

Further, sound of intensities too great for safe or tolerable human hearing can be handled relatively easily. Microphones and amplifiers can be used to take unbearable bedlam and scale it down to whatever level we wish – raising the prospect of 'hearing aids' in our increasingly noise-polluted society that work in the opposite way from current models.

As a result, broadly speaking, augmentation of our sense of hearing is possible in controlled circumstances on much the same scale as augmentation of sight.

And it is just as costly, cumbersome, and complex a proposition.

So, once again, we turn to the realm of the workable day-to-day possibility. Then we can consider these adjuncts:

→ A hearing aid with variable controls (practically speaking, capable of boosting input intensity by up to 60 decibels).
→ A portable, wide-band receiver (practically speaking, able to increase 'hearing' range about 1,000 times).
→ A cassette tape recorder (practically speaking, able to handle about 10 times the normal spans of intensity and duration).
→ A 'translator,' such as this version of 'radar':

Electronic eyes for the blind

Three transducers mounted in the bridge of a pair of spectacles enable this blind person to detect objects up to 20 ft ahead over an arc of 60 degrees. The transducers transmit and receive ultrasonic impulses which are converted into audible signals in the electronic control box held by the developer, Professor Leslie Kay of the British National Research Development Corporation. The box is normally worn on the user's belt, and the sounds it produces are fed to tiny earphones mounted in the spectacle side pieces and connected to the ears by short plastic tubes. With practice, a blind person can learn to distinguish between the loudness and pitch of sounds produced by different objects at varying distances. The device is not yet in commercial production.

The Medical Post, vol 6, no 13, June 30, 1970, p. 1

The result: As an estimate, human hearing can be enhanced about 100-fold over normal.

Now, what about improvements in the sense of hearing itself? Again, the two main aspects involve i/progress in basic standardization, and ii/progress in pushing sensory capacity forward.

Some common denominators can be established. Exact wavelengths and intensities of assorted sources of sound can be established and then compared with individual capabilities by means of an audiogram. In the same way that a first violinist will sound his 'A' to set a standard for a symphony orchestra tuning up, so humans can with standard sounds and the proper equipment test their perception and seek to educate it (the phenomenon involved in learning to 'play by ear').

So far as is known to date, no special foods or chemical substances are of much use in improving hearing ability. All that is usually stressed is the importance of keeping the external ear clean and unencumbered – which means, among other things, that there actually are some slight hearing disadvantages involved in having long hair.

As with sight, practice is important in training hearing. While humans will probably never match dogs or bats, they can work on the establishment of sensory-cerebral links that allow for the identification of single sounds in a bedlam (a baby crying during a house party, for instance) and significant improvements in range. Such are essentially learned arts – usually goaded by necessity or intense ambition.

With smell, we have something of a breather. This human sense is not directly concerned with external waves or other such intangibles. Actual substances are required to set off the sensory reaction.

As a result our examination of possible augmentations and improvements can be very tangible indeed. We need only concern ourselves with matter. (As Funk and Wagnall define it: 'That aspect of reality conceived as existing prior to and independently of the mind and to have characteristics susceptible to precise measurement in terms of extension, force, mass, radiation and energy.')

Experiments of various kinds have indicated fairly precisely the point at which the human sense of smell comes into contact with the world of matter. Two Dutch scientists, Hessel de Vries and Minze Stuiver, have summed them up in a paper entitled 'The Absolute Sensitivity of the Human Sense of Smell' (in *Sensory Communication,* edited by W. A. Rosenbluth. Cambridge, Mass.: The MIT Press, 1968, p. 167):

From an analysis of olfactory threshold data it is derived that the threshold of one human olfactory cell is at most 8 molecules for appropriate odorous substances. Analysis of frequency-of-response curves shows that at least 40 molecules are necessary to produce a sensation.

If we again turn to forms of translation, however, it does seem possible to go well beyond this point. We can use various kinds of equipment to detect the existence of virtually any molecule (or even atom) in our environment. And, if we wish, we can set up such equipment to translate this detection into a detectable smell – that is, we can use our nose to expand our perceptions. The existence of an atom of gold, for instance, could trigger equipment to present us with the necessary number of molecules of, say, horse manure to permit an olfactory reaction. In no time at all, we would become skilled technicians with a precise gold-to-horse-manure scale of measurement.

More realistically, translation involving the molecular and atomic detection implicit in smell probably makes more sense if it is double-ended. Then, equipment would be used at the scanning end to seek out molecules and atoms as before, using non-olfactory means to detect particles that *could* be sensed by smell if there were enough of them; and any that were detected would set off a response in light or sound. This approach is valuable simply because humans now are more attuned to precise reception and evaluation of data by sight and sound than by smell or taste, as we will see when we turn to problems of description and standardization of the latter senses.

Outside the laboratory, it again becomes necessary to settle for compromises consistent with the limitations of cost, bulk, and complexity. Still, the concept of translation in extending smell is not as farfetched as it may seem. A device now being used in the United States Army was described – within the limits of security restrictions – in the August 1967 issue of *Science Digest* (p. 97):

People sniffer

Even your best friend won't tell you, but the Army's Manpack Personnel Detector will. It is designed to pick up essence of human perspiration at distances up to 464 yards. The sensor is clamped to the underside of the soldier's rifle barrel and is connected to the electronic backpack by a flexible hose. If the 18 pounds of gadgetry senses key human effluent chemicals in the air currents, it sounds the alarm through an earphone strapped to the operator's head.

Scientists who developed the device first studied the way bedbugs catch a whiff of their human prey. The Army doesn't explain how a searcher tells the difference between the enemy and an unwashed buddy. A new slogan our fighting men might be wise to follow is: "A dainty soldier is a live soldier."

With such devices, it is evident that some degree of proxy improvement is possible in the range, selectivity, and possibly speed of reaction of our sense of smell. How great this improvement may be, however, will vary from individual to individual and from source to source. So, with smell it really is impossible to suggest any scale of improvement comparable to our estimates for sight and hearing.

Improvements in the sensory-cerebral smell chain itself result mostly from conditioning and precautions. Practice can foster the development of skills of a fairly high order, in part as a result of the laying down of ever-more-selective associational patterns in the brain to facilitate sophisticated identifications. But such skills remain contingent on the avoidance of foods, drugs, and infections likely to mute or shut down olfactory functions. (Have you ever tried smelling Chanel No. 5 after eating onions?) It might be noted in passing that claims for the enhancement of olfactory functions, ascribed to substances such as marijuana or LSD, are deemed to be the result of the combination of the muting of other sensory functions and outright illusion rather than actual substantive increases in capacity.

Taste, like smell, involves tangibles. The actual substances, in solution, achieve the effect – there are no waves, vibrations, wires, or tubes.

Taste is also essentially gross. The human sense of taste is about 1/25,000th as precise an instrument as the human sense of smell.

Obviously, then, there is a great deal of room for augmentation.

The principal problem we face – as with smell – is essentially semantic. How are we to exchange data on tastes (or smells) in such a way as to be predictably and consistently intelligible to one another? It is quite possible with available equipment to detect molecules of a potentially taste-generating kind at levels well below the ordinary human threshold of sensory reaction. But how are they to be described? As indicated in Chapter 2, individual reactions can be directly contradictory – even within the relatively simple parameters of sweet-sour differentiation.

So, in degree at least, with taste and smell our concern lies primarily in behavioural areas. In other words, we can arbitrarily assign descriptions and accompanying values to ever-more-finely-graduated divisions of taste- or smell-initiating substances and then set to work conditioning ourselves to operate in accordance with such assigned descriptions (explaining why, for example, many children eventually come to accept spinach). Lacking finite scales such as those of the electromagnetic spectrum, we are much more dependent upon subjective resolutions.

Once we have done that, the laboratory can come to our aid in confirming the existence of molecules or even atoms of the defined kind.

In day-to-day affairs, again, a much greater degree of imprecision applies. Precisely conditioned labelling becomes very unlikely indeed, and molecular (or even atomic) sampling equipment a virtual impossibility.

Instead, it becomes a practical necessity to settle for a combination of what might be termed cultural conditioning and a gustatory version of a people sniffer. Then it's a question of making sure that some definitions of a highly probable kind are recognized ('chili is hot') and that other definitions of a given culture ('yoghurt tastes good') are widely disseminated and shared. One might also try to put together the requisite pack of wires, tubes, filters, and what-not of a 'taste-tracker.'

At a very rough estimate, such a combination should be able to contribute to extensions of the range, capacity for differentiation, and improvements in consistency of labelling up to about ten times our present unaided sense.

Improvements in the sense of taste itself are not very impressive to date. Much of the standardization implicit in cultural conditioning has tended to be of a defensive kind. That is, instead of establishing scientific benchmarks to advance taste perceptions, efforts have tended to mute, dilute, or even remove potentially flavourful elements so that possibilities of offence can be reduced. Many mass-marketed foods and drinks bear testimony to such an approach – epitomized by bread like cotton wool, bland puddings and pie fillings, intercontinentally uniform hot dogs and hamburgers, and the mockery of 'Kentucky' fried chicken.

Some substances can help. Monosodium glutamate, for example, has been used for centuries to stimulate sensory reaction to various tastes – apparently selectively and by means of a chemical sensitizing of taste buds. In limited amounts, ordinary table salt does the same kind of thing and spices of many kinds can help to increase the detectability and intensity of many tastes.

In addition, our other senses play a part in improving upon taste data. Sight can contribute to positive or negative expectations and realizations of taste – a fact cooks recognize when they 'dress up' dishes, and food manufacturers respond to when they add artificial colouring. Smell is very closely linked and even sounds (such as Muzak) can affect taste judgments.

But, pending extended research and experimentation, taste probably must be regarded as a strictly secondary human sense. Data from it cannot be counted upon to be reliable, precise, or broad enough to serve the primary purposes of tuning in to the 'everything' of reality. Such data as are available serve mainly for shading – providing some qualified colourations to the larger and more precise pictures served up by eyes and ears. (For example, marketing research has established that grocery shoppers react more positively, and predictably, to colour than to taste or smell in most instances – one of the reasons why many large outlets actually have differently coloured lights for different sections of their store.)

With touch, aspirations to enhanced sensory capacity turn upon a mixture of tangibles and relative intangibles. On the one hand, actual objects and substances exist to demand or defy detection. And, on the other hand, we must try to deal with an array of waves, temperatures, and other elusive items.

Unaided, the average human should be able by touch alone to distinguish between weights as close as .05 grams (.0017 637 ounces) to each other, note temperature changes of .5 degrees Centigrade (.9 degrees Fahrenheit), and detect variations in texture of about a millimetre (1/25 of an inch). This capability assumes a reasonably normal range of settings – those workably close to the atmospheric, climatic, and topographic conditions of everyday human life. Outside the usual range, in circumstances of extreme cold, for example, such sensory functions may well break down completely or even reverse themselves – as with 'cold' actually being received as 'hot.'

Intensity and duration are somewhat limited too. Again in normal circumstances, a human can rely on touch sensors able at best to deal with intensities up to about 1,550 vibrations per second, with changes in the number of vibrations occurring as frequently as once about every one-twelfth of a second. (The most efficient of the sensors are found around the tongue, finger tips, upper lip, and some hair follicles.)

All this can be vastly improved upon with auxiliary equipment. Weight differences can be detected in the laboratory down to the atomic level. Temperature changes of as little as 1/100,000 of a degree have been recorded. Variations in texture have been made apparent among different electrons.

Equally, the use of film, tape, computers, and other devices has made possible a much greater leeway in taking note of variations in intensity and duration.

In sum, extensions of human touch are possible in controlled circumstances over the whole spectrum from measuring the sub-atomic to weighing a star. Touch, like seeing and hearing, can use the techniques of translation to make contact with most of what seems to exist.

Outside the laboratory, light, compact, and relatively cheap equipment can achieve fairly impressive improvements on our sense of touch. A pocket thermometer can be routinely accurate down to 1/100 of a degree. Pressure-sensitive fabrics are available that record changes in weight of as little as 1/100 of a gram. Textural variations of as little as 1/8 of a millimeter can be detected with a magnifying glass. With the proper dials attached, the duration of the stimulus can be as little as 1/1,000 of a second – though repeated actions probably can't be much faster than 1/12 of a second.

The result: The human sense of 'touch' can be augmented about 100-fold in workable day-to-day terms.

Existing sensory capacity can also be improved upon. Because most of the inputs impinging upon the sense of touch are measurable in specific terms, it is possible to run tests on individuals to determine how their actions and reactions compare. With practice (as with the experienced butcher's thumb on a scale) people can learn to adjust their sensory perceptions to match up with objectively measurable ones.

In addition, a variety of drugs and chemicals can contribute at least selectively to the enhancement of touch or the readiness of the sensors to react to touch.

More important, the human sense of touch appears to be relatively underdeveloped at present. Research associated with space programs (for astronauts who have to be trained to cope with situations where there may be no light or sound stimuli available) suggests that humans are capable of co-ordinating the several ingredients of touch in a much more precise and sensitive way than they do now. The variables of changes in temperature, pressure, duration, and intensity can be used in a learned manner to provide more detailed, more selective, and a wider range of data than any individual component. Just as, for example, a blind person develops quite remarkable speed and sensitivity in his finger tips using braille, a person trained in touch 'literacy' can aim to acquire comparable touch-sensing improvements over his whole body.

Now, let us turn briefly to proprioception-plus ... the co-ordinating aspect of our senses and their combined functions. Can we find ways and means of extending the range and effectiveness of the *collective* functioning of our senses plus our brain capacity?

Surprisingly, there doesn't seem to be very much improvement available. The present combinations of our minds and our senses have not yet been matched, let alone exceeded, by hardware of any kind of comparable compactness and capacity. Even the most sophisticated computer systems don't yet come close. The average human, it seems, is capable of almost instantaneous correlations, cross-sense consultations, confirmations, and creative insights. He or she can sustain such activity almost continuously, and in a manner permitting round-the-clock maintenance and repair that seldom interferes with the collective process. An average human is, in this sense, a device capable of *billions* of simultaneous actions and reactions all the time.

All that can be added is some slight improvement within narrow limits in the rate of performance and its predictability. A massive computer complex, for example, is useful mainly because it works relatively quickly and accurately at tasks it is specifically instructed to do. As such, it is faster than humans – *but only within its focused and directed area* (so far, anyway). It is also more accurate, when not shut down for repair by men in white coats, in the sense that it is less likely to suffer from the emotional storms, bodily ills and inhibitory conditioning that affect humans. Computers won't fight with their wives and see the world more bleakly than it is. Computers don't have hangovers blurring numerical skills. Computers don't have inhibitions and so can advise us when humans might stammer.

But, with all the advantages of computers, they don't add much to what our own bodies do, unknown to us. Experimental and theoretical evidence available to date suggests that the human mind-sense combinations involved in proprioception and myriad other activities actually retain all data received. In other words, everything a person has seen, heard, smelt, tasted, touched, *and* all the relationships and conclusions built upon such inputs, are thought to persist within him as perpetual electrical reverberations, or imprints, or neuron chains of some kind. And, since data put into machines of any kind will be much more gross overall, we aren't likely to be able to enhance human *capacity* to any significant extent.

As for *performance* ... that's a different matter. But we can improve. Most notably, it is possible to modify or eliminate human vagaries that result in so-called 'forgetting.' (The point being that humans don't forget in the sense of losing: they forget as a positive act to serve functional or psychiatric purposes.)

To augment our memory we can also use data storing and processing equipment: a pocket adding machine, a slide rule, an assortment of memo pads with reminders written in, the facilities of a shared-time computer service, files and indices. Such things can, on occasion, increase our capacity and predictability a great deal.

Now, having skipped through a simple survey of what can be done to improve our sensory-cerebral grasp of the 'everything' of reality about us, what can we conclude?

Briefly, it seems, the situation is this:

Individual humans in everyday life can avail themselves of aids sufficient to enhance their overall cerebral-sensory inputs by about 10 to 100 times their normal range. In laboratory conditions, such enhancement can be pushed much further – probably to the sub-atomic and the galactic.

Yet challenges and uncertainties remain. Since we are presuming to seek to grasp and deal with 'everything' (meaning, arbitrarily, an infinite number of variables infinitely expressed), *and* to exchange data and views on all aspects of it, we need to press on further. We need i/to consider other kinds of cerebral-sensory extension, and ii/to grapple with the nettles of language.

BETTER LIVING THROUGH CHEMISTRY?

We need to consider other kinds of cerebral-sensory extension.

We have seen that the sensory parts of our bodies are limited – even when backed up with hardware, chemical stimulations, and men in white coats. But what about alternatives to the frail senses? What about by-passes aimed directly at the brain?

As noted, there is some evidence to suggest that our brains are pretty remarkable – possessed of capacity and complexity well beyond that of our senses. And, as we will see, there is evidence to suggest that techniques and substances do exist that can wholly or partly by-pass the senses to make direct contact with brain sectors.

But, alas, some major reservations must be kept in mind. Two especially: i/our understanding of what comprises the brain and how it works is tragically sketchy, and ii/our data on how and why various techniques and substances make contact with what we think is the human brain are highly tentative. Essentially, we are still in the Stone Age of comprehending cerebral functions and alterations. This is partly because it is uncommonly difficult to get inside any portion of the brain while it is still alive, and partly because we haven't yet been able to formulate a statement of what we are looking for that can be related to practical tools and techniques.

As a result, and with appropriate apologies, what follows can only be made up of sets of relatively educated guesses. We can take note of what appears to be happening, the confirmations through repetition that appear to occur, and some theorizing that may or may not be validated at a later date. Such a state of affairs reflects the fact that – apart from measurements of minute electrical charges and discharges, alterations in chemistry, and the like – all we have to depend on is subjective description of what appears to the possessor of the brain concerned to be happening. No external human or machine has yet really been able to get directly in touch with the human mind.

Two main approaches to the brain area deserve consideration: i/mechanical and electromechanical contacts and ii/chemical contacts. (Others, such as hypnosis, we will consider separately.)

Any respectable science fiction buff is familiar with the electromechanical propositions. Tiny electrodes are implanted in brain areas to affect perception, provide direct inputs of data, and permit direct expressions by-passing the sensory system. In theory, at least, there is the prospect of the human brain acquiring dimensions of existence almost entirely on its own and of coming into unmuted and undistorted contact with other brains ... veritable legions of them ...

Actual practice isn't too far off this. It now is possible with microminiature equipment to place a tiny electrode (about a millionth of an inch in diameter) inside a cell without evident interference with the cell's usual functioning.

Through trial and error, it has proven possible in this way to affect mood, basics such as hunger, thirst, temperature, and respiration, and possibly even memory. As Albert Rosenfeld notes in his survey *The Second Genesis: The Coming Control of Life* (Englewood Cliffs, NJ: Prentice-Hall, 1969, p. 205):

One can easily imagine people in the future wearing self-stimulating electrodes ... which might render the wearer sexually potent at any time; that might put him to sleep or keep him awake, according to his need; that might curb his appetite if he wanted to lose weight; that might relieve him of pain; that might give him courage when he was fearful, or render him tranquil when he was enraged.

Further, such prospects promise the ability to by-pass at least the end organs of the senses (eyes, ears, nose, skin receptors, and so forth) and their imprecisions. So, to the extent that sensory functions can be separated from cerebral functions, we may be close to very significant improvements in the quality and quantity of impression-forming data reaching our brains and a comparable enhancement of expressions from our brains.

Of course, there are very large questions related to such potential enhancement of perceptual capacity and quality. It still isn't entirely clear how electrode contact works (some research suggests it triggers reactions similar to neuron firings, while other research hints that the reactions may, in fact, be the muting of neuron firing). Moreover, control through such direct stimulation threatens unparalleled dimensions of mind-bending by third parties (such as 'benevolent' dictators, administrators, and other kindly folk) wholly at odds with individual contact with 'reality.'

At present, about all we can do is take note of work under way and some of the possible implications. As various characters continue to

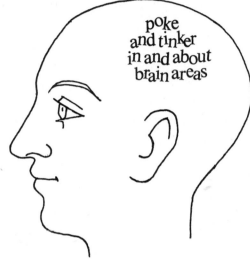

poke
and tinker
in and about
brain areas

we'd better pay attention. (That's one reason why the Admiral is very watchful when his dentist starts drilling.)

Chemical contact to and from brain areas may well be even more significant. There isn't the cumbersomeness of wires and electrodes, for one thing, and a much greater orchestration of effects can be attempted. Henri Michaux, the French writer and painter, wrote about chemical effects in *Light Through Darkness* (New York: The Viking Press; London: The Bodley Head, 1963, p. 5).

Multitude in consciousness, a consciousness which spreads until it appears to double, to multiply itself, avid of simultaneous perceptions and knowledge, the better synoptically to observe and embrace the most distant points.

The abnormal excitation radiates. Hyperacuity. The prodigiously present attention, at the height of the possibilities, registers fast and clearly. The separating and evaluating power increases in the eye (which sees the finest reliefs, insignificant lines), in the ear (which hears the slightest sounds from afar, and is hurt by loud ones), in the understanding (observer of unapparent motives, of what lies beneath the surface, of the most remote causes and consequences that ordinarily pass unperceived, of interactions of every kind, too multiple to be grasped simultaneously at other times), finally and above all in the imagination (in which visual images, with unparalleled intensity, crowd out a shriveled and shrinking reality) and, last but not least, revealing at times to the subject, in the parabnormal faculties, the gift of clairvoyance and of divination.

M. Michaux wrote as a fairly representative enthusiast. So far as he was concerned, there are chemical substances (mescaline, especially) that both improve upon sensory-cerebral functions and by-pass sensory limitations. Even some of the less rhapsodic examinations of chemical enhancement of perception and understanding seem to bear out at least part of his claims in more regular and controlled circumstances.

But remember that observations and evaluations of chemically-induced enhancement are still largely dependent upon subjective description – shakily supported by observed behaviour and the metric data of physiological condition. At best, we can deduce that some apparent amplification, augmentation and, possibly, re-organization of sensory-cerebral activities take place when humans imbibe certain chemicals not usually present in their body envelopes. We can set such deduction against observed side-effects (short- and long-term) to try to see if the results seem positive enough to merit serious consideration. Avoiding both evangelism and dire warnings, we can cast our enquiry in the form of five key questions related to communication only:

→ Does a chemical improve upon the function of the senses and brain or merely give the illusion of improved functioning?
→ Does a chemical reduce inhibitions which interfere with perception?
→ Does a chemical form part of a pattern of human socializing that fosters more open and effective communication?
→ Do the immediate or longer-term effects of a chemical tend to cancel out immediate advantages in communication?
→ Are there amounts, settings, or associations that may be sufficiently beneficial to outweigh disadvantages or disapproval about a chemical?

In approaching such mind-benders, we need not confine ourselves to the more popularized and hysteria-fostering substances. Instead, let us freeze time and select a range of substances in legal and/or illegal circulation at the time of writing. Our list:
→ nicotine (cigarettes, cigars, pipe tobacco and snuff)
→ caffeine (tea, coffee, cocoa, cola drinks)
→ alcohol (potable spirits)
→ tranquilizers
→ hypnotics: barbiturates
→ hypnotics: non-barbiturates
→ opiates (opium, heroin, morphine, codeine, etc.)
→ cocaine
→ amphetamines
→ hemp derivatives or syntheses (marijuana, hashish)
→ psychedelics or hallucinogenics
→ glue
→ amyl nitrite
All of these, to varying degrees, fall into the broad category of substances which affect sensory-cerebral activities as we know them.

Nicotine

A stimulant of the central nervous system (relatively mild in amounts absorbed from ordinary cigarettes and cigars).

Does the chemical improve upon the functions of the senses and brain or merely give the illusion of improved functioning?

Nicotine may produce some improvement in sensory perception through stimulation of the central nervous system, but of minor proportions and not in all persons.

Does the chemical reduce inhibitions which interfere with perception?

Not chemically. There may be some conditioned reduction of inhibition as result of extensive and suggestive advertising. We may be conditioned to feel more adventurous in 'Marlboro Country,' for instance.

Does the chemical form part of a pattern of human socializing that fosters more open and effective communication?

Yes, in the smoking act itself. Users gain oral gratification, something to hide behind, advantages of ritualized gestures of friendship, in offering and accepting cigarettes or cigars.

Do the immediate or longer-term effects of the chemical tend to cancel out immediate advantages in communication?

No, not so far as nicotine itself is concerned in ordinary use (though pure nicotine is deadly poison in even small amounts). Some short-term habituation occurs with nicotine (6–12 hours) but the main disadvantages lie in tars in cigar and cigarette smoking which have been linked with lung cancer, bronchial complaints, high blood pressure, and cardiac failure.

Are there amounts, settings, or associations that may be sufficiently beneficial to outweigh disadvantages or disapproval about the chemical?

Not specifically – varies widely from individual to individual.

Caffeine

A stimulant of the central nervous system (somewhat stronger than nicotine) found in tea, coffee, cocoa, and cola drinks.

Does the chemical improve upon the functions of the senses and brain or merely give the illusion of improved functioning?

Caffeine provides some improvement in sensory perception through an increase in alertness, and a masking of fatigue by stimulating the central nervous system. Effects are relatively minor and not applicable to all persons.

Does the chemical reduce inhibitions which interfere with perception?

No, apart from conditioned association with sociability.

Does the chemical form part of a pattern of human socializing that fosters more open and effective communication?

Yes, in the sense that coffee, tea, cocoa, cola drinks provide for tension-reducing oral gratification in circumstances of ritual hospitality and sociability.

Do the immediate or longer-term effects of the chemical tend to cancel out immediate advantages in communication?

Caffeine can be a factor in some cases of insomnia, heightened tension, and nervousness. Some short-term habituation occurs, together with a relatively strong tendency to psychological dependence.

Are there amounts, settings, or associations that may be sufficiently beneficial to outweigh disadvantages or disapproval about the chemical?

Optimum daily consumption ranges from 1 to 5 cups of coffee or their equivalent.

Alcohol

A depressant of the central nervous system. Effects vary with the proportion of proof spirits in the liquid imbibed and, to some extent, with the nature of other adulterants.

Does the chemical improve upon the functions of the senses and brain or merely give the illusion of improved functioning?

Alcohol in small to moderate quantities (exact amounts vary widely from individual to individual and with acquired tolerance) gives an illusion of improved sensory perception. Little evidence exists of actual and predictable improvement, however. The high calorie level of alcohol can provide some energizing 'lift.'

Does the chemical reduce inhibitions which interfere with perception?

Some reduction of inhibitions often occurs, particularly in so far as communication may be hindered ordinarily by shyness or lack of confidence. Euphoria in some cases provides a short-term offset to depression.

Does the chemical form part of a pattern of human socializing that fosters more open and effective communication?

Yes, as a result of extensively promoted and conditioned social patterns of real or imaginary conviviality.

Do the immediate or longer-term effects of the chemical tend to cancel out immediate advantages in communication?

Alcohol, over any long term, can be a factor in brain, liver, and kidney damage, obesity, and gastro-intestinal inflammations. In the short run it can be a factor in cerebral confusion. Sustained consumption in any large amounts can lead to strong habituation (up to 14 days) with severe withdrawal symptoms.

Are there amounts, settings, or associations that may be sufficiently beneficial to outweigh disadvantages or disapproval about the chemical?

Optimum amounts vary with the metabolism of the individual and the degree of his acquired tolerance.

Tranquilizers

Substances in the ataractic class of drugs which tend to depress the central nervous system and contribute to muscle relaxation. (Better known proprietary brands include Miltown, Valium, Librium, Dartol, Equanil and Stelazine.)

Does the chemical improve upon the functions of the senses and brain or merely give the illusion of improved functioning?

To the extent that tranquilizers offset 'disturbance of the mind,' they can facilitate sensory perception. Notable examples include the modification of hallucinations and delusions. Advantages are frequently to be weighed against depressant effects on the central nervous system including drowsiness and impaired vision.

Does the chemical reduce inhibitions which interfere with perception?

Yes, in the sense that cerebrally-inspired anxieties, tensions, and conditioned limits can be modified or eliminated.

Does the chemical form part of a pattern of human socializing that fosters more open and effective communication?

Not particularly, apart from effects on individual sociability that may be induced by modified inhibitions.

Do the immediate or longer-term effects of the chemical tend to cancel out immediate advantages in communication?

In long-term use, some tranquilizers can be a factor in jaundice in some persons, loss of white blood cells, skin rashes, liver damage. Short-term use can lead to diarrhoea, drowsiness, interference with vision and hearing, and dysfunction of the salivary glands. In both cases, such effects are relatively rare.

Are there amounts, settings, or associations that may be sufficiently beneficial to outweigh disadvantages or disapproval about the chemical?

Varies with the specific substance and individual. There is a ceiling above which disadvantages outweigh benefits to communication, and it seems to lie close to the range of average doses.

Derivatives of barbituric acid which act as central nervous system depressants and muscle relaxants.

Does the chemical improve upon the functions of the senses and brain or merely give the illusion of improved functioning?

No significant actual or illusory improvement in sensory perception is ordinarily experienced. Those addicted, however, may secure a 'high' of a nature, including an illusion of improved perception for a brief period. In isolated cases, a degree of agitation rather than sedation may occur, with some illusion of enhanced perception.

Does the chemical reduce inhibitions which interfere with perception?

Not to any significant extent, apart from some relief of tension and anxiety prior to sleep.

Does the chemical form part of a pattern of human socializing that fosters more open and effective communication?

No.

Do the immediate or longer-term effects of the chemical tend to cancel out immediate advantages in communication?

Yes. Barbiturates are addictive with withdrawal symptoms including convulsions and even death. Chronic intoxication seriously interfering with perception can occur within a few weeks of consumption at levels as low as six times normal therapeutic dosage. The drug is a factor in kidney damage and with addicts is characterized by abrupt and extensive mood changes.

Are there amounts, settings, or associations that may be sufficiently beneficial to outweigh disadvantages or disapproval about the chemical?

No.

Hypnotics: Non-Barbiturate Sedatives

Generally substances such as methylpentynols, ethchlorvynols, glutethimides, methylprylones and ethinamates (Oblivon, Placidyl, Doriden, Nodular and Valmidate in proprietry terms) which are central nervous system depressants, muscle relaxants, and anticonvulsants.

Does the chemical improve upon the functions of the senses and brain or merely give the illusion of improved functioning?

Little actual improvement in sensory perception is gained, except in some circumstances when the chemical is used to calm a highly excited patient. Some illusion of enhanced perception has been claimed.

Does the chemical reduce inhibitions which interfere with perception?

Not to any significant extent. Some success has been recorded with minimal doses but not to any degree comparable with tranquilizers.

Does the chemical form part of a pattern of human socializing that fosters more open and effective communication?

No.

Do the immediate or longer-term effects of the chemical tend to cancel out immediate advantages in communication?

Yes, though to a lesser degree than with barbiturates. Side-effects include nausea, skin rashes, some habituation and withdrawal effects after prolonged use, hypotension, and circulatory complications. As one authority notes: 'It is a matter of time before they are misused by the unstable.'

Are there amounts, settings, or associations that may be sufficiently beneficial to outweigh disadvantages or disapproval about the chemical?

No, apart from some possible but yet-to-be-established treatment employing minimal doses.

Opiates

Actual or synthesized derivatives of opium (opium, heroin, morphine, codeine, demerol, percodan, and a variety of cough syrups) act as central nervous system depressants, muscle stimulants, and relaxants.

Does the chemical improve upon the functions of the senses and brain or merely give the illusion of improved functioning?

This class of chemical frequently gives an illusion of improved sensory perception, often to the point of hallucination, delirium, and delusions. Except in circumstances of extreme pain, cardiac asthma, and dysentery, where relief of symptoms can restore perception closer to normal, no actual sensory gains are known to occur.

Does the chemical reduce inhibitions which interfere with perception?

To some limited extent in the sense of enhancing euphoric predispositions or aspirations for a brief period. More commonly, these chemicals tend to contribute to inhibitions by reason of their illegality and the current flavour of social ostracism towards non-medical users.

Does the chemical form part of a pattern of human socializing that fosters more open and effective communication?

Only in the very narrow sense of community and contact with other users, at the expense of the general community.

Do the immediate or longer-term effects of the chemical tend to cancel out immediate advantages in communication?

Yes. All the substances are addictive to some degree and characterized by withdrawal symptoms including nausea, allergic reactions, delirium, and convulsions. Even short-run use is often accompanied by constipation, respiratory complications, loss of weight, and temporary impotence.

Are there amounts, settings, or associations that may be sufficiently beneficial to outweigh disadvantages or disapproval about the chemical?

None so far as enhanced communications are concerned.

Cocaine

A central nervous system stimulant, vasodilator, and muscle stimulant derived from coca leaves and most commonly used as a local anaesthetic (Benzocaine, Novocaine, Tetracaine).

Does the chemical improve upon the functions of the senses and brain or merely give the illusion of improved functioning?

Initial effects tend to give the impression of heightened sensory perception. There may be some actual improvement – sharply qualified, however, by accompanying euphoric and delusional effects.

Does the chemical reduce inhibitions which interfere with perception?

Inhibitions are sharply reduced to a state close to uncontrollable excitement. (The phrase 'drug fiend' is said to have been applied first to cocaine users.)

Does the chemical form part of a pattern of human socializing that fosters more open and effective communication?

Aspects of violence, paranoid delusions of persecution, anxiety, and ultimate depression in the cocaine cycle tend to rule out any credible patterns of social facilitation.

Do the immediate or longer-term effects of the chemical tend to cancel out immediate advantages in communication?

Long-term effects are usually serious, including toxic psychosis, extreme irritability and proneness to violence, skin rashes, and depression. Short-term effects of anxiety and depression virtually cancel out initial feelings of well-being and euphoria.

Are there amounts, settings, or associations that may be sufficiently beneficial to outweigh disadvantages or disapproval about the chemical?

None. Apart from clinical use as a local anaesthetic, the chemical seems to have no workably tolerable level of use and in its abuse tends to be solitary and anti-social.

Amphetamines

A stimulant of the central nervous system and the circulatory system, providing the main active ingredient in diet and 'pep' pills (Dexedrine, Benzedrine, Amphos, Amphetone).

Does the chemical improve upon the functions of the senses and brain or merely give the illusion of improved functioning?

The illusion of improved sensory perception is very strong during the initial period of use – characterized by wakefulness, a sense of euphoric well-being, sharpened vision and hearing, and a sustained ability to concentrate. Actual improvements are less clear, though greater energy and pace of perception do seem to be probable effects.

Does the chemical reduce inhibitions which interfere with perception?

To the extent that the chemical increases the sense of engagement and the level of excitability, some reduction of inhibitions can occur.

Does the chemical form part of a pattern of human socializing that fosters more open and effective communication?

Not usually. Excessive users ('speed freaks') tend towards violence and instability ill-suited to workable social interaction.

Do the immediate or longer-term effects of the chemical tend to cancel out immediate advantages in communication?

Yes. Amphetamines are psychologically and often physically addictive with prolonged use and are accompanied by side-effects such as insomnia, hallucinations, hyperexcitability, irritability, toxic psychosis, depression, and paranoia. When taken at the same time as alcohol, they can contribute to a multiplier effect of serious proportions. There seems to be a lot of truth in the slogan, 'Speed Kills.'

Are there amounts, settings, or associations that may be sufficiently beneficial to outweigh disadvantages or disapproval about the chemical?

Some advantages in perceptual ability and communication skill can be secured with relatively intermittent use at dosages of up to **30** mg a day.

Hemp: (marijuana) derivatives or syntheses

A psychotomimetic agent which affects thought processes and perception and may be a central nervous system depressant (although this is not yet wholly clear experimentally).

Does the chemical improve upon the functions of the senses and brain or merely give the illusion of improved functioning?

The illusion of selective improvement in sensory functioning is very strong and may coincide with actual improvement (or the muting of some senses to the benefit of the remainder). Taste, hearing, and touch have been cited as most commonly deemed to be enhanced. Less frequently, sight may seem to improve.

Does the chemical reduce inhibitions which interfere with perception?

Yes, to the extent that euphoria and the reduction of psychiatric blocks frequently occur. Such gains, however, are modified in many cases by alterations in the sense of time and space, diminished memory functions, and less effective co-ordination.

Does the chemical form part of a pattern of human socializing that fosters more open and effective communication?

Yes, in that the chemical fosters some group feeling by reducing ego drive. Ritualized gestures of friendship seem associated with its use as well. These advantages are qualified by aspects of near-paranoia related to the drug itself and its status as an illegal substance.

Do the immediate or longer-term effects of the chemical tend to cancel out immediate advantages in communication?

No. No immediate side effects of great significance have been extensively verified. Excessive use appears to contribute to depression, possible psychological habituation, lassitude, and occasionally, psychosis. Side effects can include nausea, bronchial complaints, and, occasionally, violence. Much confusion exists, however, in the absence of controlled studies; it is possible that routinely retailed tales of abuse may be based on individual psychiatric predispositions rather than the drug itself.

Are there amounts, settings, or associations that may be sufficiently beneficial to outweigh disadvantages or disapproval about the chemical?

One experiment in Amsterdam provides drop-in centres for marijuana users (mainly 15- to 25-year-olds) who police and regulate themselves. About 1½% of the potential clientele has been attracted, and experience so far indicates that the consequences of excessive use, legal difficulties, and alienation from the community have been sharply reduced. Communication benefits, on the part of senders and receivers alike, seem to be minimal, however.

Psychedelics

Substances affecting the central nervous system (as stimulants and depressants), the circulatory system, and muscular co-ordination. Most common are LSD and related compounds (LAE, STP, nutmeg, morning glory seeds) and psilocybin, peyote (or mescalin), and DMT.

Does the chemical improve upon the functions of the senses and brain or merely give the illusion of improved functioning?

Illusions of improved sensory functioning are very strong at various times during the course of apparent effects (which may persist up to five days intensively). Many claims have been made for actual improvements plus versions of 'expanded consciousness.' Clinical data are not yet wholly clear.

Does the chemical reduce inhibitions which interfere with perception?

Yes, in many cases. To varying degrees – depending on the circumstances and the substance used – such prospects can be offset by so-called 'bad trips' in which anxiety, panic, or outright paranoia or schizophrenia swell inhibitions.

Does the chemical form part of a pattern of human socializing that fosters more open and effective communication?

This is still a debatable issue. Advocates assert that insights, openness, and personal ease are fostered to the point of making effective communication probable in most cases. Doubters argue that non-clinical use tends to foster excessive subjectivity to the point of active escape from reality.

Do the immediate or longer-term effects of the chemical tend to cancel out immediate advantages in communication?

Short-term effects can include nausea, triggering of psychoses, anxiety, impaired co-ordination, and, possibly, chromosomal damage. Long-term effects have not been extensively documented though extensive personality change, it is fairly generally agreed, is a frequent effect.

Are there amounts, settings, or associations that may be sufficiently beneficial to outweigh disadvantages or disapproval about the chemical?

Varies with the individual. It seems reasonable to note, however, the comment of D. C. McClelland of the Harvard Center for Research in Personality (the man who originally brought Timothy Leary to Harvard) on psychedelic *researchers and subjects.* He remarked in 1961 that they are characterized by 'Dissociation and detachment ... (2) Interpersonal insensitivity ... (3) Omniscience, religious and philosophical naivete ... (4) Impulsivity ...'

Glue

The active agents are central nervous system depressants found in hydrocarbon solvents (commonly acetone).

Does the chemical improve upon the functions of the senses and brain or merely give the illusion of improved functioning?

No improvement upon sensory perception occurs. Some illusion of improvement may occur in isolated cases.

Does the chemical reduce inhibitions which interfere with perception?

Some reduction of inhibitions is possible from its action as a central nervous system depressant (the effects are similar to those of wood alcohol).

Does the chemical form part of a pattern of human socializing that fosters more open and effective communication?

No, apart from the activities of small groups of dedicated users who tend, in turn, to become progressively more alienated from all others.

Do the immediate or longer-term effects of the chemical tend to cancel out immediate advantages in communication?

Emphatically yes. The substance is highly toxic. Any prolonged use, or even breathing-in of a large amount at one time involves serious risk of permanent brain damage and liver and kidney damage. Judgment and co-ordination are affected adversely.

Are there amounts, settings, or associations that may be sufficiently beneficial to outweigh disadvantages or disapproval about the chemical?

No.

Central nervous system depressant, vasodilator, derived from amyl alcohol.

Does the chemical improve upon the functions of the senses and brain or merely give the illusion of improved functioning?

No. As a coronary dilator it would ease sensory mutings or malfunctions resulting from attacks of angina and some other diseases of the heart, and so possibly restore sensory perceptions to more normal ranges.

Does the chemical reduce inhibitions which interfere with perception?

Its role as a central nervous system depressant includes some reduction of inhibitions.

Does the chemical form part of a pattern of human socializing that fosters more open and effective communication?

No. The substance is not suitable to most aspects of social use because it is primarily an anaesthetic.

Do the immediate or longer-term effects of the chemical tend to cancel out immediate advantages in communication?

It is not especially toxic, though effects of repeated vasodilation might lead to complications in some cases. In the short-run, effects tend to be slightly cumulative.

Are there amounts, settings, or associations that may be sufficiently beneficial to outweigh disadvantages or disapproval about the chemical?

Variations in amount, setting, or association would not outweigh perceptual disadvantages.

In addition to these items, a fully comprehensive canvass of contemporary chemicals would include such elements of exotica and esoterica as bananas, hydrangea leaves, catnip, ether, cleaning fluids (carbon tetrachloride – *very* dangerous) and yohimbine. In the absence of valid data or wide circulation, these are left to your imagination or dismissal.

Finally, we come to a wrap-up question and its implied demand for some conclusions about chemicals and communication. Is there a chemical-free circumstance in contemporary society and, if not, how best can a workable pattern be arrived at?

So far as people in any numbers are concerned, it now seems uncomfortably evident that a chemical-free society is beyond our collective reach for quite some time to come. Interrelationships between the effects and defects of humans and the aims, activities, apparatus, and aspirations of contemporary society seem to be such that chemicals of some kind have become necessary adjuncts to life. We need them to help us perceive, to help make our perceptions bearable, and, from time to time, to blot out perceptions that we cannot stand. Do you know anyone who does not use at least one of the chemicals we have examined?

As a result, the challenge shifts to one of orchestration rather than elimination. We are called upon – individually and collectively – to figure out **optimum patterns** of chemical use.

From the point of view of communication – the fostering of ability to deal as thoroughly and as frequently as possible with an infinite number of variables infinitely expressed – these guidelines would seem to apply:

i/Stimulants are preferable to depressants because they do not usually interfere so much with receptivity.

ii/Potential habituation – physical or psychological – is to be avoided if at all possible.

iii/Enforceable law is best not broken. Awareness and ability to be aware both appear to suffer in direct proportion to the extent that an individual or society is concerned with concealment or preoccupied with fears about nighttime door knocks.

iv/Profound suspicion should be applied to observations and conclusions reached during times when a chemical – any chemical – has been imbibed. (For instance, the first draft of this litany was pitched out until the caffeine and nicotine wore off and, lo and behold, four errors were avoided.)

v/Individual tailoring is preferable to group-think. There is little point in using a chemical because others do: valid use serves an *individual* need or purpose.

vi/Discernible need ought to precede use – any chemical leads to a net loss or alteration of perception. Resort to one is justifiable so far as communication is concerned *only* when an omission, frailty, or brief need for oblivion can be seen and justified.

vii/Minimum amounts to achieve predetermined goals are preferable to open-ended consumption.

viii/Recurrent canvass of alternatives to chemicals is desirable. You may recall, for example, that even the most dedicated California acid-droppers eventually concluded that the purposes of their acid-dropping were really best served spiritually and intellectually rather than chemically.

ix/Non-clinical use is best treated with reserve – fusty, fussy, and expensive as they often are, clinicians do have training and experience with the human animal. Those that demonstrate caution, care, concern, and discretion can be lifesavers.

In sum, all our experience to date of any verifiable kind makes it clear that there is no chemical route to better communication that provides lasting, consistent, or especially excellent results. At best, chemicals can be of some use, some times, for some people.

In spite of all the qualifications, however, we can see that some aspects of sensory-cerebral extension are currently or potentially possible from various electromechanical and chemical augmentations. Or so it seems.

We can also see something else ... ever-growing difficulty in formulating and sharing data, impressions, arguments, and exhortations. As we are fulfilled or frustrated by our own eyes and minds, by attachments to them, by electrodes, or by chemicals, we tend to find greater and greater difficulty in conveying to each other what we perceive.

Now is the time to try to deal with one important aspect of such difficulties.

ON MAKING CONTACT

To this point, we have a fairly convincing case before us to support profound modesty about being human ... and to temper any hopes of ever really knowing what is going on. Our general catalogue of capacities – ordinary and augmented – is sufficiently flawed or unpredictable to make it quite clear that we constantly, routinely miss inputs of many kinds.

Moreover, some of the contents of this same general catalogue make it quite clear that inputs we do miss can lead to consequences that can be disturbing, damaging, or even fatal.

What then?

Individually, we cannot achieve omniscience. No way. But omniscience (or something darn close to it) remains a goal. The infinite number of variables infinitely expressed that comprise our assumed definition of 'reality' will persist in expressing themselves whether we perceive them or not. Just as you don't have to see or hear a bullet for it to kill you, failure to perceive a variable in the cosmic orchestration can be comparably unnoticed and comparably fatal.

We cannot afford the luxury of individual frailty. Survival demands more knowledge and skill than one individual is capable of perceiving, acquiring, or expressing. We must pool our information and experience. We must add to our ordinary sensory-cerebral capacity, and seek to foster means for its continued and rapid growth. You, me, Sarah Minge, Harold, the Admiral ... all sorts and shapes of humans ... are challenged to utilize everything available to reduce human incompleteness.

All right.

But this means contact.

This means shared understandings. This means intelligibility. Sarah Minge can scream

at 140 decibels, for example, but you or Harold or I or someone (not the Admiral ... he's deaf) has to receive a 140-decibel 'HELP' signal *and understand it* before the massed array of pooled technological, chemical, physical, and intellectual human talent can be brought to bear on her difficulty. Otherwise, poor Sarah may as well have muttered 'gribble' or given up entirely.

Clearly, then, it is necessary now to pause to consider contact in its many dimensions. Hopefully, with some judicious mixing of dogma and heresy we might emerge equipped to facilitate contact and understanding in our own interests.

How?

Let us try by testing out what we mean and can do with three key aspects of contact: i/languages, ii/links between languages, and iii/verifications of both languages and their links.

OK. What is language?

Words? Gestures? Settings? Objects? Silence? Symbols? Sounds? Space? You name it ... it's probably language.

This suggests that language in its broadest sense is a vehicle for expressing reality. Such a vehicle can be used by and among humans and also by and among other beings (porpoises, for instance) and even machines (such as computers or automated factory equipment) or between people and animals or people and machines. In sum, language can be said to encompass the *expression* of any of the infinite number of variables infinitely expressed in, at, or about us.

The vehicle becomes identifiable as language by being expressed. It is taken note of and facilitates contact as language when we, or other beings or machines, perceive the expression. It succeeds as language of contact to the extent that the cumulative perception matches up with the actual expression.

But that is no great help. We can weasel out by saying language is 'everything' – at the price of getting hoisted yet again on the problem of perceiving and describing 'everything.'

Let us turn instead to building blocks, and try to climb our way, a step at a time, from some agreed-upon specifics to something close to 'everything.'

Once again, then, what is language?

That's our present quest. We are reversing our usual process. Instead of starting with 'everything,' let us dump an assortment of objects and experiences on the table and ask ourselves what they are and how they relate to language. Hopefully, this approach will eventually make it possible to work our way back up the ladder to some tentative consideration of the 'everything' role of language.

First, let us examine one of the most concrete forms of language. Among other things, language may be discerned in the *manifestation* of an object or activity. Reasonably simply, such manifestations are acknowledged when we perceive the sounds, shapes, or other *shared* sensory impressions evoked by such an object or activity. But, surprisingly, there really aren't too many examples of manifestations that do evoke shared sensory impressions on anything like a universal scale.

The Admiral may rumble 'Damned nonsense' and point to his favourite oak tree as a reasonably universal manifestation, for instance. But, upon reflection, even he is likely to acknowledge that the clearcut 'oak tree' manifestation he has in mind triggers a number of different responses in different people and beings:
→ a grandmother's soul to some pantheists.
→ a large obstructing 'weed' to a suburban developer.
→ a lavatory to his dog Winston.
→ an item in an ecological system to a biologist.
→ a source of 1,000 board feet to a lumberman.
→ a home for, among others, an elderly owl.
→ a ??????? to the manifestation itself (and what do 'oak trees' call themselves?)

At best, we can get an idea of the possibilities of inherent and universal manifestation from some symbols and gestures. Maize and other cereals, for instance, all seem to share the manifestation of qualities of fruitfulness. Tilting your head with your hands palm to palm against your ear and your eyes shut seems to signify 'sleep' almost everywhere. The symbols of the international traffic code, now that automotive culture has become international, are perceived in a similar way fairly widely.

This, in turn, suggests what probably happens most of the time in human use of language. Instead of objects and activities being language merely by existing, they acquire identity of a relatively universal kind when language is *attached* to them.

In other words, we create labels for the manifestations. The Admiral's use of the words 'oak tree' then comes to stand for certain specified combinations of quality that he and many, many others over an extended period of time have learned to agree upon. One part of the label will express the 'treeness' that is commonly discerned. The other will express the 'oakness' that provides additional data to narrow the field.

How this comes about can be seen by observing the Admiral dealing with Harold on the day when Harold tried to carve a heart and Sarah's initials on that same oak tree. Roused, the Admiral marched from his porch and struck Harold smartly over the head with a rolled-up copy of *The Financial Post.* Returning to his rum, he reported: 'That'll teach him ... *whacked* the fellah over the head.'

'You ... *what*?' responded his housekeeper.

'I *whacked* that young fellah over the head!'

'What's *that* mean?'

(Whereupon the Admiral picked up his still-rolled copy of *The Financial Post.*)

whack!

The housekeeper understood.

In short order, as demonstrations of this kind are given, experienced, and observed, 'whack' comes to be a shared label for an activity. It becomes unnecessary to demonstrate further: the label is enough and requires much less exertion, as well as saving wear and tear on the newspapers.

Created labels that, through usage, become relatively universal provide most of our language for expressing our perception of finite objects and actions. Experiences, observations, and descriptions built up from the base of present and past labelling are mixed and through repetition acquire qualities of precision and communality.

Sometimes, as evidenced by acronyms such as laser (standing for *l*ight *a*mplification by *s*timulated *e*mission of *r*adiation), the very process of labelling is described in the word itself.

Furthermore, as the road signs suggest, such language need not be verbal or written. Gestures, variations in posture, facial expressions, changes in tone, and selection of trappings to go with such expressions, all comprise important parts of language. The human index finger, for example, can be used soundlessly to convey the meaning of a magnificent range of objects and activities.

So much for the easy parts. Any object, event, or action that can be experienced *at first hand* doesn't pose too many problems. In its finite aspect at least, a rose is a rose is a rose ... As with the admiral's 'oak tree' we can move from the general concept of 'roseness' to ever more specific concepts such as 'red,' 'perfumed,' 'Crimson Glory'' 'located in Sarah's front yard,' 'fourth from the left when you face the sidewalk,' and so on. (Surely you've located the damn thing by now!)

But when emotions, ideas, and other abstractions, or finite objects that are outside the range of one's own experience (such as aardvarks), are the subjects of language, we start running into difficulties.

For instance, I may wish that you could freem my blobbet since it's porgle *or* you may have gleeps in mind. We may have very clear *internal* understandings of the emotions, ideas, abstractions, and distant delights this situation involves. But how are we to share our understandings and be sure that the precise detail of what is meant is understood?

It's not easy. Just as 'sex' to a college admissions officer means whether the applicant is male or female while 'sex' to a psychiatrist includes the range from courtship to copulation, many of the expressions of our emotions, ideas, abstractions, and unshared experiences are, at best, approximations. 'Peace' can mean non-violence, or enforced agreement in a demonstration, or even a battle. January is 'summer' in Australia and 'winter' in the eyes of a North American. 'Beauty' can mean ... well, you name it.

In some cases, we have settled for imprecision.

now has become a concept label, so vague as to be almost totally adjustable to purpose, place, circumstance, and the current advertising campaign at work. So have many other words, gestures, postures, and expressions. Either the aspiration is simply too great to express or the understanding of it is too demanding to be widespread.

When we settle for imprecision, in turn, we must acknowledge a very sharp reduction in both the extent and the intensity of contact. While contextual factors such as purpose, place, and circumstance will serve to fill in gaps, it is possible to drift along in an essentially internalized manner, with each person adding his own private details, in his own mind, to fill in gaps left by common agreement to be imprecise.

So long as such private understandings don't come into conflict with one another or with finite labels we depend upon, this needn't matter too much. For example, Simon and Garfunkel indicate the workability of shared incomprehension in their recording of 'Dangling Conversations.' In that instance two old people (at least in their forties) talk about how they really don't communicate:

You're a stranger now to me
Lost in the dangling conversation
And the superficial sighs
From the borders of our lives.

(From Columbia 45 rpm 4-43728 'The Dangling Conversation' by Simon and Garfunkel) © 1966 Paul Simon. Used with permission of the publisher

We can even function adequately when not only comment but also aims differ, so long as they remain non-conflicting. Sarah Minge is 'in love' with Harold in the sense that she aims to fill lonesome voids in her life and is profoundly surprised and grateful that Harold is willing to spend time with her. Harold, on the other hand, is hypnotized by the prospect of readily-available carnal knowledge, which he excuses on the grounds that he is 'in love.'

Where we run into trouble is when internal understandings do come into conflict with each other or where specific and unpleasant results begin to flow from understandings that had seemed safely generalized and intangible. One person may have an internal understanding that 'beauty' includes goldenrod and skunk cabbage. This can lead to profoundly disturbed relations with hay fever victims, or with people with unduly sensitive senses of smell. Similarly, there is likely to be trouble when the generalized, intangible proposition 'peace' is translated into 'the war that will end war' as H. G. Wells pointed out in 1914 in his anti-war book so entitled.

(The first world war, like so many of its predecessors and successors, was claimed to be fought for 'peace' rather than commercial advantage, territorial aggrandizement, and political dictation. It was to be the last war – the war that would end war. As the substance of the actual aims of the hostilities became evident, the claims to be fighting for 'peace' wore pretty thin.)

We are compelled to acknowledge that, although imprecision may be harmless some of the time, there are occasions when it is absolutely essential to be **precise.**

Troubles too often arise from misunderstanding or misinterpretation.

Take the imprecise association of the word 'phosphate' with the sinful concept 'pollution,' for example. A person says 'phosphate' and right away the legions of environmental decency salivate and ring alarums. But practically speaking, in specific terms, the situation is much more ambiguous. One person's pollution (phosphates in detergents) may be another person's fertilization (phosphates in farming) or another person's cooking (phosphates in baking powder) or another person's rust preventative (phosphates used to coat iron). Without even considering some of the other pejorative aspects of the topic (social, economic, medical, and other needs on a cost-benefit scale), it becomes apparent that we need to find ways of assigning greater precision to our abstraction of 'pollution' as assigned to 'phosphate,' so that it can become a set of concepts appropriate to needs, threats, and balances between them.

Abstractions can be dangerous. Unless we seek to regulate language in precise terms it will tend (as it has in the past) to become an obscuring fog rather than a tool of reality.

What means do we have then to understand abstractions or finite objects outside our own experience?

There are three notable means – regulation, analogy, and empiricism. They are not wholly separate from one another and may actually be combined in many instances, but for the sake of simplicity, we'll take them one at a time.

1/Most often today, we start the language-making process with regulation. In the creative sense, someone will take an object, action, or idea and assign a label to it quite arbitrarily so that henceforth people will have an easy and precise way to refer to the object, action, or idea. (Of course, this works only if everyone else agrees to accept his label.) The Abbé Canavilles of the Royal Gardens in Madrid christened a hybrid flowering plant from Mexico with the name 'dahlia' in honour of the Swedish botanist, Andrew Dahl, who pioneered its introduction and use in Europe (oddly enough, with the aim of its being used as food rather than decoration). The Abbé said, in effect, 'That's a dahlia.' Others, reading his book, said 'Yes.' Thereafter a concept label existed.

Most of our experience with regulated language is not creative, however, but second hand. Rather than make up our own individual languages and suffer from problems of unintelligibility or continual explanation, we turn to dictionaries and related compendiums and accept the regulations set forth there. In such a way, provided the repository of rules is of some merit (not containing, for instance, 'God: See Love' and 'Love: See God'), we gather a fund of assigned meanings that provides us with language used by others and allows us to check out our own language as well.

Regulation is especially useful when the other two language tools falter. As we will see, there are limits to the use of analogy and empiricism. But, as any bureaucrat will confirm, regulations can be devised for anything.

2/Analogy involves drawing parallels. It is a technique often used in formulating language of regulation. It can also provide language on its own by drawing on our observations and knowledge of previous regulations.

With analogy we seek to build from existing experiences and language to new ones. We say, 'happiness is a warm puppy,' for instance, and provided everyone involved in the exchange has owned a puppy – and enjoyed it – or knows someone who has had such an experience, we have begun to gain an understanding of the strange new word 'happiness.' Yet we are still a long way from any complete or precise understanding of happiness. If we were to stop now, as too often happens, we might think we knew what 'happiness' meant – until we met it in a totally different context and had to start over again.

As we encounter more and more analogies indicating what happiness is, however, the once unintelligible abstraction becomes progressively clearer. Carefully, and usually fairly slowly, we build an inverted pyramid of shared language, extending outwards and upwards from our own relatively clear, accurate, and tangible experiences into the world of the unknown and intangible. (If you'll pardon the analogy.) So long as the language units are related accurately and are compatible with one another, the scheme works fairly well. If we slip into false analogies, however ('Zilch's Soup is like mom's apple pie'), portions of the language pyramid may well collapse.

3/Empiricism involves observation and experimentation, and frequently analogy and reference to regulation as well. If, over the course of examining several hundred uses of an abstract or intangible language label, certain reasonably clear and common denominators can be charted, then it is possible to set down a shared meaning justified by usage. When Harold's nephew came home with an unidentified blob and a worrisome label for it, his worried parents rushed the blob to the lab. There, careful testing designed to exclude some possibilities and confirm others gradually narrowed down the range until, finally, it was identified as ... lemon jelly (and not the germ warfare gel the nephew claimed). In just this way, language used for ideas, emotions, abstractions, and unshared experiences can often be given shared meaning.

A good language empiricist acts rather like a Martian ethnologist visiting earth for the first time. He notes, from his bank of tape recordings, printed matter, films, monuments, and other artifacts collected from various places, that there is a word of a somewhat abstract nature – say, 'truth.' He checks the ways in which it is used. He draws analogies with words already given sharable meanings. He looks to such regulation-defined words as he has to hand.

Gradually, certain common themes become apparent. His report might read as follows:

Truth (trooth; pl. –dhz), n. Quality, state of being true or accurate or honest or sincere or loyal or accurately shaped or adjusted, as *the t. of the rumour is doubted, there is t. in what he says, may depend on his t., wheel is out of t.*; what is true, as *have told you the (whole) t., the t. is that I forgot, am a lover of t.* (or. *T.* personified), *fundamental tt., home tt.* (unpalatable facts about oneself), GOD's *t.*, GOSPEL *t.*; *in t.* (literary), *of a t.* (archaic), truly, really; *to tell the t., t. to tell,* formulas introducing confession.

(And, at that time, he would have matched the third edition (1934) of the Concise Oxford Dictionary, and in fact would have used one of the methods followed by dictionary-makers themselves.)

To this point, then, we have gathered an aggregate that suggests, step-at-a-time, what 'language' is. As we lay it out, it indicates that 'language' is made up of individual words, sounds, symbols, gestures, objects, and settings which
→ manifest an object or activity
→ represent the manifestation of an object or activity
→ generalize an imprecision
→ create shared and precise meaning by analogy
→ create shared and precise meaning empirically, or
→ create shared and precise meaning by regulation.

That's one version of what language is, anyway. And in describing it in this way we arrive at our second major consideration – the links *between* languages. You see, what you have just waded through is not only an effort to grasp and indicate what 'language' is; it is a specific example of the importance of such links. My version or 'language' about a set of concepts has been very clear to me (and to Sarah, Harold, and the Admiral), possibly clear to you, and probably fuzzy and infuriating to professional philologians, linguisticians, grammarians, and the compilers of dictionaries.

How then are we to manage to bridge the many gaps in understanding, agreement, interest, degree of precision, intention, and mode of expression – not only between English and 'foreign' languages such as Japanese and Urdu, but also between people who share the same language groupings – such as neighbours or even one's own family.

(At this point, we should acknowledge parenthetically at least that there are wholly private languages entirely beyond the scope of bridges, definitions, or any other communication links. Sarah sometimes uses words in special and personal ways, mixing interior poetry, ignorance, personal emphasis, and inflections, and a variety of non-verbal tuning. Such highly individual language has not any primary interpersonal communication function and, frankly, is much too idiosyncratic for consideration here. Let us merely acknowledge that individual languages mean that there cannot ever be any one language that we all can share and, equally, there is no real possibility of total 100% communication of what we formulate individually and try to pass on.)

The effort involved in considering

links   between   languages

is the opposite side of the coin from the effort involved in formulating a definition of language. In seeking to define language, we seek – in the main – means to take a perception or conception of some kind in one person's mind and find a way of expressing it that will permit it to come into being in other people's minds. In seeking to link languages, we seek to ensure that the expressions that result can be re-expressed or played back in recognizable form.

In other words, language is Sarah Minge conceiving of and expressing her concept of 'I love you' to Harold.

Links between language are those procedures whereby Harold attempts to grasp the conception and formulation offered by

Sarah. They are also the attempts of any others in receipt of the communication from Sarah (including us) to manage clear and precise understanding.

Now, how can receivers of any and all kinds try to effect links between languages?

There are many means. We can use (1) 'translation,' (2) expanded experience, (3) assortments of wishful thinking, (4) attempts to catalogue and accommodate cultural variables, (5) the use of 'third-party' languages such as numbers, (6) attempts at other-direction.

1/*Translation* in the sense that is meant here includes more than the usual trading of words or gestures in one language for their equivalent in another. It demands efforts to match up meanings by relating intent, impact, and relativity. For example, the 'language' of one person may consist of such a scenario:
Sarah Minge, *as she perceives herself* (not too flattering a perception, alas, except she's proud of her tiny feet), *in a setting that affects her* (immediate effects of wine, candlelight, soft music; longer-term effects of lonesome apartment, dull job, nagging mother, and training in calculating personal prospects), *in a formulation that she has been taught a meaning for* (by magazines, TV, school, etc.) *says* (in mixture of words, posture, facial expressions, and nervous gestures of assent):

Then comes translation. Harold (to whom the sentence was offered as an evening's pearl), you, and I are seeking language links. We need to get to the nub of what that scenario really means to Sarah – and us – as we determine its intent, impact, and relativity. So ...

In an orchestration reminiscent of the co-ordinated muscular and mental skill involved in adjusting to a tennis serve, we start a series of translation scans. We note, as clearly as we can, Sarah Minge herself. We note the setting. We note the words, posture, facial expressions, and gesture.

We say to ourselves 'Now, if I were Sarah Minge, what would this extraordinary statement mean?'

And we add, almost inescapably, some extraneous and internal data of our own (such as alternatives to Sarah, perceptions of ourselves, our own sense of settings, and a host of other unpredictable imponderables).

What we come up with will be a 'translation.' It may work out as a straightforward perception of '*I love you*' much the same as that formulated by Sarah in the first place.

It may work out as 'I love you' blessed or menaced by wedding bells.

It may work out as 'Yes!' or 'I'm distracting you from those evil designs by talking nervously,' or 'Here is an invitation to a philosophical discussion,' or (if ordinary translation is involved too) 'Je t'aime.'

'Translation' is by no means a perfect way of linking languages. There are bound to be flaws in the process, probably inherent flaws. But since some useful links are fostered by it, it is better than nothing.

As with language itself, 'translation' is most likely to be accurate and effective when dealing with shared experience, or with perceptions that are tangible and relatively simple. As we move along the scale to the more abstract and complex – to emotions, ideas, and unknowns – 'translation' becomes progressively more daunting and, probably, more inaccurate.

2/Expanded experience almost speaks for itself. Language links grow as we grow. The wider our horizons of past and present perception are, the more extensive and precise they are, the less we have to rely upon 'translation.' When it is possible to say to oneself, 'I've been there,' in referring to place, activity, idea, or emotion, then the link between languages comes close to being the sharing of language.

In such a way, Harold, you, and I may actually have experienced a scenario very much like the one experienced by Sarah Minge. Because of that experience, we can come relatively close to Sarah's actual language throughout ... perhaps even moving our lips in sympathy.

3/This raises the function of wishful thinking. Often unconsciously, we seek to operate language links in terms of what we *want* the language we are receiving to mean, rather than what it does mean. We actually create a scenario and assign it to the person using language.

Sometimes, of course, we're close enough to get by. Sometimes it doesn't matter. And sometimes it can be disastrous.

4/Cataloguing and accommodating to cultural variables is an aspect of language linking that is difficult but, when successful, highly rewarding. European-North American party habits furnish an interesting illustration.

Roughly speaking, Europeans tend – because of their cultural conditioning – to talk to each other at a distance about six inches to one foot closer than North Americans. They feel that contact is best made at that range and at it they feel most comfortable.

North Americans, however, aren't used to that degree of proximity. Their cultural conditioning tells them – quite inaccurately in most cases – that language exchanges at European nearness are made only in circumstances of anger, hostility, or extreme intimacy.

So, at a party where guests are standing about nibbling canapés and quaffing refreshments, there is apt to be an

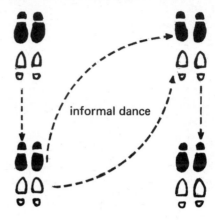

informal dance

in progress. The North Americans, uncomfortable at the unaccustomed proximity, keep moving back a step. The Europeans, seeking normal language contact, keep stepping forward. Almost unnoticed, the party is a gathering of people busily shuffling their way round and round the room.

Sensible cataloguing and accommodating to cultural variables deals with just this kind of problem. Language links are fostered as individuals teach themselves that, in this case, North Americans aren't stand-offish or Europeans aren't pushy and aggressive. The awkward ritual dance ends and, among other things, people stop falling over wayward footstools.

Essentially, such efforts are focused on the acquisition of cultural data (the fact, for example, that sports fans whistle when cheering in North America, but whistle when indicating disapproval in Europe) and on the use of such data in 'reading' the user of a language. When the data are sufficient and accurate and our reading competent, it becomes possible to turn any given output scenario into a received version that is useful.

5/Third-party languages play a part in cultural cataloguing; as well they serve as language links on their own. Latin, for example, has been used essentially as a third-party language ever since its living qualities vanished. Among other things, it has enabled doctors throughout the world to exchange precise information of a pharmaceutical and diagnostic nature in terms relatively free of the cultural 'static' of their own native languages.

Third-party language in this sense is not simply an effort to slip out of subjectivity. Most of us, naturally enough, do tend to modify or disguise subjectivity when we seek contact via language. We sometimes do this by using the grammatical third-person forms, such as 'one [really meaning "I"] would suspect that Sarah has marriage in mind.' But third-party language in the sense we are considering here is not disguised subjectivity; it is language of as bloodless and non-cultural a kind as possible, usually designed to be bloodless and non-cultural because it seeks to cross over the boundaries of passions and cultural assumptions.

The obvious advantage of third-party language links lies in their quality of removing, or at least downgrading, the demand for extensive 'reading' of cultural and subjective data by the language recipients. Instead, the language *user* takes on this task by putting his or her expression into third-party terms *before* setting out to make contact. Sometimes, in fact, a person can become sufficiently skilled at the third-party forms to skip the first-language step entirely (as in the case of cardinals chatting in the Vatican in elegant Latin).

As we will see in Chapter 11, some wondrous things can be done with third-party language. Ten-digit numerical codes, for example, can be used to collect and catalogue information of astonishing precision and complexity. Yet at the same time there is constant danger that recourse to third-party language will result in evasion of some very important aspects of contact. Simply because such languages are impersonal, non-cultural, and bloodless, they cannot help but introduce these same qualities into formulations and exchanges of information using them.

Already we have seen evidence of this. In contemporary society, a person **you** can become a **number**.

Your triumphs, tragedies, emotions, aspirations, past, present, and future can all become numerical designations. Unless great care and even greater range and complexity are accommodated in such third-party designation, there is very real danger of losing actual parts of yourself. Consider, for example, a situation like this:

'Hey Joe, we've got a 47-12, give him a 562 and send him to 423 for 0056,' may well be the formulation of the registration of a person for university admission. Translated, it comes back in day-to-day language as a graduate (**4**) of a state secondary school (**7**) with first-class standing (**1**) in biology (**2**). In turn, 47-12 is given an undergraduate (**5**) honours (**6**) standard first-year academic program (**2**) and sent to the departmental representative (**4**) dealing with uncomplicated enrolments (**2**) in standard courses (**3**) where he will be offered no comment on his program (**0**), no comment on other academic offerings (**0**), a list of required texts (**5**), and a standard fee form (**6**). Here, even though hypothetical, we can see the difficulties clearly. For instance, 47-12 (that may be you, remember) may despise biology, despite the first-class standing, but be unaware of possible alternatives. The standard first-year honours program may contain an optional course (say, Religious Knowledge) much better replaced by another one for that specific person. The departmental representative assigned to uncomplicated enrolments may be a new member of faculty who is unaware of options or alternatives and is too insecure to be interested in students in hundreds as human beings. Failure to comment on other academic interests may save time but fail to unearth this student's great keenness and capacity for, say, mathematics. And the standard fee form may be misunderstood as a binding contract for poor 47-12 that he cannot – when he does become aware he is dissatisfied – get out of for a year.

In sum, third-party language can be a qualified blessing.

6/Finally, there are the versions of language link provided by other-direction. In these circumstances – all too common, alas – the language-user reverses ordinary practice and assigns to his words, posture, expressions, gestures, and other language forms the meaning that his recipients seem to be using. The language link becomes a bid by the language-user to identify with the receivers.

An other-directed Sarah Minge would say 'I love you' only when her perception of Harold or you or I indicated that it was expected and appropriate *in our view.* Constantly asking, in effect, 'How am I doing?,' such a version of Sarah would seek answers from outside rather than from herself *and* the outside. And only to the extent that Sarah was *actually* all things to all people and highly skilled in the expression of all things to all people, would she be effecting productive language linkage.

Extreme forms of erroneous other-direction are fairly commonplace. Some of the more notable blunders of academic research, for example, have arisen from field studies in which those being studied set out to tell the researchers what they thought the researchers wanted to hear, whether it was accurate or not. (This is one reason why non-directive questioning techniques were devised. Field workers would ask, for example, 'Do you eat your babies?' The natives being studied would muse upon the answer they felt the questioners were looking for, or expected, and reply, 'Yes.' A year later, a fat monograph would report that 96% of the Ululanders questioned eat babies.)

However, when magic moments do occur and inner actuality does match with perceived expectation, selective other-directedness can be a most useful link. If Sarah actually does contain the assorted ingredients of an 'I love you' combination within her and sets out to pick the moment when it, by being directed by Harold or you or me, becomes a commonly intelligible contact ... **WOW!**

Now, what about the third aspect of contact: iii/verification of languages and of their links?

Almost the first thing we must do, even before attempting verification, is to scale down our expectations and assumptions. We have seen that the human animal is imperfect. Techniques and devices used by human animals are fallible too. At almost any moment and in almost every circumstance, flyspecks of error obscure and confuse our efforts to express language and perceive with language links.

This leads us to an aspect of verification that is too often ignored. Because of error, we must temper each step in the process with an understanding that the bids for contact, *and* our own evaluations of them, are operative only as probabilities or possibilities. They will even contain elements or qualities within them that may run directly counter to the intent being assessed.

So, a first step in verification is qualification.

We don't ask what the absolute and total purpose of a language expression is, we settle for queries about overriding aim or predisposition. We don't seek measurements of the exact language link system, we look for practical approximations of its most common and extensive qualities. And, whenever possible, we acknowledge that we may be measuring the wrong aspects or asking the wrong questions in the verification itself.

This pushes us back one more step from our central concern of knowing 'What is going on.' It underlines the probability that, just as the sensory-cerebral system of the human is imperfect, the data riding on it tend to be imperfect too.

All right. With such reservations in mind – and they are very important to keep in mind – what further about verification?

Part of the task of verification can be done purely mechanically – the more finite and material the subject, the more likely mechanical means will suffice. For example, computer systems can be set up to respond to the wave patterns of an assortment of key words spoken by one person. This works because both the meaning and the expression of some parts of human language are sufficiently finite to permit rather precise measurement. The meaning part can be turned into a third-language code calling for some kind of response, and the expression part can (as long as it is the same person each time, at present) set up electromagnetic wave patterns that are consistent enough to trigger the mechanical response. In this way, the operator can speak some words – 'start' or 'stop' or 'multiply' or 'divide,' plus a few object words as needed – to start a computer operating. The output can be verified by simple monitoring – as long as the meaning can be sketched out clearly enough and the mode of expression is reasonably consistent. (Remember 47-12!)

Another use of the mechanistic approach is found in content analysis. In its assorted forms, content analysis is i/a tool to match up expressions with the people likely to have used them (on the basis of past performance, vocabulary, historical accuracy, and the like), and ii/a means of lending sufficient tangibility to a language expression for it to be checked against the action, object, emotion, or abstraction it seeks to represent.

Such analysis has been used, for instance, to attempt to confirm that Shakespeare's plays were written by Shakespeare, and not (as some people argue) by Sir Francis Bacon. Great chunks of the writing attributed to each of these authors were examined for particularly distinctive stylistic patterns, and then compared for significant similarity.

Less seriously, except for those actually convinced, forms of content analysis were responsible for the argument in October and November 1969 that Paul McCartney of the Beatles had actually been dead since 1966 – despite his records and personal appearances. As the music journal *Rolling Stone* described the tale:

Evidently it got its start when somebody first noticed that there's a voice saying "Turn me on, dead man," on "Revolution No. 9" when played backwards.

This called for some "research" into earlier and later Beatles. On *Sgt. Pepper* it was noted that there is a hand over Paul's head on the cover (a Greek or American Indian sign of death), and on the back cover his back is turned. The guitar on the grave on the cover is left-handed, just like you know who.

On *Magical Mystery Tour* on the inside there's another hand over Paul's head. He's wearing a black carnation, although the others wear red ones. At the end of "I am the Walrus" somebody says, "I buried Paul." The walrus on the cover is the only personage there in black, and, as everyone knows, "the walrus is Paul" (source: "Glass Onion," *The Beatles*).

On *Abbey Road*, Paul is out of step with the other three on the cover, and are his eyes closed or not? The rumor says they are and that this is his funeral procession. Fred LaBour, writing in the Michigan Daily, University of Michigan paper, says John looks like an "anthropomorphic God, followed by Ringo the undertaker, followed by Paul the resurrected, barefoot with a cigaret in his right hand (the original was left-handed), followed by George, the grave digger." He points out that they are leaving a cemetery.

Rolling Stone, no 46, Nov. 15, 1969, p. 6

In effect, the mechanistic approach to verification is an attempt to reduce constructively the human factor in the process when this would seem to minimize rather than add to the probability of error. Sometimes, alas, human elements in the use of language verification merely contribute to a monumental waste of time or even error – as would be the case if we worked through all the possible semantic, social, economic, spiritual, and ideological implications of the 'Stop' on a stop sign every time we came to one.

We use much the same approach as the mechanistic one every day when we sift and evaluate the flood of routine data input all around us. Our structure of habit, for instance, is mainly a system for turning our perceptual system on 'automatic' so that it will tend to function relatively unthinkingly and uniformly when presented with familiar language and other cues. Such habit can provide important assistance in the verification of language and language links simply because significant variations in the habit-triggering inputs will not ring true. We get a kind of mechanical warning system service on the one hand, and the freeing of our sensory-cerebral systems for other activities on the other.

For example, good driving or flying involves the application of automatic scanning habits that trigger responses when something in the procedure is out of kilter. A pilot's good, and largely 'automatic' pre-flight check will flip out of 'automatic' only when the setting or behaviour of one of the instruments or pieces of equipment doesn't respond to his mental check-list as it should – possibly saving a life in the process.

Similarly, our attention level rises when an individual word or phrase doesn't fit in its context. Many newspapers and news agencies, for example, insist that writers use the order of expression 'now is' (instead of 'is now') because if there is a mistake in typing or typesetting, 'not is' is much more likely to catch the attention of editors (and so avoid lawsuits or other bothers) than 'is not.' Nothing can change a sentence's meaning more readily than a 'not' where it's not wanted.

Reliance on habit patterns, reasonably enough, is wholly contingent upon the assumption that the patterns are valid and open to actual verification. A habit that triggers

errør, érør, error or RAGE, RAGE, **RAGE**

at the sight of words or other language expressions such as 'long hair' or 'capitalist' or 'intellectual' or 'hard hat' or 'people's democracy' isn't really a verification process at all. It is a kind of mental shorthand that by-passes verification in favour of generalized, rather categoric, and frequently unthinking emotional outbursts. Such 'feedback' is in fact anti-communication, introducing, as noted in Chapter 1, static into the system.

So, in addition to habit, we need to consider other aspects of verification. We need to consider the individual and collective applications of empiricism, analogy, and regulation – those same techniques that were involved in the formulation of language in the first place.

Much of the necessary and useful verification of language and language links results from empirical effort – observation and experimentation repeated a sufficient number of times to permit cautious assumptions of probability about language and language links. The Admiral keeps muttering

megalomania

at certain times of the day. We observe this muttering and note that the word is used consistently in connection with individuals making grandiose claims in what might be called 'the insanity of self-exaltation.' Harold, as he emerges from the Admiral's sitting room, white-faced and shaken, tends to tell Sarah that 'the Admiral is going on again about madmen ...'

And, of course, we check ourselves. A glance at the newspaper page the Admiral has flung on the floor reveals that, true enough, 'the insanity of self-exaltation' is being manifested in terms of John Charles Grabbit's plan to buy the NHL or Count Luigi Grope's insistence on 25 Playboy bunnies at his table at the same time or President Ferdinand's decision to run for election simultaneously in Israel and the United Arab Republic.

In due course, we test out various sets of situations sufficiently often to establish a high degree of probability that when the Admiral mutters 'megalomania' and/or when Harold reports 'he's on about madmen again' and/or when we see a crumpled newspaper article about Grabbit, we are in the presence of the concept of 'the insanity of self-exaltation.' Both language and language link are saying the same thing.

Empiricism can also be used for verification of a defensive kind. Observation and experimentation can confirm that there is a considerable gap between the language and its ostensible language link. We note that the Admiral turns purple every time Sarah says 'peace.' And, with time and care, we can eventually discover that he is not a warmonger: the problem lies in the fact that Sarah means 'non-violence' and the Admiral thinks she means 'surrender.'

Verification by analogy involves asking ourselves what the word or phrase or other aspect of language being tested can be related to that is already proven. Often used in conjunction with empiricism and regulation, analogy can indicate what either or both of the expression and perception are like.

For example, Sarah (still at it) expresses

Verification for her can include analogy: 'love' ... like 'prefer your company,' 'enjoy hugging,' 'think you are beautiful, intelligent, and gentle,' 'feel an affectionate devotion,' and 'suffer symptoms of flushing, trembling and nervousness that I don't feel with anyone else.' She has discovered these items to be symptoms of love before and by analogy applies them to her relations with Harold.

Harold (also still at it) perceives 'I love you.' Verification in his case can include analogy substituting 'love' with 'am wild with desire,' 'enjoy hugging and ...' 'think you are beautiful, intelligent, and gentle,' 'feel an affectionate devotion,' and 'figure she wants me to (gulp) marry her.'

Such analogies, clearly, can help to indicate the ways and extent to which the language and language links are functioning in common. They can also provide useful clues for relating Sarah's and Harold's concepts to those that are possibly more universal (both regulatory and empirical) concepts of 'love.'

Regulation can also be used for verification of language and language links. A judicious study of numbers and estimates of authority can indicate that given bits of language and language link are accepted with a common meaning. In one case, there will be a version of consensus (80% of the language-users and language-receivers agree). In another, there will be acknowledgement of authority (if Mr Audubon says that is a striped grebe ... it's a striped grebe).

Here we find that Sarah's 'I love you' includes 'feel an affectionate devotion' ... and ... wait for it ... so does Harold's. When we turn to consensus, we find a recurrent pattern of relating 'love' to 'feel an affectionate devotion' on the part of a great majority of the users of the word. And, from our dog-eared book of regulations, the dictionary, out pops 'feel an affectionate devotion' too. So, Sarah, Harold, you, and I can all cite regulation as our input and authority for assuming that a measure of 'feel an affectionate devotion' can be assumed to apply to both the language and language link.

Mind you, there are some problems here. Sarah also says she 'loves' chocolate ice cream. Does this, by regulation, mean 'feel an affectionate devotion' too? Yes. And, alas, it indicates that Sarah is making sloppy use of language. On checking, we find that her analogies don't stand up to either empirical or regulatory verification. We find, in fact, that Sarah, in this case, is using highly subjective language that, although it just might scrape by via Harold's

96 language linking capability, won't pass either consensus or authority (dictionary) ... at least not until some changes are made.

Verification by regulation (aided by analogy and empiricism) serves much the same kind of function as a referee or judge. In the final analysis, language and language links depend upon decisions if they are to function at all as relatively universal means of contact. (Imagine the total confusion on the part of those who honestly worship and love objects if they were to hear Sarah say, 'I love ice cream.' According to them, she would be 'feeling an affectionate devotion.' And then ... for her to *devour* the ice cream!!!) Without decisions of some kind – and of course they can be amended or modified from time to time – language and the processes used for language links would run the risk of losing their meaning. Remember when 'giant economy size' actually meant *giant economy size* and we didn't have to achieve the meaning with 'super-jumbo' and so forth?

Let us sum up. To the extent that our aim, in seeking to know what is going on, is to facilitate contact, we are committed to the perception of how habit responses are triggered, what habit responses we share, and what they mean. And we are involved in a scale that necessarily includes a large number of people and a reasonable period of time.

Well then ...

Individually, we have seen, we lack the capacity and predictable competence to operate very well as monitors of multitudes of events involving many people and extended time periods. It seems to be becoming evident that we need to consider various forms of *pooling* of language and language links.

In other words, we still cling to the hope of getting close to some 'reality' – that old infinite number of variables infinitely expressed – but we also begin to acknowledge that, with the materials known and available, we can't guarantee the results.

Our individual senses are imperfect.
Our augmentations of senses are imperfect.
Our languages are imperfect.

There remains the possibility that through repetition, cross-reference, care, and a portion of luck, we may with our varied combinations of perception actually be able to chart some facets of reality accurately. We may manage close-to-infinite expression of some variables, for instance. In such careful and concentrated groping, it may well be that collective efforts will prove to be helpful.

So, let us turn now to pooling in practice – to the systems of communication that we have about us to serve collective purposes. We can check out their capacities and competences, and seek to see what we gain.

We can begin with the so-called mass media – print, radio, TV, and film.

PRINT

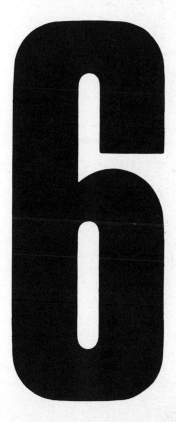

With the help of the Most High at whose will the tongues of infants become eloquent and who often reveals to the lowly what he hides from the wise, this noble book Catholicon has been printed and accomplished without the help of reed, stylus or pen but by the wondrous agreement, proportion and harmony of punches and types, in the year of the Lord's incarnation 1460 in the noble city of Mainz of the renowned German nation, which God's grace has deigned to prefer and distinguish above all other nations of the earth with so lofty a genius and liberal gifts. Therefore all praise and honour be offered to thee, holy Father, Son and Holy Spirit, God in three persons; and thou, Catholicon, resound the glory of the church and never cease praising the Holy Virgin. Thanks be to God.

Colophon of the *Catholicon,* printed by Johann Gensfleisch zum Gutenberg in Mainz, 1460. Quoted in S. H. Steinberg, *Five Hundred Years of Printing* (Harmondsworth: Penguin Books, 1955), p. 19

Gutenberg was greatly excited by print. Not only did it ease the eye strain of some indifferent handwriting, it made possible the exact reproduction of data in one form for dissemination over a wide area at roughly the same time.

Humans could not help but benefit – in numbers and in the predictable quality of what reached those greater numbers.

What Gutenberg didn't entirely forsee, however, was the explosion of print of the 19th and 20th centuries ... to the point where it became *the* vehicle for the expression and exchange of information and ideas throughout the world.

Print became a great pooling device. On the one hand, the imperatives of the Industrial Revolution resulted in mass literacy. People had to be able to read in order to use the instruction manuals, heed the urban offers of wondrous employment, follow the dictates of distant sales managers, and fill in time as their work days shrank to as little as twelve hours.

On the other hand, machines and processes came forward to foster the ever-more-rapid preparation, reproduction, and distribution of printed material. Typesetting machines, rotary presses, the typewriter, newsprint and fast-drying inks, rotogravure, and more recently lithographic offset printing of pictorial material, and a host of other technological developments combined to create a capacity to serve – and even court – the new millions of readers, the possessors of mass literacy.

The turkey and a hungry man had been brought together. For the first time in human history, relatively simultaneous contact with data became a possibility for millions of people. Individuals acting and reacting together could take giant steps ... far beyond the scope of their simple or augmented sensory-cerebral selves. The results could be standardized in print – clarified and simplified so as to serve the common denominator of human perceptual capacity.

More important, the principle of proxy was firmly established on a mass scale. Humans found that some of their limitations could be modified or sidestepped. Sight no longer was restricted to simple individual or binocular range: it became the *collective* sight of many hundreds of pairs of eyes in many hundreds of places – all seeing at roughly the same time. So too with the other senses.

What we got with print (and later, to a degree, with other media) was a highly useful combination. Existing language, cast in alphabetic (as opposed to symbolic) terms, was married to a form of expression that was able to reproduce its characteristics on a relatively universal scale. This, of course, meant that some of the characteristics of alphabetic language itself (linearity, in particular) were carried forward and certain additional characteristics inherent in print were added.

What resulted was a proxy agent combining the alphabetic version of language (remember we noted in Chapter 5 that language also includes gestures, sounds, and other qualities) with means of widespread dissemination in a standardized form.

(It is rather important to remember that a combination is involved here. The examinations and evaluations of print that follow do not attempt to separate aspects that are purely alphabetic-language from those that are purely print. Print is taken to be one of the expressions that encompass alphabetic-language characteristics. By dealing with print, we deal by implication with alphabetic-language qualities, although these same qualities may be found to varying extent in language as used in radio, TV, film, and other expressions that follow.)

Note that a principle of proxy – of

MASS PROXY – is involved.

Proxy means 'agency of substitute or deputy.'

Mass proxy, for the purposes of our enquiry, involves many substitutes or deputies acting on our behalf.

In other words, we do not do much of the seeing, hearing, feeling, tasting, or touching ourselves. Others do it for us. *And* their account of each cerebral-sensory experience comes to us via mass media – in this case print.

Well then, what about such proxies? What about the human and other substitutes or deputies?

What about the print itself?

Clearly, we have to check. Blind surrender to the principle of proxy could be a grave mistake. Either the people or the print – or both – acting on our behalf could be faulty. Either or both could also possess in their very natures misleading or distorting qualities.

Let us try to step outside the bounds of our ordinary (and frequently unquestioning) familiarity with print and its agents. Let us

try to forget the grandfatherly qualities that tend to encourage us to take print and its agents for granted.

Instead, assume that print and its agents are upon us for the first time (as was the case, it is said, with the Chinese in the 6th century). They are offering (among other things) to act on our behalf – to facilitate the pooling of human perceptions so that we may better know what is going on.

What characteristics – superb ... and sinister – are we being offered?

On the superb side, there are some undeniable advantages. Probably most important is the relative permanence of print. Since we have faulty and frequently faltering senses, it is very handy indeed to have an expression that will sit there for all the time we need to focus, sense, and seek to understand it. For example, if for some reason you have made a pact with yourself to read this paragraph, you don't really have to worry too much. It will still be here after you blink, blow your nose, go to the bathroom, take a coffee break, have a nap, come back from hospital, or whatever else your frail human condition conjures up to plague you. Try it and see.

Furthermore, such relative permanence is the handmaiden of an associated set of advantages. It allows you to check back on facts (and so make a leaky memory bearable). Even better, it allows you to leap ahead (and so ease the agonies of suspense). Whereas words spoken or otherwise briefly presented tend to make perception an all-or-nothing challenge,

print sits there

– ready to be sensed and reviewed as much and as often as necessary.

Print is also relatively orderly. To be used effectively, ideas, images, arguments, descriptions, and all the other expressions humans may put into print, have to be sorted out enough to be cast into separate and distinct words and, most of the time, sentences. This isn't dictated by whim or fancy, the very mechanics of print demand such order and finiteness because the machines can't function otherwise. At least, this is true of traditional methods of typesetting and composition, and even the increased flexibility now possible is available only at a premium in cost so far.

For our faulty and faltering senses, such order is a positive blessing. Some of the selection, weighting, simplification, and clarification of data is done for them – reducing, if the job is done properly, the risks of human error on the part of the receivers. Anyone who has ever tried to assemble a thingamajig from a mail order catalogue without good printed instructions can testify to these advantages.

At the same time, print is reasonably flexible. Variations in type size and shape, in arrangement of words on a page, and in the use of filled and blank space, can assist the expressions of an impressive variety of nuances of meaning, emotions, emphasis, or assumed importance.

For example, this collection of words not only represents a showcase of type resources but also a reasonably wide range of emotions and meanings.

Such flexibility further facilitates perception. Print that helps set a mood or indicates emphasis provides relatively clear cues or guidelines. It can help the reader function with even somewhat less personal sensitivity than normal (for example, when he has a bad cold or is over-tired), or, conversely, it can enhance his sensitivity by directing his senses in their concentration. (Print says, for example, 'Brain, this is a love story ...' Brain then can concentrate on its love memories, love senses, and love organs.) Typography can enhance such effects.

Print is also relatively universal in that it is able to present its content as a common denominator. The first and millionth copy of the print presentation will be the same, apart from some slight wear and tear on the plates. All the words, punctuation, page numbering, footnotes, illustrations, and arguments will fall in exactly the same place and order.

This is very important. As a consequence, it is possible to stabilize the stimulus or message that is transmitted. Everyone using the same item of print will be receiving the same output. And while variations will persist in the conditions in which this output is received, and in the use and comprehension applied to it, some common observations can be made (such as, 'There is a misprint on page 276'), and all readers may be able to draw on a certain amount of common language.

Furthermore, print is inherently self-disciplining. Everyone has a threshold below which he or she cannot absorb the meaning and message of print. If *anything* in the chain from eye to mind tends to wander, then the communication process shuts down. Print ceases to be a process for conveying impressions and fades into the background ... indistinguishable from all the other static present.

This means that print contains a built-in demand for attention of a kind not present in any of the other basic procedures we examine. As a result, there is a much better than usual prospect that senses organized to receive the communication will be as well organized as possible, and, in turn, will pass on as accurate a series of mes-

sages as possible. The situation won't be perfect or of uniformly high standard, but it *will* tend to be better than usual.

For example, ask someone to read this paragraph to you and jot down what you think it said. Then read it yourself and make similar notes. Unless you are a very unusual person indeed, the notes from your own reading – with attention focused by the discipline of print – will be fuller and more accurate than those from someone else reading to you – when your senses are freer to wander.

Similarly, print has the built-in advantage of adjustable demand. Unlike other extensions of the senses, print does not require the reader to match its pace. Print has no pace. It just sits there. Readers can make print work to their pace, instead of the other way around.

Permanent ... orderly ... universal ... flexible ... self-disciplining ... variable in pace ... those are the primary advantages of print in our communal attempt to make reality manageable. But, like all pleasures and advantages these days, positive characteristics are offset in part at least by disadvantages.

First of all, as has become a popular refrain, print is *linear.* Just as the mechanics of print can be praised for their order, they can be damned for their requirement that words, sentences, ideas, and emotions be presented one at a time and usually in rows and columns.

Each   word   has   to   be   set   down   in   its own   place   and   no   other   word   can   be placed   there   or   there   will   be   a   blot   (oops) black blob that no one can read or understand. Equally, the mechanics of print have traditionally required that the print be set in lines. When a line is printed this way, the typesetting is relatively simple and straightforward, but if
you   this,
write a   like
line

you give the typesetter a headache and increase the cost and complexity. Further, lines that run in neat columns, one below the other from top to bottom of the page, again serve the mechanical preferences of print, whereas if you put one line here

>   and another line here
>   and another line here
>   and yet another here
>   and still another line here,

you aggravate the costs and complexities even more.

Of course, *habit* is a very significant ingredient in this situation. Everyone is taught to read in a linear way, from the 'Run John run' stage up to Fanny Hill. Everyone moreover is encouraged to expect and follow standards of neat rows and neat columns. (Remember those primary school gold stars for neatness and the use of margins?) To a certain extent, even if print were routinely freed of the constrictions on its format of cost and complexity, its consumers might very well continue to insist on physical linearity.

But this is not really what Marshall McLuhan and others mean when they talk about the linear nature of print. They are more concerned with content. By its nature print tends to express physically a beginning (where the printing starts) and an end (where the printing stops). No matter what you do, there is no really effective way to get around this.

Various writers have tried to avoid or modify linearity – e. e. cummings, James Joyce, Ezra Pound, and McLuhan himself, to name a few – but their experiments have had but qualified success. Not only are problems of cost and composition involved, but there also seems to be high reader resistance. Print consumers keep insisting on formats that they are familiar with and which don't take too much time to read.

So, with mainstream mass media, there really is little practical leeway. Either the print is there or it isn't. Some variations are possible with lightface and boldface type, and variations in type size and style, but the inexorable fact of some kind of beginning and some kind of end still remains.

Consider this space, for example:

(See, my invisible aside prior to this sentence doesn't exist so far as you are concerned. For your purposes, this sentence began with 'See' and all the gestures or curses, or loving phrases, or indecent suggestions, or strange rumbles that went before don't exist. And in just the same way, this section, for you, will end when the bracket is closed ... *not* when I finish my additional comments in the invisible space afterwards!)

Now, even when working in terms of trying to scale reality down to manageable size that we can cope with, such linearity *is not a help.* There is a great deal of evidence and a considerable probability that reality is not – even in approximation scaled down – at all linear. As suggested in Chapter 1, reality involves a fantastic range of *simultaneous* variables of every conceivable kind, size, shape, and dimension (plus a few others that aren't conceivable too).

Consider love again.

In print, the best that can be hoped for is for Sarah to say

I Love You

and maybe follow this with, say, 60 pages of purple prose amplifying on the shades, degrees, qualification, dimensions, and details of what is encompassed in 'I love you.' But, *note this,* it will be purple prose following. There is just no way for poor Sarah to express the simultaneous, multi-dimensioned, tangential armada of variables as they occur at just the one instant. In fact, by the end of her 60 pages of purple prose, Sarah may have actually changed her mind because Harold has fallen asleep. Or her senses may have become totally and differently engaged by a great gastric heave. Or an irate Admiral in a rumpled dressing gown may have appeared to break the expression off after only 12 pages.

In this sense, then, print tends to *remove us from reality.*

In addition, such linearity – with its inescapable flavour of beginning and end – serves to *condition expectations* in a way that is opposed to reality. The more a person is led to expect beginnings and ends from print, and the more that print plays a central part in efforts to express and perceive reality, the more a person comes to believe honestly that reality involves beginnings and ends.

But does it? We don't know the absolute answers, but within the absolutes, we have, again, a great deal of evidence that suggests that many, many parts of our day-to-day reality don't involve beginnings or ends at all. For example, with very few exceptions, it is impossible to say that any familiar thing really began at any specific

point. Print may say, or at least imply, that something began when Sarah said 'I love you!,' but we know (and so does Sarah if she pauses to consider objectively) that many of the ingredients leading up to the statement go back to the whole spectrum of experiences and conditionings involved in Sarah, Harold, their parents, their communities, their ancestors and so on. If Sarah's great-great-great-grandfather hadn't been enchanted by a beautiful Iroquois maiden in 1848, he would have gone on to Australia (and died in a mine disaster before marriage). If ... and so on ... with every possible beginning actually contingent upon something relevant, even important before it.

Equally, what *ends* with Sarah's statement?

So, in this sense too, print's quality of linearity laced with beginnings and ends tends to *remove us from reality.*

Now, we can take a bit of a breather with some of the simpler disadvantages of print. Obviously, print suffers from several structural disabilities that aren't characteristic of the real world.

→ Print doesn't move ... the world does.
→ Print is silent ... the world isn't.
→ Print (so far as regular content is concerned) is tasteless, touchless, and odourless ... the world (gasp) isn't.

These limitations become important when the central element in the particular reality being perceived requires one of the missing dimensions. For example:
Print can say 'the speed of sound' but this doesn't workably convey anything close to the full sense of acceleration or motion.
Print can say 'a standing ovation' but this doesn't workably convey the substance of that sound or make it comparable to other sounds.
Print can say 'unwashed hippie' but this doesn't workably convey the sense of either stench or liberation (depending on your point of view) involved in the actual odour.

Experience, of course, can help modify such disabilities. If the reader has experienced the dimensions of the speed of sound, or a standing ovation, or an unwashed hippie, the words in lifeless print have vitality and meaning beyond the page. But it is only a qualified gain. The print itself remains inert. The more perception must depend on that fundamentally inert expression rather than on the actual sensation, the more contact with reality is diminished.

A very good example of this is provided every Monday in North American newspapers. Almost without exception they print a report on week-end accidents, something like this:

Weekend Accidents Claim 74
Ontario Toll On Roads 13

By The Canadian Press

At least 74 persons died accidentally across Canada during the weekend, 52 on the highways.

A Canadian Press survey from 6 p.m. Friday to midnight Sunday night, local times, also showed 14 drownings, five fire deaths, one person electrocuted, one killed in a fall and one in an airplane crash.

Quebec reported 22 fatalities, 19 in traffic, one fire victim, a drowning and the plane crash victim.

Ontario had 16 deaths, 13 on the highways and three drownings.

British Columbia had six traffic fatalities and three drownings.

Alberta recorded eight deaths, four in traffic, three by drowning and one person killed in a fall.

Six persons died in highway mishaps in Saskatchewan, where one person was drowned and one was electrocuted.

In Newfoundland, four children died in a fire and one person was killed in a traffic accident.

Nova Scotia had a single traffic fatality and two drownings.

Two persons died in traffic accidents in Manitoba and one person drowned in New Brunswick.

No fatalities were reported in Prince Edward Island.

The survey does not include industrial accidents, known suicides or slayings.

The Ontario dead:

SUNDAY

Garnet Gordon Schmidt, 16, Arthur, in a three-car accident near Arthur, 20 miles northwest of Guelph.

Thomas Locke, 17, and Michael Edward Beatty, 18, both of Owen Sound, and John Frederick Connors, 19, Stoney Creek, when their car went off the road and rolled over four miles west of Owen Sound.

Joseph Mailleur and an unidentified boy, both 6 and from Cornwall, when they fell off the boat they were playing in on the Cornwall canal.

SATURDAY

Mathew Caris, 23, Warwick Township, and Louis Parsons, 18, Watford, in a car-truck collision near Watford, about 20 miles east of Sarnia.

Stephen Brothwick, 18, Sarnia, in a two-car collision in Sarnia.

James Edward Furlong, 19, Dunnville, when his car went into a ditch.

Irene Filiatrault, 52, North Bay, when her car rolled over at North Bay.

Harold Dean Null, 32, Mishawaka, Ind., and an unidentified woman from Bolivia, in a two-car crash just east of Woodstock.

Welby Neil Jamieson, 20, St. Catharines, when the car in which he was a passenger struck a tree near Brockville.

Margaret Veronica McNish, 43, Kirkfield, Ont., in a two-car crash near Glen Arm, 40 miles northwest of Peterborough.

Howard Vance, 22, Ottawa, when his sailboat capsized during a race on the Ottawa River.

Kitchener-Waterloo Record, June 22, 1970, p. 15

The reality of what the print expresses is quickly lost. Most people aren't regularly involved in accidents – some never are. Few people actually know the victims, or the location of many of the accidents. Very soon, what starts out as a reality involving pain, anguish, loss, folly, and destruction diminishes to the proportions of a box score – a minor diversion. Our senses, instead of being aided and enriched in their perception, are dulled. Reality, instead of being scaled down to manageable proportions, is

almost wiped out.

The consequences grow over time. Since print tends to persist as our principal medium of record, the initial inadequacies tend to be perpetuated and enhanced. The survivors die or disappear, the first-hand memories fade, the other more ephemeral records (such TV videotape, recording tape, and even film) are disposed of or deteriorate. Print looms ever larger as the account of events in all their multiplicity. Scholars burrow away in newspaper and magazine archives, dig up pamphlets and printed broadsheets and many tend – from the natural consequences of extended exposure – to take the print accounts more seriously.

Not infrequently, this means that history and understanding are both substantially reshaped to conform with the print version and the print emphasis. And so the reality ceases to be the retained truth: the frail and faulty account in print takes its place. We no longer settle for a scaled-down version of reality, we accept a reshaped version – an alternative reality – instead.

The Great Man approach to history exemplifies this at its most extreme. Although contemporary scholars are beginning to try to move away from chronicles based on kings, the nobility, and others in the narrow world of printed documents, their efforts are limited by the ephemerality of the alternatives. Oral history is essentially a 20th century phenomenon – apart from a few tribes that have managed to keep clear of print. Relatively few artifacts, buildings, clothes, or even games have survived to provide data. The whys and whats of average, representative people either died with them or lingered in distorted fragments. Print has secured huge advantages for its versions of our pasts.

Related to this limitation are the special problems encountered in trying to express abstractions verbally, and particularly in print.

As we all know from direct and sometimes embarrassing experience, there are some things, events, experiences, ideas, and other communications that just can't be expressed adequately in words at all.

General labels are about the best we can do: intuition, 'sense,' 'feel,' unconscious perception, hate, love, freedom, and the like.

That's the problem. While the actual dimensions of reality seem to contain an important measure of wordless variables, there is no way for print to convey more than the vaguest hint at best. The rest of the reality is lost.

Consider, for example, the great fumbles made in the late '60s in trying to convey the substance of 'soul' in music. Some people who made the effort settled for a check list of those with 'soul' and those without it (and, curiously, the lists varied and often conflicted). Others erupted into clouds of vague nouns and adjectives, in the hope that by sheer weight of cumulative connotation the meaning would begin to trickle through. Still others turned flatly fatalist ('Like, you've either got soul, man, or you haven't ... you know ...').

Mind you, it is not fair to blame print entirely. Print is based upon letters and words – upon language. If the language underpinning print is faulty, vague, or absent, then print will suffer accordingly. The only difference will be that language can be in other contexts clarified, amplified, and otherwise supported by gestures, wild sounds, aspects of 'atmosphere,' and similar immediate sensory cues; print cannot be so enhanced to anything like the same extent. It may utilize drawings and tables and pictures but little else. Print, then, is cast in the role of a somewhat limited accomplice of language and, inevitably, its incapabilities mean that *our grasp of reality suffers.*

An Arbitrary Guide to Soul

Fortunately, soul is not the exclusive possession of good guys who are losers, or even of bad guys who are winners. As a guide to further understanding, here is a totally arbitrary gallery of familiar figures from legend, history and the arts, who by their works or hangups are either elected to the Valhalla of Soul (YES) or relegated to Straight City (NO):

YES		NO	
Aaron	Luther	Moses	Calvin
Bonnie	Marat	Clyde	Robespierre
Bottom	Melville	Titania	Hawthorne
Billy Budd	"Mona Lisa"	Fletcher Christian	"Nude Descending
Aaron Burr	Napoleon	Alexander Hamilton	a Staircase"
Charlie Brown	Oedipus	Orphan Annie	Wellington
Catherine the Great	Molly Pitcher	Frederick the Great	Jocasta
Holden Caulfield	Pocahontas	Andy Hardy	Betsy Ross
Charlie Chan	Pogo	Sherlock Holmes	John Smith
Cleopatra	Pope John XXIII	Julius Caesar	Daddy Warbucks
Coleridge	Baron von Richthofen	Wordsworth	Pope Pius XII
Dickens	Teddy Roosevelt	Thackeray	Kaiser Wilhelm
Disraeli	Rosencrantz	Gladstone	Franklin Roosevelt
Dostoevsky	and Guildenstern	Turgenev	Hamlet
Dracula	Rousseau	Superman	Voltaire
Fagin	Shakespeare	Oliver Twist	Bacon
Faulkner	Sitting Bull	Hemingway	Custer
Homer	Snoopy	Vergil	Sandy
Fanny Hill	Socrates	0	Plato
Captain Hook	Strindberg	Peter Pan	Ibsen
Julia Ward Howe	Swift	Francis Scott Key	Pope
Huck Finn	Thoreau	Tom Sawyer	Emerson
Don Juan	Tom Thumb	Casanova	P. T. Barnum
Thomas Jefferson	Tonto	George Washington	The Lone Ranger
Jesus	Nat Turner	St. Peter	John Brown
Job	Whitman	Jeremiah	Longfellow
Kierkegaard	Mary Worth	Hegel	Prince Valiant
Lawrence of Arabia	Christopher Wren	T. E. Shaw	Frank Lloyd Wright
Leatherstocking	Ferdinand	Daniel Boone	The Wright Brothers
Robert E. Lee	von Zeppelin	U. S. Grant	

Time, June 28, 1968, p. 48

To this point, we have examined print as an impersonal process. We have noted the characteristics that apply to this process, including linearity, relative permanence, and limited range of sense-stimulation related to content. Now it is time to add people and some of their characteristics to the process.

There is an important distinction involved here. Apart from the consequences that derive directly and almost automatically from the inherent nature of print, print takes on some characteristics and colourations *as they are assigned to it.* These additional and variable qualities are primarily the work of people. Print doesn't tell lies ... lies are told in print. Print doesn't censor or bias itself ... censoring and bias are applied to print. Print doesn't select itself ... print is selected.

It is the

people-print combination

that requires attention if we are to go beyond the purely functional characteristics of the transmitters alone. This calls for a brief examination of some familiar propositions:

→ The people-print combination is especially vulnerable to censorship.

→ The people-print combination is subject to economic pulls and pressures.

→ The people-print combination is beset with value judgments.

→ The people-print combination tends to be past- rather than present-oriented.

Such propositions, of course, don't apply everywhere all the time. Rather, they indicate possibilities that attach themselves to print when people are added. They will be applicable to varying degrees depending on the specific blend of the specific people and the specific print process involved in specific communications.

Consider people-print and censorship for a start. With print comes the recurrent fact of fixed physical position. Most commercial printing operations are still too heavy, too complex and delicate, and too unwieldy to be readily transportable. It is relatively easy to track down and supervise the products of mass media printing. The people involved possess other vulnerabilities. While a dictator won't get far seeking to imprison, terrify, brainwash, or exhort a printing press, he can do rather well with people. It is the proud boast of behavioural science that, given time and equipment, any person can (usually) be converted or (alternatively) silenced. And you can usually locate the printer (or at least bar him from his tools) by locating the printing press.

The spectrum of possible censorship is much wider, however, than the old-fashioned idea of a censor (paid by the government, or the owner) blue-pencilling offensive or 'dangerous' passages. More common today, at least in our immediate experience, is the more efficient procedure of self-censorship by anticipation and conditioning. The *New York Times,* for example, accepted self-censorship of information about the Bay of Pigs fiasco in Cuba on the grounds that the 'national interest' was at stake. British publications accept the principle of 'D' notices calling for voluntary suppression of material on 'security' grounds. Publishers everywhere muzzle their presses in response to regulations about such topics as 'obscenity' and 'sedition,' as hazily outlined – and seldom tested – in criminal and related law.

Depending upon motive and point of view, such censorship may be good or bad – but that's not the point. So far as an individual's perception of reality (warts and all) is concerned, any censorship distorts reality.

Such an assertion acquires a little extra bite, perhaps, when one recalls the point made in Peter Watkins' book and film *The War Game* in 1967:

On nearly every single aspect arising from the threat of a nuclear war which has been indicated in the last twenty pages of this book there has been practically a complete silence in the press and on television during the last ten years in Great Britain
Silence on the entire theory of the nuclear balance of terror, and where that theory might one day fail
Silence on the strategic worth and cost of Britain's own nuclear weapons system
Silence on Britain's resources in terms of grappling with full-scale evacuation and other emergency measures
Silence on the entire system of regional seats of government and the post attack administration
Silence on the probable effect of a mid-range nuclear attack on Britain, and silence on the effects of nuclear weapons themselves
Silence ...

Peter Watkins, *The War Game* (London: Sphere Books and Andre Deutsch Ltd., 1967), p. 36

CENSORSHIP

Out, Damned Spot!

Readers usually don't know what they're missing, but every newspaperman knows about the office taboos—words that can't be printed and sights that can't be shown. The Chicago Daily News, a reasonable paper in other respects, used to paint out the nipples of male wrestlers and other shirtless athletes. The Atlanta Journal supplies shirts. Before passing an ad for the movie *The Love Makers*, in which Claudia Cardinale reposes on the chest of Jean-Paul Belmondo, the Journal daubed a tunic on Belmondo. In Southern California, where semi-nudity is a way of life, the Los Angeles Times does its best to spare readers what they can see on any beach.

The Scandinavian Airlines System recently submitted to the Times a full-page ad that had already appeared in other newspapers and magazines. It showed an inviting, bikini-clad blonde above the caption: "What to Show Your Wife in Scandinavia." But it clearly was not what to show your wife in Los Angeles. Before running the ad, the Times censor scrupulously amended the blonde's anatomy to conform to regulations. He removed her navel.

What to show your wife in Scandinavia

UNBOWDLERIZED SAS AD

What to show your wife in Scandinavia

RETOUCHED AD

What not to show in Los Angeles.

Time, March 6, 1964

Economic pulls and pressures mix the people-print combination in slightly different ways. In somewhat simplified terms, the mixture arises from the fact that on the one hand there is finite cost involved in any print process and on the other hand there is a limit on the funding that people can or will make available.

These expressions will vary enormously in practice, from tatty processes to technological triumphs, from vicariously evangelistic patrons to state subsidy. But, whatever the specific relationship may be, it will come down to a bid for costs to be met combining with a willingness to put up the cash or materials.

The *requirements* involved in matching up the demands of print with the willingness of potential revenue-producers are the points at issue. From the print side, the requirements are those that affect the actual physical output – quality of paper and ink, excellence of typeface, capacity and excellence of press, and so on. To a workable degree, there is a reasonably close correlation between cash resources poured in and technically superb product coming out.

From the people side, the requirements are those arising from the purpose of the print – information, circulation and sales, argument, evangelism, recreation, and, occasionally, the reconstruction of reality regardless of expense. Here the abundance, security, and certainty of the resources to be assigned depend on the way in which the print purpose relates to resource-holding purpose.

It is much more likely, then, that economic pulls and pressures will tend to work in favour of big, well-heeled units (private and public) as opposed to small, impecunious units. Such units – be they advertisers, subscribers, sponsors, or states – will call the tune. The extent to which such tunes are muted, modified, or re-written versions of reality will be the extent to which print's presentation of reality suffers.

In practice, fortunately, the economic consequences of people-print tend to have a partly self-correcting element built into them. Relatively few print organizations can cater entirely to the whims of one side of their existence without risking serious damage to their overall purposes. Toadying to the advertisers at the expense of circulation can lose enough circulation eventually to stop the presses or disenchant the advertiser. Wooing subscribers at the expense of advertisers can disrupt primary financial support (few newspapers, for example, cover much more than basic production cost from subscriptions and newsstand sales: it's the ads that cover the remaining overhead, frills, and profits). Prostration before government can alienate advertisers *and* subscribers with similar consequences. And excessive hostility towards government can lead to loss of information, subsidies, and, occasionally, heads.

Moreover, in the sense that J. K. Galbraith popularized (in *American Capitalism: The Concept of Countervailing Power.* Boston: Houghton Mifflin, 1952), there are countervailing influences – alternative outlets. The publication of House of Commons debates verbatim, for example, helps to offset some of the special-interest description of Parliament that might otherwise pass unchallenged. When really in doubt, you can wade through *Hansard* to see what was really said and in what context (subject to some editing on occasion). The publishing industry as a whole – thousands of books and magazines – affords a very wide spectrum of views that, in total, come closer than any simple publication to a portrait of reality. All you need is the time and money to muster such a spectrum.

But, whatever the balance works out to be, the chances of reality being offered regardless of economics are very slim indeed. Some occasions, some editions or issues, some places, may be marked by the suspension of economic influences, but these will be few, infrequent, and brief.

Both censorship and economic pressures tend to implant value judgments in print. As weapons or coercions, they serve to enforce or encourage compliance with largely external values – those of the state, the market place, the controlling interest, or one section of the community.

But there is another aspect of value judgment that comes to bear in the people-print combination, one that is more prosaic and taken for granted in day-to-day operations.

Selectivity.

The linearity of print, the one-at-a-time order of its expressions, and the physical limits of space that can be used in a linear fashion, all conspire to encourage selectivity and differential emphasis.

People, for their part, tend to act (consciously or unconsciously) in a selective way. Even when not affected by censorship or urged on by economic pressures, the people preparing material that is to become print perceive and emphasize 'everything' selectively – just as everyone else does.

Consider a beauty contest, for instance. Let us say that five different print persons attend such an event with the object of preparing material for use in many different print outlets. It would not be entirely improbable to suggest a cast like this:

Rhymer Blank, general reporter, 41, significant for our purposes for his devout dedication to flesh and his sniggering mind.

Pamela Prim, women's editor, 38, significant for our purposes for her conviction that clothes make the woman, for women.

Walter Layout, magazine writer, 28, significant for our purposes for his current article in preparation on 'Can you tell him from her?'

Augustus Dollar, financial writer, 56, significant for our purposes for his 'Marketplace' series, planned to include 'The cash nexus of contests.'

Idle Dreamer, author, 37, significant for our purposes for his book in preparation on the theme of beauty (fictionalized).

Now, even though all these people are conscientious, experienced, perceptive, and honest, and even though they attend the same happening at the same place, it is certain that selectivity and emphasis will come to apply to their particular people-print combinations.

For instance:

___

SCARBORO LOVELY NAMED MISS COOL
by Rhymer Blank

Halifax – Pert, buxom Sharon Starlet of Scarboro wiggled off with the 1971 "Miss Cool" crown today with a display of poise and skin that left 27 rivals wrinkled with envy.

The 19-year-old model drew a standing ovation in the final walk-through of the contest that displayed arts more than enough to make up for an earlier mediocre showing in the talent category.

Said Sharon "...

___

Bare Look Back In '70s Styles

By Pamela Prim, Women's Editor

Clever cutting and the use of body paint brought some fashion surprises this week to the ordinarily dowdy "Miss Cool" contest.

Every effective entry in this year's gala featured bias-cut bikinis and accessories and the interesting use of mauve and orange body paint to accent pattern themes.

The winner, Miss Sharon Starlet of Toronto, was typical of the trend-setters with a ...

___

The Question is: CAN YOU TELL HIM FROM HER?
by Walter Layout
Birddogger's staff writer

A silky blonde head was the first to catch my eye ... groovy ... shoulder length. Nice outfit too: Fitted magenta tunic with chartreuse pants. So, I asked him: "...

Marketplace
by Augustus Dollar

It happened in 1929 and it looks like it may happen again. Clothes and the stock market may well be combining again to touch off a recession, perhaps even a depression.

That, at least, is the message from Halifax this week in the annual Chamber of Manufacturers' Miss Cool contest. In the words of contest organizer J. Howard Dapper of Maritime Fabrics: "The girls have averaged at least a half a bolt of cloth in every wardrobe over last year's entries. Nude to the waist was out completely and hemlines were back down to mid-thigh. It is about as drastic a change as we've seen since the late '20s."

"We're already selling ...

Their first glances were ironic. He was, as usual, wedged into too small a space beside Agatha, looking anywhere to avoid the angry ... the perpetually angry ... set of her jaw. She, with the languidness of the unformed, was turning slowly on the runway, softly sweeping the room with her eyes.

At one instant, and only for one instant, their worlds met ... Paul's inarticulate plea bringing a tiny frown to blemish her inhumanly perfect expression, her hauteur conjuring a profound impression of measured calm that wrenched with an exquisite agony.

Then ...

None of this involved censorship (except for the editing out of some of the language used by the promoter when he got the bar bill). Little of this was primarily related to economics (except to the extent that each print expression was directed to specific audiences, advertisers, or subscribers). The event was common to all the five perceivers, who shared workably similar perceptions if not preoccupations.

What happened was the people-print combination of values. Each of the five perceivers selected and emphasized and had his selection and emphasis aided, even encouraged, by the print medium he was working with.

Each of the five selected and emphasized one small segment of the reality of what occurred, according to his value system at the time. All five segments (plus several hundred others) would have to be put together for even a glimmering of what the reality was.

Even without the convenience of the relatively clear categorization values involved in the fictional example, it is probable that similar – though less obvious – differences will apply every time people seek to describe anything in print. The print will tend to organize and assign priority to expressions (something has to be first); the person will tip in the flavours of his or her own perception. And, of course, it is possible (indeed common) for further confusion to be supplied by all the other people involved in the print operation: editors chopping and adding according to their perceptions, headline writers, designers, linotype operators, proof readers and so on.

For us, this can add up to diluted or distorted reality.

You still doubt it? Here is what print itself has reported about the situation on occasion:

Item: Head in the New York Post, January 17, 1967:

Report Mao Gains In Power Struggle

Item: Head in New York World-Journal-Tribune, January 17, 1967:

Mao Seen Losing Struggle In China

Item:

REPORTING
Listening with One Ear

The message seemed clear enough to the New York Times. GUEVARA CALLS U.S. DRIVE ON CUBAN TRADE A FAILURE, read the headline above a story based on a televised interview between Ernesto ("Che") Guevara, Fidel Castro's Minister of Industry, and American Broadcasting Company Reporter Lisa Howard. But the Associated Press, which was also listening, caught quite the opposite pitch. Guevara, the wire service reported to its subscribers all over the world, "concedes that the U.S. economic blockade 'has been a serious drawback' to the island's Communist regime."

Who was right—the A.P. or the Times? In the answer lay a journalistic lesson on the danger of listening with only one ear and getting only half the story. Both the Times and the A.P. were right—both were also wrong. Each seemed to have tuned in on only that portion of Che Guevara's interview that suited their contradictory themes. Castro's man had, in fact, been indulging in a little Cuban doubletalk—as came transparently clear in any thorough reading of the interview. Extracts from A.B.C.'s tape:

Miss Howard: How seriously is the economic blockade affecting the Cuban economy?

Guevara: Obviously, it has been a serious drawback.

Miss Howard, bringing up the shipment of British buses to Cuba: Do you feel these purchases represent a failure of the United States' blockade?

Guevara: Yes.

Time, April 3, 1964, p. 63

The suggestion that the people-print combination tends to be past- rather than present-oriented does not imply that 'past' is automatically bad. As a result of this quality, however, print may over-emphasize rules, attitudes, values, and practices from the past at the expense of those of the present reality. This involves not only rules of syntax, but attitudes towards happenings. Print itself

contributes a mechanical influence to such a state of affairs by virtue of the fact that once cast, the material is fixed in time and space. This introduces a time lag ranging from an hour or two in the case of newspaper print through one to six weeks with magazine print, to as much as three years with some book print.

People, moreover, compound this predisposition with failures – of themselves and of their organizations. With relatively few exceptions, practitioners in print work on a survivors' club basis. The green but contemporary youngster is put to routine apprenticeship tasks under the watchful eye and pencil of successive editors until his performance and attitudes are deemed to be reliable. Too often, while necessary skills are acquired, equally necessary ideas and perceptions of the present are muted or lost. Chronological age or years of service don't always indicate whether or not a person is out of date, but they frequently tend to. And with the ever-more-rapid change in practices and values of our society, such a tendency is enhanced.

The people-print combination, then, cannot help but distort reality to some extent. The processes of selection, emphasis, and expression become coloured by the standards of the past. Existing realities are twisted into the old moulds, loaded with pejorative phrasing, or ignored entirely.

Well, where are we at? From viewing and reviewing print as a device for scaling down reality to manageable and intelligible proportions, we end up with yet another spectrum of plusses and minuses.

On the positive side, we do get order, permanence, universality, flexibility, and variable pace from print. This suggests that print portraits of scaled-down reality will gain in coherence (since our own cognitive functions get a better chance to work), communality, and consistency.

On the negative side, we suffer from linearity, limited sensory engagement, immobility, loss of abstractions, and vulnerability to censorship, economic pulls, and pressures, value judgments, and past-orientation. We perceive that print comes ultimately from people much like ourselves and so is as flyspecked in its perceptions and expressions as we are.

What we probably end up with is the conclusion that while print doesn't add very much of a *qualitative* nature to our perceptions of reality, it does serve important quantitative functions. Print brings us information, attitudes, ideas, and speculation from areas outside our immediate grasp. While not exactly perfect in its efforts to encompass and express such information, attitudes, ideas, and speculation, print does enhance our range, add to data, and give at least the illusion of a partly orderly world.

Those, then, are the characteristics of the proxies of print and its agents. Our perception of the 'everything' of reality will be affected by some or all such characteristics whenever we allow them to act on our behalf.

Or will it?

If we rely solely upon print ... probably yes.

But we don't have to ... not even when dealing

in mass terms.

There now are other proxy agents willing and available to be used. Radio, TV, film – all the processes and agents that can provide large numbers of us with simultaneous data on people, events, and ideas. We can augment and correct the problems of print by referring to them. We can opt for one of them in outright preference. We can consider a total orchestration.

Let us continue an investigation of proxy possibilities.

RADIO

Our chronicle [about broadcast media] will involve statesmen, mountebanks, teachers, salesmen, artists, wheeler-dealers, soldiers, saints, reporters, propagandists – and others. The tower builders reached for heaven, each in his way.

Erik Barnouw, *A Tower in Babel* (New York: Oxford University Press, 1966), p. 5.

As the 20th century dawned, somewhat tremulous with the hopes of the perfectability of Man, the liberations promised by Science, and the worship of Progress, it seemed inevitable that something would be added to supplement print as a means of proxy communication.

On the one hand, haste and leisure created a growing demand for innovation. Profits and power accrued to those who could shave a few minutes or even seconds from the information chain. Enchantment or narcosis were sought by people unaccustomed to the filling of time freed as the world moved forward to the twelve ... then the ten ... even the eight-hour working day.

On the other hand, the last great age of tinkering was under way. In garrets, basements, garages, home laboratories, and the few primitive industrial research establishments, individuals with real and imagined competence, with dreams and delusions, were busying themselves with the great adventures of scientific discovery. In a veritable torrent, devices and gadgets and systems were being put forward to solve specific problems (such as the mechanized butchering of hogs) and, more important, to explore possibilities of new marvels – like electricity.

And so it was in 1901 that a somewhat eccentric Canadian in the employ of the Weather Bureau of the U.S. Department of Agriculture – Reginald Aubrey Fessenden – managed to superimpose the effect of the human voice on a continuous wireless wave, so that it was capable of being broadcast using a telephone microphone and received by a primitive detector. By 1906, on Christmas Eve to be exact, Prof. Fessenden had progressed to an actual broadcast consisting of a violin solo (by Fessenden himself), a selection from the gospel according to St Luke, a recording of Handel's Largo, and, finally, a brief speech including Christmas greetings. This effort was heard by operators aboard United Fruit Company ships more than 1,000 miles away.

the age of radio

had begun.

(Mind you, in fairness, one should also mention Nathan B. Stubblefield of Murray, Kentucky, who is said to have made a voice broadcast as early as 1892 and to have given public demonstrations in 1902. Stubblefield, about whose life little is recorded, died of starvation in a lonely shack in Kentucky in 1928.)

Radio marked the first revolution in proxy communication after print and a significant extension of the human senses. Not only were some of the disabilities of print dispelled, but new advantages were gained. Once launched and through its initial teething, the medium of radio came to be a direct and well established rival to print.

What have we gained? And at what expense? How has radio helped or hindered our perception of 'reality' in its attempt to perceive on our behalf?

First of all, radio loosened the linear straitjacket of print. No longer was it necessary – for purely mechanical reasons – to restrict output to orderly, one-word-at-a-time, one-line-after-another presentations. Radio physically allowed two people to talk

at the same time

or mixtures of voices, wild sounds, music – in fact, any wave-making stimulus – to be heard *simultaneously*. The bedlam, disorder, frequent incoherence, and vitality of reality can, in large measure, be presented as they actually are. And, to the extent at least that volume can be matched in quality, amount, or form with individual preference or capacity, these qualities of simultaneity can be tuned to individuals. The message received is not common to everyone.

Of course there are still some disabilities in radio, as we will see, but this new freedom was an important step forward. In radio, the illusion of order need not be imposed so relentlessly where it does not apply; the absoluteness of beginnings and ends can be eased, for the medium can run non-stop; the essential demand of verbalization for coherence is removed; the impersonality is diminished. Much, much more of the raw material of reality can percolate through. At the same time the principal advantage of print is retained: radio extends our senses beyond our physical reach.

It is even possible to take out some of the middlemen. Print must filter all its expressions of reality through the senses, perceptions, selectiveness and descriptive capacity of another person. Radio needn't. Radio can take you, the listener, right to the unscreened, unorganized source of sounds and leave you to put the pieces together. When this happens, and works, it is more exciting than print. And you are saved the inevitable compounding of error that occurs when anything is strained through two human sense chains instead of one.

Consider an average riot, for example. A print account might very well go like this:

AKRON (AP) — City officials, backed by 450 National Guardsmen with orders to shoot, clamped a 9 p.m. curfew on Akron yesterday following racial disturbances along a few blocks of a predominately Negro area.

The curfew in this rubber centre of 304,000 was to last until 6 a.m. today Mayor John Ballard said at a special Council meeting. He declared a state of emergency.

Nearby Barberton and Cuyahoga Falls imposed similar, curfews.

Gen. Sylvester Del Corso, Ohio Adjutant-General, said at a news conference the troops sent in by Governor James A. Rhodes are armed. "When we order someone to stop and surrender himself, if he does not stop he will be shot."

The emergency law prohibits sale of guns, ammunition and incendiary devices including gasoline. Maximum penalty for violation is $100 fine, 30 days in jail, or both.

During the special meeting, a Negro minister accused police of racist activities. A Negro leader and Police Chief Harry Widdon got into a heated exchange over what happened when police used tear gas early yesterday.

Police said the gas was used to break up crowds on the street after store windows were broken by roving bands of young Negroes. There was some looting and fire bombs caused minor damage.

A 16-year-old Negro, Leo Stegall, was hit in the shoulder by police gunfire. Officers said he ran from a store that was being looted.

Mayor Ballard said the disturbances may have resulted from police breaking up a fight between Negro gans in a park Wednesday. He said the Negroes turned on police. Detectives said older youth in cars urged younger teen-agers to throw rocks and break windows once the trouble started early yesterday. Ballard asked for National Guard help about 3 a.m.

Police had the situation under control by daybreak, arresting 23 juveniles and 19 adults.

118   But a radio account, so far as it can be expressed in print, can be very different indeed. *In addition to* all the data in the print offering, radio can express these dimensions:

→ The sound of the actual fight between police and the gangs.

→ The sound of the 'older youth in cars' urging younger teen-agers to throw rocks and break windows once the trouble started.

→ The sound of looting and fire bombs and the sound of police breaking up crowds on the streets.

→ The sounds of the special council meeting, including the Negro minister accusing police of 'racist activities' and the 'heated exchange' between a Negro leader and Police Chief Harry Widdon.

→ The sound of the mayor declaring a state of emergency and announcing a curfew.

→ The sounds of the curfew in practice.

If the process is reversed, a similar and revealing contrast is offered. In this case, the first item is a transcript of part of the running commentary from the Montreal-Detroit hockey game played in Detroit, March 7, 1971:

... around on the boards ... to Lapointe ... out to Richard ... back to Tremblay as they handle the puck beautifully ... (Public Address: Last minute of play in this game) ... the centre to Houle ... ahead to Richard ... less than a minute to play ... Richard in front to Lemaire ... HE SCORES!!! (Crowd roar) ... Jacques Lemaire set up beautifully! ... and, Jim, the Canadiens must have had possession for about a minute!

This was a print account of the whole game:

Two for Big M

DETROIT (UPI) — Frank Mahovlich scorched his old teammates for two goals yesterday afternoon in leading Montreal Canadiens to a 4-1 National Hockey League win over Detroit Red Wings.

John Ferguson and Jacques Lemaire also scored for Montreal. Goalie Rogatien Vachon's chance for his third shutout was spoiled in the final period when Arnie Brown scored for Detroit.

Frank Mahovlich's 23rd goal of the season, a power-play score, was the first shot on goal of the game. He converted a perfect pass from Yvan Cournoyer.

His 24th goal of the season gave the Canadiens a 3-0 lead at 11:19 of the third period. Jean Beliveau fed him an excellent lead pass on a breakaway and Mahovlich beat Detroit goalie Roy Edwards cleanly.

Frank's brother, Pete, set up Ferguson at the 63-second mark of the third period and Lemaire's 26th goal came in a power play with 53 seconds to play.

Toronto *Globe and Mail,* Monday, March 8, 1971, p. 16

Despite potential pitfalls, direct, sustained, live contact can be maintained with events *as they happen* in a manner impossible through print. At its best, radio manages to extend our senses and scale down reality in a very useful manner.

Even emotions get a better chance to filter through. The actual sighs, giggles, hiccups, hmms, and snorts of human existence can be transmitted directly – with no need for words or other awkward approximations – to set a scene and mood vividly and compellingly. The context becomes much clearer. The listener can hear in the voice of a statesman the bad cold which might explain some of his bad-tempered text.

Gentlemen

an...ah...ah...CHOO

this means WAR!

Now, you may be wondering, in a reasonably puzzled way, how on earth such claims for radio match up with CXXX, your local rock or country and western outlet. You may feel that Hector Nasal, CXXX's hot-shot announcer-news reporter-sports broadcaster, actually witnesses and understands world events as much as James Reston or other senior reporters do for the *New York Times.* Or you may suspect that such 'actuality' sound as is provided on CXXX and hundreds of other radio stations like it is scanty, rigged,

and too often used misleadingly in commercials.

And if you think the latter, of course, you'll be quite right. In relative mediocrity and distance from reality, radio right now is as bad as or even worse than print. Some of its faults are inherent; some result from the same frailties that plague other media.

Let us consider the inherent disabilities for a start. First, it is clear that radio lacks the full dimensions of our collective senses. Radio can bring *sound* in many dimensions but it cannot capture sights, it is limited in conveying motion, it is tasteless and odourless. When senses other than sound are paramount for expressing reality, radio becomes a lame duck.

So what? ... Well, consider these circumstances:

→ Colour, unfortunately, has become one of the survival issues in the world today – an issue desperately in need of greater perception and understanding. Radio cannot show us, other than in inadequate word pictures, what colour means – racially, psychedelically, or artistically.

→ Taste and smell are senses that, by virtue of their very close link to reflexes such as vomiting and bodily bliss, are highly evocative, both emotionally and intellectually. With topics such as pollution, slum clearance, war, famine relief, and, alternatively, beauty and love becoming near obsessions in our world, radio is hard pressed to convey much credible reality. Instead of generating the surges and spasms of true sensory reaction and experience, the tasteless and odourless vehicle of radio tends to deprive us. If you will recall your last successful (or unsuccessful) party, you might agree that even the sound of nausea pales in contrast with smell and taste.

Second, radio is also inescapably ephemeral. With few exceptions, the offerings possible on radio are presented once and then disappear into the cosmos. If you miss a sound, a word, or a phrase, you can't easily turn back to it – as you can with print.

The action is over.

Furthermore, radio dictates the pace – not the listener. There is no easy or workable way to slow down or speed up individual reception of broadcast happenings to match individual capacity.

The mixture of assets (non-linear, immediate, wide-spectrum sound, direct contact, simultaneity) and liabilities (ephemeral, sensory limitations, set pace) inherent in radio add up to an interesting speculation – that radio, unlike print, is a mood medium rather than a fact carrier, and a limited one at that.

That is to say that within its competence and capacity, radio serves primarily to provide us with the general sense of a reality rather than the careful and detailed substantive outline. When expressing a happening in words, radio cannot by its pace and volume provide material that very many people will be able to perceive or digest verbatim. The listener will instead get a general 'feel' of the 'reality' which he then can use in concert with other senses and sense extensions to flesh out his awareness. When radio is non-verbal, depending mainly on sounds and music, the presentation will be even more mood-dominated.

The bedevilling part is that

it doesn't always seem to be that way.

Especially in those gripping circumstances when a major world event, a sports highlight, or a local crisis (such as a weather forecast on the morning of a picnic) focus our attention, we tend to come away with the feeling that what was said and sounded *is* – etched on our minds. But it seldom is. The general flavour is likely to be there (H-Bomb on Cuba, Winnipeg 42 – Hamilton 23, rain and fog) but the factual content will almost certainly be more diffuse than

that obtained and retained through print. It may even be reversed.

The classic example is Orson Welles' famous broadcast of 1938 in which, in a play written as a dramatic news report, he described the invasion of the earth by Martians. The show was clearly labelled as fiction and the label was repeated during the program. But several thousand listeners still convinced themselves of the reality of their general impression of a Martian invasion. (Even when a recording of this program was played in 1967, and despite radical changes in radio techniques that dated it horribly, a listener phoned in to an Ontario station to ask if Highway 401 was safe to drive on!)

This tendency to generality is reinforced by the lack of a safety valve we met in print. Radio has no clearcut threshold of perception or non-perception. Print demands attention to be at all intelligible. Radio is characterized by a spectrum of intelligibility. As every car radio vividly demonstrates, there is a rather grey area in radio where reception isn't perfect but still is bearable. As reception slides down the scale the sounds get progressively weaker and fuzzier ... as does our perception. So too with the listener, whose attention can wander while his ear traps some part of the message.

Those who seek to achieve effective communication by radio are very aware of such physical or mental 'static.' Because they know that message material can be lost, they build in safeguards. These usually take the form of repetition and simplification – be it commercials or news headlines.

This causes further damage to reality. With each simplification, dimensions and variables of reality are lost. With each repetition, aspects of attention are lost. The very generality being battled tends, in the end, to be reinforced.

For example, take radio newscasts. In a representative five-minute offering, typical of the 'news on the hour every hour' variety, eight to twelve news items are usually broadcast. It is commonplace for such items to be of roughly equal length, resulting in simplifications (and suggesting that Vietnam and a beauty contest are of roughly equal significance), and it is also commonplace for items to be repeated verbatim several times, hour after hour. Many, many explanations and important details and qualifications, associated with the realities of the happenings described, lose out to such simplification. (Try describing an event in Southeast Asia and its reasons in 75 words and you'll see why.) Moreover, repetition tends to fuzz interest and reaction (as with the contrast between the tense attention given by millions of people to the first moon landing and the ... yawn ... most recent one).

So much, then, for the device known as radio – a mixture of promise and paucity that in itself is limited in its ability to serve the cause of linking people to reality.

Now for the combination:

people-radio.

Much as with people-print, the people-radio combination takes the dispositions and predispositions of each component and brings forth an array of effects and defects both unexpected and, occasionally, sad. The principal items in the array can be listed as follows:

→ The people-radio combination is vulnerable to censorship and distortion.
→ The people-radio combination is unduly subject to economic pressures.
→ The people-radio combination is prey to loaded value judgments.

As with print, too, these qualities don't necessarily apply all the time to every radio presentation. There are, and hopefully will continue to be, honourable exceptions. But for our purposes some awareness of what can (and too often does) go wrong remains important because our concern is with the reliability of perception of reality. Let us take the points in order.

The people-radio combination is more likely to suffer from censors and regulators than the people-print combination. This is mainly because the people-radio combination is regarded as being more dangerous and more pervasive.

The device of radio in itself is enough to give anxious politicians and administrators the cold shudders. Radio in its various forms (AM, FM, and short wave) can range over thousands of miles, untrammelled by borders, customs posts, or local regulations. Whereas a newspaper or book or pamphlet has to be moved physically to reach an audience, distribution by radio is virtually effortless once the watts are cranked up.

Radio Moscow casually leaps across the North Pole to provide easy listening in the Canadian North. (I heard it on a transistor radio hanging from a nail in an Indian's tent on the Mackenzie River, for example.) The Voice of America uses home-based and other transmitters to penetrate Soviet fastness (I heard it there on a taxi radio at Sochi on the Black Sea). Even the CBC's International Service manages to serve European audiences on its shoestring budget (providing me a Grey Cup game in a proper British living room one year).

Moreover, almost anyone can potentially make use of radio. Only the technicians must have special skills, reasonably parallel to those demanded of printers. For the other functions of broadcasting there is no requirement of literacy, and no need of apprenticeship. To a paranoid ruler this means that everyone about him is a potential source of radio expression of lies, treason, pornography, or incitement to civil disobedience.

There is another argument cited for censorship and other controls. This is the claim that radio broadcast frequencies are public property since they are disseminated through the public air. In the same way that the activities of aeroplanes in the air are subject to close and careful scrutiny in the public interest, the activities of broadcasters are deemed to deserve attention as well. This is reinforced by the relative scarcity of frequencies that can be used for broadcasting, which suggests that something of a privilege has been granted to those who are assigned a frequency, and that satisfactory performance can be demanded as the price of such a privilege. (Freedom of the air waves has been tried. In the pioneer days of radio virtually anyone with the yen to broadcast could do so. The interference and occasional bawdiness that resulted brought regulations into force post-haste.)

Political concern about the dangers of radio is coupled with relatively easy application of censorship and other controls. Stations can be located and seized, or, if they are beyond the government's power, their electromagnetic output can be jammed. Individuals can be arrested, fined, imprisoned – even shot on occasion. Although radio is more flexible and portable than print, the fact remains that any attempt to maintain regular and sustained communication by this medium involves enough immobility of equipment, and predictability in broadcast times and frequency, to serve the purposes of control. For example, the Canadian Radio and Television Commission felt sufficiently confident about its ability to oversee Canadian radio that it promulgated regulations requiring (as of January 1971) that AM radio stations broadcast a minimum of 30% Canadian music.

And, in fact, the governments of every nation on earth do apply controls. Some settle for purely technical surveillance, insisting on the proper operation of equipment. Others add political prescriptions: they may outlaw unidentified political appeals, ban dramatization of political themes with paid actors, or prohibit access to certain parties or groups. Some apply the sanctions of the criminal code with regard to sedition, obscenity, libel, fraudulent advertising, or incitement to violence. Other make special regulations encompassing such laws and adding positive requirements of community service, contributions to the creative arts, or 'responsibility.' Some even make broadcasting a state monopoly in whole or part, so that there is a chance to oversee staff and programs directly.

As with print, all such attempts to provide advice, guidance, and curbs upon the people-radio combination can be in everyone's best interest. At the same time, the extent to which such limitations apply is a measure of the extent to which reality is muted or sugarcoated for the receiver.

The people-radio combination is even more vulnerable to economic pressures than to censorship. Either directly (from advertising itself) or indirectly (from tax or licence dollars in government-sponsored systems) the people-radio combination is wholly dependent for survival upon outside revenues related to estimated audience support. There are a few eccentric exceptions, but most radio stations and staffs must be able to demonstrate over a reasonable period of time that they have either a mass audience or a small but high-quality audience. Otherwise the sources of economic support will turn to alternative outlets.

As a result, the people-radio combination tends to seek to provide those aspects of reality that are popular rather than pertinent. That way lies audience – and audience means survival, growth, and well-being. Thus, in North America, we have witnessed the phenomenon of

'formula' radio.

→ stations and staff providing nothing but the top 10, or top 100, or top 500 tunes on the popularity charts (which are categorized, in turn, into rock, country and western, the middle-aged 'sound,' and so forth)
→ stations and staffs offering only news or only sports (seeking quality or special interest as their claim to survival)
→ stations and staffs identifying with ethnic groups or religion (including one station that is 'Serving God and Fighting Communism 24 Hours a Day').

The heights of economically-inspired inspiration call for all-girl announcing staffs, or for special 'personality' disc jockeys such as Murray the K, whose immortality was linked to a first-name relationship with the Beatles.

In short, there is a very evident area of the people-radio combination that qualifies or denies reality for the sake of audiences.

The other aspects of economic pressure are more shadowy. They involve the use and possible misuse of commercial time, and other related pressures by sponsors, either private or public. The key again is dependency.

Even if your particular favourite station and staff deliver audiences, they need not necessarily be sure of economic survival. They may espouse ideas, attitudes, or ideologies that are contrary to those cherished by the sources of economic support. They may fail to promote other ideas, attitudes, or ideologies strongly enough. They may even harbour individuals that aren't approved of. So support starts to dry up. And what does a survival-minded people-radio combination do? It can perish bravely, or it can give a little or a lot. Nothing need be said or written out in an agreement, yet the offerings of your favourite station and staff can change and, miraculously, the support of formerly frosty economic sources can grow. And everyone can live happily ever after.

Note the suggestion that *everyone* can live happily ever after. Herein lies probably the most ominous effect of the anticipation or expression of economic pressure.

'Everyone' includes you.

Now you may wonder at this. 'What do you mean,' you may assert, 'I know what I like and if I don't get it I'll ... I'll switch to another station.' But wait. What you need to ask yourself is whether *you* really *decide* what you like in the versions of 'formula' radio you listen to, or whether it is decided for you. And if economic pressures seem to work with one station, why won't they with others – perhaps most of the available ones in your community.

That's the catch. Sure, we all *think* we are exercising free choice and thus forcing people-radio to serve us. But, given the mind-numbing saturation of some kinds of offering and the appearance at least that such pervasiveness *must* represent general acceptance, isn't it conceivable that the shades and emphases of tastes may in fact be more orchestrated than responsive? Did you discover the Beatles or were they presented – massively – to you? Did the Doors creep across the threshold of acceptance by word of mouth, station-by-station evaluation or did they leap full-blown from anonymity to international reputation?

Consider the case of Richie Havens, for example. In an article in the *New York Times,* these observations were made:

> "I wanted to be a surgeon, but I dropped out of high school six months before graduation. I sang on street corners in Brooklyn with the McCrae Gospel Singers. I worked as a Western Union delivery boy—man, I delivered some heavy telegrams. I packed sweaters, made dolls, and was a $3 portrait painter down on Sixth Avenue in Greenwich Village, opposite the Waverly Theatre.

> "When I was 19, I started singing in the basket houses on MacDougal Street. We called them that because the singers don't get paid in those coffeehouses; you pass a basket after the set for tips. And how much you make depends on how good you are at the pitch. You know, stuff like, 'I live in Washington Square Park. . . . I got eight kids.' I used to do 12 sets a night, 40 minutes each, scrambling from one joint to the next. I sang solo, with combos, did guitar accompaniment—anything. You can come out with $70 on a Friday night if you really scramble and know how to pitch."

How does a talented singer get out of the basket houses?

> "Albert Grossman, my manager, used to come down to MacDougal Street to hear the talent, and he dug me for a whole year before I went uptown to his office and he signed me on. It was funny when Johnny Carson called me an overnight success on his show. Man, I paid my dues on the street."

> A singer doesn't just cut an album these days, it is packaged for a total image.

New York Times, July 21, 1968

Once again, the ways in which a star is born are not necessarily bad or good – that's for individuals to decide. The Richie Havens story, and hundreds of others like it, do suggest, however, a tinkering that cannot help but distort people-radio's efforts to relate reality to us. And when economic preferences or concerns don't coincide with the preferences or concerns of reality, reality is likely to suffer.

Next, let us turn to the susceptibility of radio to loaded value judgments, beyond the influences of censorship and economics. The medium itself is open to abuse because of its qualities of immediacy, total reliance on sound, adjustable volume (and emphasis), and, to a degree, ability to change formats and content quickly and easily. People involved in radio enhance these inherent characteristics and add others because of their own egoism, technical agility, limited personal accountability, and personal selectivity.

Four main, though probably inadvertent, kinds of value loading can result from people-radio combinations. First, there is the phenomenon of spurious

This involves the careful orchestration of music, talk, sound effects, and script material so as to give you, the listener, the impression that the communication being offered is for you directly or, at most, for your special group. This is something akin to disguising a dentist's office as a brothel – difficult but very effective when it works.

Such efforts are *always* illusory. Programming on any radio station is actually public programming: anyone and everyone with a transistor set can sit in. Further, only the very grossest kinds of audience specialization are economically feasible.

Immediately, therefore, one can see that radio offerings orchestrated to suggest person-to-person communication are invariably loaded and distort reality.

Even discounting the fraction of the misconception self-induced by eager listeners (such as the willing widow who *wants* to believe that Elwood Glover or Max Ferguson is talking directly to her), an extensive area of value-loading is left that is induced by people-radio.

This technique is especially significant when recognizable and possibly defensible loading is used as a vehicle for other influences. A program may contain music that you enjoy; it may even give you the impression of being offered by someone enough in tune with you to be like you or close to you. But along the way, mixed with the familiar and acceptable intimacy that is created, there can be sly coaching on attitudes, ideas, and activities in the world. And because the basic format registers 'acceptable' to your receptors, the coaching can register 'acceptable' too.

Similarly, in more formal areas of communication such as news programs, the illusion of familiarity and personal contact with a regular newscaster can increase the credibility rating of what he or she is saying. (Sometimes, ironically, this can go so far that the newscaster convinces himself of his central role in securing the material which he is reading – although almost always it is supplied to the station by a news agency – and he may then begin to adopt postures about it for his own satisfaction.)

One notable Canadian instance of the potential impact of such spurious intimacy is provided by the colourful and much-admired Gordon Sinclair. By his own admission, he derives much of his success from i/inserting his personal value judgments into broadcast material (at the expense of young radicals, civil servants, and other pet hates), and, ii/somehow convincing a loyal band of listeners that he is talking directly to and for them. Since radio, unlike print, tends to make a participant instantly recognizable by his voice, and much that is emotionally pejorative comes out in sound, such relationships are much more possible and likely over the airwaves than in newspapers. 'Reality' suffers accordingly.

This leads naturally to the second dimension of people-radio value-loading – selectivity. Everything that is presented by the people-radio combination has to be selected from a next-thing-to-infinite amount of records and happenings. And both the people and the device introduce value-loading into the process.

Radio tends first to influence the selection of material by its built-in abilities and disabilities. A communication accompanied by compelling sounds, for example, will have a greater impact than one that is silent or unintelligible. The sounds of war and gang-busting seem to be made for the capacities of radio – guns, planes, screams of the dying, tension and excitement everywhere. The sounds of tranquility, on the other hand, are much more difficult to convey by radio – contented contemplation, pauses to think, a growing field of wheat, ease, fullfilment, and relative silence every(yawn)where.

Or again, a value weighting attaches to the various sounds of voices, regardless of content. A politician with a stutter or a high voice or a sonorous style suffers in contrast with the polished and rolling bass of a rival – even though the man with the odd voice may in fact be more intelligent, better informed, and more conscientious.

Thus, the medium itself imposes a value scheme that is often false or irrelevant. When people are added, the situation escalates in two important ways. First, the innate value-loading of the medium is emphasized by the addition of anticipation, which may either rule out some sounds and people in advance, or emphasize them for detrimental purposes. (How can you criticize *someone you don't get to hear* stating his controversial case, or evaluate the work of an excellent poet when all he is interviewed about is hockey during intermissions?)

Second, the conscious or (more often) unconscious value judgments of the people doing the selecting will come to bear. The radio person will tend to select some items and programs and exclude others on the basis of his own range of tastes and distastes. Since such selectivity will be applied *before* broadcast, there will only be negative evidence of it so far as the listener is concerned. Such evidence is difficult, often impossible to detect. (How can you criticize someone for *not* telling you something you *don't know* is going on?)

This area of value-loading clearly is related to the previous speculations about economic influence. The extent to which selectivity can be dictated by the characteristics of the medium, and applied by the individuals involved in the medium, provides an indication of how much our conception of reality can be substantially influenced. Some undue emphasis and some omission will almost always occur. Every instance will tend to warp our perceptions.

The third kind of value-loading derives from another problem that the people-radio combination shares, in part, with the people-print combination. This is the difficulty of dealing with abstractions. The areas of abstraction that suffer will be somewhat different (after all, you can actually express 'soul' sounds on radio) but not entirely so.

The most obvious area that suffers is purely visual abstraction, including much good modern art. The people-radio combination affords only sound as a vehicle (and to be fair *some* sound approximations of modern art have been successful); immediately the limitation becomes punishing. People in the medium may be able to help a bit with inspired words or selections of other sounds, but still ...

Similarly, what of concepts such as **death** or **truth** or **freedom?**

All have certain verbal and sound qualities, but all also have visual, visceral, and eclectic qualities as well. Either the words and sounds will be used as awkward approximations, at the expense of dimensions of accuracy, or, more often, the abstractions will be replaced by something concrete. Death, then, is turned into a kind of mockery by becoming the sound of a bullet thudding into a body cavity, or a sigh, or a squawk. Freedom is turned into a pattern of rituals involving ballot boxes or sit-ins. Truth becomes little more than an assertion. Radio, alas, seems as inhibited as print in expressing abstractions.

Something very dangerous indeed is posed by such disabilities. As a human race we brood and sense inarticulately that abstractions really do contain much of the essence underlying our behaviour and patterns of belief. We ignore them at our peril, because action cues and emotions within us persist repeatedly in provoking some of our most savage and creative outbursts in the cause of abstractions. A glance at the tapestry of our collective histories, at our principal provocateurs from Machiavelli to Marcuse, at our technological triumphs, or at our towering edifices of theology, testifies to the central role of abstraction.

So, it can be argued that the degree to which the people-radio combination (or any other proxy agent) fails in trying to express abstractions in the proportion and context of the human condition is a measure of the degree to which reality is *both distorted and muted.*

In Western society especially, one can suggest that the prevailing modes of materialism, for all their blessings, are in part a consequence of patterns of communication which find themselves unable and/or unwilling to seek to express abstractions. One can also suggest that some of the current dislocations apparent in our material nirvana are also a result of such failures. In the same way that for want of a horseshoe nail the battle was eventually lost, for want of balance between materialism and abstraction we humans may be lost.

As Peter Viereck sums up succinctly:

... And when anti-materialism gets publicised like toothpaste, when religion gets wrapped in cellophane, then commercial materialism wins its biggest triumph of all: a triumph in the name of anti-commercialism. In every city's 'put Christ back into Christmas' campaign, the carols blare their anti-materialist reminder the loudest from the mechanical loudspeakers in the busy department stores. Is it accidental in our society or is it typical that precisely our most money-avid industry, the cinema, includes a firm whose motto is 'Ars Gratia Artis'?

Synthetic food pills we already have. Why not synthetic culture pills, synthetic souls?

The Unadjusted Man (New York: Beacon Press, 1956)

Finally, there is the value-loading in the people-radio combination that relates to immediacy. For anyone, undue stress on immediacy can be unfortunate.

Immediacy is a hallmark of the people-radio combination for fairly obvious reasons. The medium itself is instantaneous. Unlike print, which goes through a number of stages of production, much of radio is presented as it occurs, at the precise moment that it occurs. Live action, live performers, live sounds permeate the whole fabric of the medium. With sometimes stunning impact, radio can take a listener virtually anywhere for a portrait in sound as it is being painted.

The people associated tend, not unreasonably, to seek to take advantage of this characteristic of the medium. For reasons of healthy sloth, they are tempted to favour programming based as much on *now* as possible because little in the form of preparation or homework is involved. For reasons of prestige and competition, they stress immediacy as a counter to the appeals of print (relatively slower) and television (somewhat slower and more cumbersome) – their prime rivals.

The result is a people-radio combination stressing the world as it is happening ... stressing **TODAY**

... stressing action.

So ...? Can this be anti-reality? Isn't reality the world as it is happening?

Here we end up with a yes ... but. Certainly contact with the world as it is happening is central to perception of reality. There is even a bonus in so far as people-radio can provide indications of such happenings through the sounds of the happenings themselves.

But there is also a problem of balance and emphasis. A sickening feast of 'now' can dangerously eclipse both the past and the future. And there can be reaction to such a surfeit that can be destructive.

From a stress on immediacy can come the discounting of individuals – even of generations – because they are not part of the immediate here and now.

We are told that 25 per cent of all the people who ever lived are alive today; that 90 per cent of all the scientists who ever lived are living now; the amount of technical information doubles every ten years; throughout the world, about 100,000 journals are published in more than 60 languages, and the number doubles every 15 years.

Don Fabun, *The Dynamics of Change* (Englewood Cliffs: Prentice-Hall, 1967), p. 5

But wait a minute.

Sure, the here and now are important – that's where our body envelopes are. But an awful lot of the past and future are important too.

Take, for example, our here and now ways of life. For many people the emphasis – rightly or wrongly – is on materialism. The Good Life is a home of your own ... love is a mink coat ... beauty is a $35,000 sports car ... integrity is a AAA credit rating. In (rarely) possession or (mostly) aspiration we seem to measure the road to humanness or heaven in firm, tangible, material things. And so long as the stress is on here and now, such standards of measurement are likely to continue. Apart from a miserable and frequently invisible handful of eccentrics, who's to disagree?

Yet if you go back a bit – or look ahead a bit – the pervasiveness and inviolability of such a here and now tends to get fuzzy. There

was a time, for instance, when the soul transcended everything material. There was a time when humans dictated terms to machines rather than accepting the reasonable (do not fold, bend, punch or mutilate) or unreasonable (nine reminders *after* paying for the subscription!) edicts of machines. There may be a time when affluence or havoc will raise the status of non-materialism again.

To the extent that radio – and other media – overstress the here and now (in part as a reflection of ourselves), they introduce rigidity, mute alternatives, seize up senses of a continuum of life. Individual here and now topics balloon out of all proportion to dominate landscapes while they last. A Congo crisis recedes (with the basic issues unresolved) before the onslaught of urban rioting which gives way to wails about a population crisis which are eclipsed by furore about Chinese nuclear threats which are muted by inflamed navels (from too much contemplation) about an American presidential election which fades before concern about a regional blizzard which gives way to uproar about skirt lengths which is vanquished by outrage about poverty which is cut off by a space launching which trickles out of sight in the face of NHL playoffs. Monitor a newspaper or newscast at three-month intervals and you can compile a list of featured and forgotten topics of daunting dimensions.

Alternatively, because some humans are stubborn enough or reactive enough to become ornery, over-emphasis on the here and now of the human condition can also lead to foolish discounting. Just because a topic or issue is taken up by the people-radio combination, it becomes unacceptable.

We see this all the time. It may take the form of the unduly switched-on individual spending all his or her time scrambling madly to stay ahead of the here and now, and gaining a fine crop of psychic scar tissue in the process. Or it may appear in the switched-off individual who adopted his or her posture in 1948 and is going to stay that way, think that way, be that way till the last breath trickles through grey lips.

What about radio and its agents as a proxy for us then?

As with print, this is a mixed bag. Clearly, quantitative functions are discharged very well indeed. The average day's total of radio emissions is quite staggering. Individual range and capacity of sensory perception are both multiplied many, many times. The radio proxy can and often does serve to bring us closer to an idea of what is going on.

Qualitatively, however, the evidence suggests disabilities comparable to those of print. There are distortions and omissions in the inputs provided by radio such that our perception of the 'everything' of reality will be imperfect. We need to be wary in relying solely on radio as a proxy agent ... or even upon a print-radio mixture.

Now, let us turn off our transistors and take a look at the next proxy candidate – the great eye of television.

TELEVISION

8

Once upon a time ... many riots and world crises ago ... there was no television. The flickering medium that now bathes us in its universal light didn't exist as a process, system, proxy agent, or device for mass consumption. The technical parts were scattered about, almost casually, in assorted laboratories in Britain, Europe, and North America – toys that were idly played with. Practical people saw no real future for them, singly or collectively. Potential addicts were blissfully unaware.

Almost incredibly in hindsight, the world actually went on, day to day, largely untroubled, uncurious, and unconcerned about the absence of a proxy agent that could bring reasonable approximations of actual events anywhere in the world to millions of human sensory-cerebral systems.

How television came about, in fact, provides a tale about as comic, gripping, improbable, and overblown as much of the medium's actual fare. Many of the ingredients of the story are of some importance for our estimation and evaluation of television as a proxy agent providing reality inputs for us.

What was required was a remarkable combination of accidents. Just as a fish, hunger, the right bait, suitable tackle, and a fisherman have to combine at one precise instant to result in a trout breakfast, many varied ingredients had to come together to make television a mass medium.

One ingredient was the **technology.** Like the lures in a hobby shop, it had been available for some time before extensive uses for it were found. As early as 1884, a German scientist named Paul Nipkow had figured out and fabricated an experimental system actually capable of transmitting pictures – murky but recognizable. Others followed. By the 1920s most of the major technical bugs involved in translating light waves into electrical waves and back again had been worked out. A few experimental stations actually went on the air, and by 1939 – when television development was temporarily halted by the assorted intrusions of the second world war – prototype television service was already available in Britain and the eastern United States.

At any rate, the technology as it did develop didn't add up to a mass medium available as a proxy agent right away. Other ingredients and accidents were required.

For a start, there had to be money or its equivalent to underwrite all the expensive talents and facilities required for more than experimental and limited production, transmission, and reception. There also had to be a supply of people with the training and abilities required to operate and maintain the facilities. There had to be an audience too – at least in potential – so that the consumption and exchange implicit in a mass proxy agent could come about.

And, possibly most important of all, there had to be social circumstances such that the medium, once established, could grow and prosper. (As Sarah Minge often says, 'There's no sense in marketing a better mousetrap if there aren't any mice.')

Ordinarily, the coincidence of five factors of such scope is out of the question. Competing demands, available goods and services, established social policies and practices, and the weight of simple inertia conspire to diminish the prospects for all but incremental or marginal changes at any given time. Virtually all the major changes in the human condition that have occurred – Christianity, the automobile, collective bargaining, medicare, mass literacy ... the lot – have come about over protracted periods. Seldom has there been a single moment when, magically, massive turnabout has occurred.

Well, at the end of the second world war, such a magical moment *did* occur. The result was mass television. (Don't let this shred your faith in magic – remember there are good witches and bad ones.)

So, turn back in time to 1945, and observe the unfolding of a

MAGICAL MOMENT.

There was money. Consumers, particularly in North America, had pockets bulging with the fruits of compulsory wartime savings, service gratuities, high-wage defence jobs, and the new increments of the welfare state. They were ready, cheerfully and massively, to buy – and if the offering was something a little different and more interesting than the dreary products of wartime austerity, so much the better.

Investors were eager too. Their wartime risks had brought some healthy returns and the next concern was to sock some of that bonus capital into items that would earn and grow even more. Obviously, at least for the moment, wartime industries were out: what about some new action, say in electronics?

Manufacturers were almost frantic. Many had switched to full-time military production. Peace had stopped those assembly lines. So, what next? ... Find us a business where we can use the equipment and skills we have with little serious changeover! ... Television you say? ... Great!

(And, as Buckminster Fuller, the noted scientist and theorist, has observed, there is a natural compatability between armaments and communication: '... both the communications and transportation industries have benefitted by the general systems controls adapted to weaponry systems – simply because mails, telephones, telegraphs, wireless, railroads, ships, autos, and trucks were and are themselves vital parts of the operational weapons-delivery and support systems.')

There were skills. The second world war had been a complicated war employing the most advanced technology of its time. Thousands of men and women received training of a kind and sophistication never before known. These same thousands, now released from the demands of death, represented a trained, yet-to-be-employed, pool of talents over the whole spectrum of television production – actors, newsgatherers, make-up artists, writers, producers, camera operators, stage hands, lighting experts, audio experts, set and scenery designers, technicians, tube makers. Even when all the demands of radio, print, film, and the like were met and all the guarantees of a return to the old job were honoured, many skilled people were still left over for something new.

There was an **audience.**

The second world war had shaken up the whole of North American society. Some almost incidental legislative enactments had added to the upsets. Existing media had been going through some patchy times. The companies that produced television shows and manufactured television sets embarked upon a major promotion campaign. Consider these factors as they occurred simultaneously:

→ The war brought a marriage boom and, in turn, a soaring birth rate. That meant thousands of families – new families – with screaming kids, overcrowded or makeshift homes, and the rigours of retraining or new education financed by veterans' benefits or savings. It also meant more stay-at-home entertainment, or getting a babysitter before even planning a night on the town (if you could lure a babysitter in). Either way, wouldn't a TV set be helpful?

→ A tax levied on night clubs (in part as a reaction against the idea of wartime profiteers carousing while the boys were dying) hit hard at clubs with live entertainment and dancing. The result: many entertainers were out of work (and so were available for TV), fewer places were available for people to go to for entertainment (so why not stay at home and watch TV).

→ Vaudeville was dead. As a result of film (which we discuss next) most of the variety palaces of North America had sickened and died. Again, actors and entertainers were available for TV because of fewer alternatives open to perform before live audiences.

→ Movies weren't, at that stage, better than ever. For one thing, the industry had fallen into the hands of bankers as a result of some colossal mismanagement and profligacy, and the money-men were stressing safe formula productions at the expense of risky, creative ones. In the mid '40s, until British, French, Italian, and Scandinavian filmmakers revived the medium with fresh ideas and approaches, the film industry was rather tired – and at precisely the time when the cheapness and convenience of TV was to become apparent.

→ Print had reached some basic outer limits. For one thing, there was the limit of literacy – several million North Americans thirsted for something that didn't include reading in its price of admission. In addition, the print generation that had brought about the rise of the mass circulation newspaper and magazine (with new formats and ideas in the 1920s) was aging. As the performance of giants like the *Saturday Evening Post* indicated, there was just enough hardening of the editorial arteries to provide a juicy opportunity for a rival medium.

→ Radio was still largely in the grip of its transition from a primarily print-oriented operation – staffed by many print people, and operated as talking print – to a medium of words and *sound*. Nor had the transistor yet appeared to boost the mass market.

→ Persuasion was being applied. One recent estimate, made in the presence of a Radio Corporation of America vice president and not denied by him, suggested that RCA alone invested $50 million in the promotion, not production, of television in the late 1940s.

→ People were living longer. What do you do with an aged granny (at home or in the rest home) to keep her quiet and happy all day long? Wouldn't something like TV be a blessing?

And finally, there were basic social changes as the television age opened. The upheavals of the industrial revolution, two world wars, and the depression of the 1930s, plus, if you want, the stunning impact of the arrival of the atomic era, had combined to progressively atomize what were formerly unified and finite aspects of individual existence – community, occupation as a craft, church, morality, rule of law, thrift, truth, individual self-reliance.

Literally and symbolically, people were separated from one another and subdivided within themselves. There was the impersonality of the city, the assembly line, and mass slaughter. There were massive shifts of population tugging people out of settled communities into new, unfamiliar, and impersonal surroundings. There was the spread of regimentation in the growth of armed forces, huge industrial establishments, transit systems, and distant administrative procedures. Many people in the mass became relatively faceless, anonymous, interchangeable, standardized entities.

In turn, such invisible people were sliced up within themselves. In the course of a lifetime ... a career ... even a day, a person came to play more and more different and partial roles. One fragment played, for example, the role of son or daughter. Another played the role of employee or student. Another played the role of utility company customer. Another played the role of political party supporter. Another played the role of hobbyist. And so on. From a pattern in which the individual was a relatively whole and complete person acting and reacting in a central, integrated environment which was relatively consistent and co-ordinated, people shifted in the century after 1850 to radically different patterns. They literally flew apart psychically to become a succession of different versions of themselves in different settings – *often actually inconsistent with each other.*

The key here lies in the change of self-perception that is inescapably involved. While you perceive of yourself as approximately one distinct and unified entity in tune with an ordered universe, you draw upon those extensions of perception that reflect, serve, and reinforce such unity. But if your own unity and distinctiveness dwindle, the need and desire for comparable unity and distinctiveness in extensions of perception can dwindle too.

And this calls for something like television: a kaleidoscopic, restless, ever-changing medium to mirror the new fragmented man, to provide escape, non-linearity, anonymity in a mass, and pleasurable emotionalism. As a speculation, at least, we could argue that even if there hadn't been the hardware and economic accidents, the basic social circumstances of the post-1945 world demanded some kind of medium like television.

Thus, as an additional item in the catalogue of proxy extensions of the senses, television leapt almost overnight from tinkerer's toy to everyone's adjunct. For it to assume massive proportions took about five years. (That's a conservative estimate.)

What have we got this time?

So far as any improvement in our ability and capacity to perceive reality is concerned, we once again have a mixed blessing and curse. Let us examine the ingredients in more detail.

To begin with, try setting up a representative television operation in your mind:

First, a receiving set (black and white: colour comes later). 133

This gives you a piece of equipment capable, in North America, of providing for the reproduction of about 365,000 bits of an image in an area of about 400 square inches. Such bits, in turn, can be graduated from black to white to provide for the shades of contrast in the composite picture. The picture as a whole provides your eyes with roughly half the amount of information that the eyes alone are capable of perceiving when focused directly on an object.

Such pictures are changed 30 times a second – a rate somewhat faster than the eye can perceive. As a result, you get the impression of continuous movement with the ingredients of each individual picture overlapping with those of previous and subsequent pictures. (The whole remains intelligible as a perceptible impression because most of the actual bits don't change from picture to picture – probably only about 10% in fact change on the average.)

In short, as you sit viewing (the ideal place is directly in front of the set at a distance equal to about eight times the height of the picture tube), you are using a sense extension that provides you with a reasonable approximation in black and white of what you would perceive if you were there in person.

Next, the transmission chain.

This consists of the various links between your set and the point where the telecast material originates. It includes all the devices used to convey the modulated carrier waves which provide the picture and the sound that you see and hear. Within about a 100 mile range, the main link will probably be the air through which the emanations from a transmitting tower (roughly 50 kilowatt power for the picture wave and around 35 kilowatt power for the FM sound wave) are conveyed. Increasingly, this link is being supplemented or even replaced by a coaxial cable connection which either takes advantage of a community antenna to improve reception or actually ties in directly with the originating point. If greater distances are involved – as with network programming – there will probably be microwave links employing more concentrated directional beams than ordinary transmission or, occasionally, satellite links through space using precision dish antennae.

This electronic linkage is where physical loss of picture and sound quality is usually likely to occur. As distance increases, as the number and varieties of interchange multiply, as external interferences from other sources such as thunder storms, aeroplane engines, and power mowers add up, the strength and accuracy of the signal reaching your television set tends to diminish. The picture tends to get fuzzier, criss-crossed with static, or prey to rival signals. The sound tends to get weaker or more uneven.

Some of these effects may be offset by various devices to boost signals and screen out extraneous impulses picked up along the way. But, as many a red eye will testify after a hockey telecast, some occlusions and intrusions will persist. As an estimate, one can assume that even in the best areas of transmission and reception, something like 10% of the original television signals will be lost in this process.

In practice, 90% provides picture and sound reasonably close to what our senses demand. Still, as a first qualification in our assessment of television as an extension of our senses, it becomes apparent that what we see at the receiving end is not an exact copy of what is observable at the sending end. It is a somewhat diluted approximation (as, of course, it is with radio as well).

Finally, the sending system.

The remaining combinations of hardware and people which stand between the viewer and the occurrence are provided at the sending end. These combinations are by far the most complex because they include a mixture of technology and judgment. Technology provides television cameras (or their equivalent if film or tape is being inserted into the system), lighting, sets of scenic selection, microphones, and a control room fitted out with devices to select, mix, switch, and pass on various versions of the occurrence. Judgment comes to bear in the selection of which aspects of the technology to use, which to combine with others, and which to discard, and which versions of the occurrence similarly to use, combine, or discard.

Necessarily, the raw information introduced into the television system is going to be affected very significantly at this stage. Because some selection of available equipment has to be applied, patterns of differential emphasis will tend to emerge. Because each technological unit in the complex has its own strengths and weaknesses, such emphases will be compounded. So far, no one has done any objective studies on the effects of the many decisions implicit in such emphasis and selectivity, but it seems clear that effects do occur. A celebrated instance, for example, involved Richard Nixon in a series of television debates with the late John F. Kennedy during the 1960 U.S. presidential campaign. By accident or design, Mr Nixon was so lighted in the television studio and had a skin so seen by a television camera that he seemed to have a very heavy five o'clock shadow. In our North American society such an unshaven appearance is associated with villains. As a result, it is suggested that Mr Nixon lost the debates – and the presidency of the United States – before he opened his mouth to speak.

At any rate, the simplified three-stage system just described encompasses television *as most people know it today.* Now, with it in mind, let us circle the medium and consider what it all adds up to.

On the positive side, we probably do gain a certain extension of our senses from television. We can be taken to places and events quite directly and, once there, can be presented with reasonable indications of what is happening. Moreover, such indications will not be entirely linear, but will include a number of simultaneous visual and aural dimensions.

Further, the intrusion of the interpreter will tend to be limited. Unlike print or even radio,

television can let events speak and show for themselves.

It affords immediate, first-hand contact with both eyes and ears. No commentator in the world can intrude to effectively deny what you can see and hear yourself, and few will even be tempted to try. Even when attempts are made, there will be the difficult challenge, 'Let us see for ourselves.'

Television can also be wholly immediate much of the time. So long as the originating equipment can be installed (sometimes difficult, so far), events, individuals, and ideas can be presented as they are at the immediate moment. Like radio – though perhaps less easily and less often – television can take us almost anywhere in the world and let us hear *and see* what is going on. In fact, by virtue of superior ranges of lenses and microphones, we often end up with a fuller perception of an event, individual, or idea than we might get if we were there in person. A TV camera, for example, can focus close-up with a zoom lens on events up to half a mile away – our ordinary visual close-up range is about 10 feet. A 'shotgun' microphone can single out and pick up a conversation at a comparable distance – our ears lose acuity at about 100 feet. When

you consider that there will probably be several cameras and several microphones in use at any one time, the advantages start to add up impressively. Football games, space shots, political conventions, and wars all provide impressive demonstrations of such advantages in practice.

Television also provides a sense of focus, engagement, and intimacy that most other media lack. Very early it was discovered that crowd scenes tend to wash out into a sea of grey on the TV tube. As a result, the medium quickly switched to a primary concentration on small segments, on close-ups – on dimensions suitable to the 400 square inches of picture being provided. Immediately, this meant an emphasis on focus: any event, idea, or other expression had to be scaled down and selected.

This can be very useful. Such scaling down and selection – if done well – serves to reduce the number of variables in the event, idea, or other expression that we have to grapple with. Instead of our having to sort through a fuzzy grey picture of 13,476 hockey fans to spot Aunt Ida, the TV picture will give us a batch of, say, 40 fans, with a plump, gesticulating Aunt Ida leading the attack on the referee. This, of course, can be misused as well, but we'll save that for later.

Engagement is provided by the mixture of picture size, motion, and sound on the one hand and our eyes and ears on the other. In the way that a good carnival pitchman always talks and moves at the same time in order to hold his crowd, TV talks and moves in a partly darkened room and holds us. As we all know so well, it is seldom that animated conversations, games, or other live activities survive the pull of a reasonably good TV offering. Engaged, we turn to the electric eye and commune.

Now, for positive purposes – such as telling us survival information, passing on warnings, conveying important and exact instructions – such a quality of engagement is also an advantage. It means relatively undivided attention and the bonus of contact that goes with it.

The sense of intimacy is somewhat akin to that of radio – though much less valid. Partly because the workable limits of an average set and general social practice both tend to make TV viewing a one, two, or three person activity, and partly because telecast material usually is built around a host or narrator, people get a sense of close personal contact with what is going on. The picture takes you right there, a familiar face is on hand to explain and amplify, the setting in which you are watching is personal and uncluttered (except in some bars). Not surprisingly, it is quite tempting to assume that the TV is being offered for you or your special group – and that there aren't 40 to 100 other people in and around the set behind Johnny Carson and there isn't an audience of millions.

This too can be very useful at times. To the extent that a sense of intimacy fosters acceptance, and acceptance in turn means more ready awareness of the reality of our human condition, we benefit. It can mean, for example, the difference between remembering and not remembering to take a polio shot, the difference between continuing a bit of bigotry and allowing for a different point of view, the difference between perceiving and not perceiving. Just as we tend to make extra efforts and allowances for friends, we can be coaxed by TV's suggestions of intimacy.

And, finally on the positive side, there is a function of television that is often deplored and decried. This is the combination of ease, amusement, escape and/or adventure that makes up the sinful concept of entertainment. At the risk of trial for heresy, one can suggest that effective perception of reality actually *demands* entertainment and is *facilitated* by entertainment. The demand part is involved, primarily, in the processes of rest and rejuvenation that everyone must have to make optimal use of mind and senses. To the extent that television rescues minds and senses from excessive preoccupation with debts, death, taxes, and the like, it is a positive boon. The facilitation stems from the function of alternate avenues. If, while relaxed and unthreatened, we are able to allow ideas and information into our heads that would otherwise be re-

jected, we gain a bonus. Among primary school children, for example, it has been found that a great deal of important, significant, useful, and creative information has been picked up via television simply because it isn't in the stuffy context of a classroom or cast as an obligation. Equally, people who have trouble reading or working in large groups repeatedly demonstrate that as an alternative to print and study groups the avenue of TV is an invaluable high road.

But, as with the other media we have examined, there are some modifications or qualifications attached to the apparent advantages afforded by television as an extension of our senses. Even without the shrillness of professional critics, it is apparent that the medium – like the others, or even more so – contains some inherent defects that can and do distort the portraits of reality it provides.

One distortion, however, needs to be set outside of this context. This is the distortion involved in efforts to offset the *innate* defects of the medium, made for the sake of approaching reality. It is a distortion, for instance, to vary the lighting, camera angles, and microphone placement used for different individuals – say, political candidates. But such distortion, when perceptively used, can actually serve to present a more accurate version of each contending individual than would any single system used for all individuals in common. The 'tailored' system can modify the artificial emphasis inherent in each of the devices of television to allow the viewer to hear and view more of the individual as he or she really is. The argument here is difficult, but persuasive:

One must sometimes falsify an immediate dimension of reality in order that the larger whole can approach reality.

The case of Mr Nixon is again a case in point. Modification of the lighting and make-up used with Mr Nixon in his debate with Mr Kennedy would not have changed either Mr Nixon or Mr Kennedy. What they said to each other, and what they really looked like, would have remained close to what the people watching in the studio observed. All that would have been removed was the distortion provided by the reaction of lights and TV camera on Mr Nixon's face – a reaction not evident on Mr Nixon in the flesh. More difficult, perhaps, would be the case of Canada's prime minister, Pierre Elliott Trudeau. He suffers from the opposite problem – he is so photogenic that it is almost impossible to portray him on film or television as he really is. He looks younger, sportier, and (apparently) more lovable than he does in the flesh. And so, the challenge to the medium in this case is to artificially age, mute, and de-emphasize the TV picture of Mr Trudeau until it assumes qualities and appearance more in line with his actual self.

Now, even assuming the best, what reservations should we persist in having about this pervasive new proxy medium? The most evident ones involve problems of cost, cumbersomeness, selectivity, value-loading, artificiality, and what might be termed psychiatric time-bombs. Let us muse on each of these in turn. (People-TV is a consideration too, as with the other media, but by now we should be able to combine the considerations for the sake of simplicity and avoiding tedious repetition.)

The costs are enough to make you weep. Even when aspirations are limited to a dull, normal television channel, the bill for plant and equipment alone is apt to run from $800,000 to $1.5 million. Actual operations will cost an additional $600,000 to $1.6 million each year. And, if the channel turns to all-colour presentations – as most have now – these figures jump to a total of $1 million to $3 million for plant and equipment and $675,000 to $2 million for operations. Note too that, unlike many production processes, the plant and equipment used in television have short life-spans – averaging about five years maximum in most cases. In today's television broadcasting, an average station with average equipment, average staff, and average programming represents an expenditure of roughly $1 million to $3 million a year.

Right away you have troubles. Quite apart from the relative scarcity of channels and licences, cost alone limits consistent access to television broadcasting facilities. No one – public or private – is going to be able to get a station of his own without some way of nailing down an awful lot of money. One may well ask who is likely to be able to get one to three million dollars a year. An anarchist? a teenager? a housewife? a professor? a student? Not on your life! Harsh reality and the evidence in every country where there is television make it very clear indeed that to get that kind of money you have to turn to government – or the marketplace.

Accordingly, you have to be either politically acceptable (not necessarily politically partisan – more to the point, in tune with the broad philosophy and day-to-day convenience of public administrators) or able to demonstrate economic rectitude. There will have to be a payoff of reasonable proportions – in electors' acquiescence, or dictator's satisfaction, or dollars rolling in. Within a certain leeway, the allocation of the scarce resources that money represents will have to return demonstrable results that can compare with a great many alternative allocations that had to be ruled out to allow for the television channel.

If it is a political allocation, the competition will involve some hard decisions and challenges. Does the $1 million to $3 million produce better political results than might have been secured from spending the same money on health care, education, roads, national defence, unemployment insurance, or, perhaps most important, the direct wooing of voters? Is the fragile fabric of community consent strengthened by the outlay? And, at the same time, are the human greeds, ambitions, prejudices, and preoccupations of political overseers at least checkmated?

If it is a question of the marketplace, equally rigorous tests apply. Would the $1 million to $3 million earn more in mortgages? Or in a flier with Acme Grobbets, Inc? Does the allocation support the principles of the marketplace? Are the comparably human greeds, ambitions, prejudices, and preoccupations of investors served well enough to gain the advertising, the stock purchases, and the bank loans required?

Almost inescapably, the medium will tend to become somewhat imbalanced by such considerations. While it may aspire to portray reality as exactly and completely as possible, it will have to curb such aspirations with sensible financial considerations affecting its very existence. The revenue base – public or private – will have to be protected.

So?

So, nothing over any sustained period can be tolerated – no person, no program, no policy, no portrayal can be tolerated – if it means that the funds necessary to get and stay on the air are threatened. State-run or state-financed stations, for example, cannot be expected to carry sustained attacks upon the principle of rule of law, simply because states of every political complexion all depend upon the principle of rule of law to function. They will not (and cannot) consciously tolerate serious erosion of such a principle and, if necessary, will deprive a state-run or state-financed station of revenue (or even legal existence) if it persists in challenging such a principle – even if the current reality of actual events does in fact involve negation of rule of law.

Similarly, 'private' stations relying upon versions of the marketplace will be sensitive to the preferences of advertising agencies and investors. They cannot be expected to take wholly happily to campaigns to nationalize beer companies or the automobile industry, to promote any serious lack of confidence in stock markets, or to advocate policies and practices by individuals or governments that will wither their revenue roots. Like governments, marketplace operators do not usually have a death wish.

But it is not only the financial sponsor whose interests must be watched. Protection of that revenue base is frequently dependent upon audience. Directly, to the extent that its advertising rates depend upon a guaranteed number of viewers, and indirectly, to the extent that it is politically sensitive to voter acceptance of publicly-financed undertakings, a television station or network has to be able to deliver audience if it is to obtain survival revenue.

Not unnaturally, then, really radical or revolting or creative or experimental programming – of a sort likely to lose viewers in any significant numbers – tends to suffer. Much of the 'wasteland' flavour of television programming, in this sense, can be ascribed to the 'wasteland' qualities possessed by, *or ascribed to,* viewers. To protect and enhance their revenue base, television operators, like those in radio and print, depend a great deal upon audience acceptance or what they think the audience will accept.

Yet, in the grimy world of reality, many radical, revolting, and creative or experimental aspects exist. It is not breach of confidence to suggest, for instance, that the very people who make up television staffs actually use language, engage in behavioural quirks, support ideas and ideologies entirely at odds with what they permit themselves to present in programs. The dulcet 'One Moment Please' on the picture and sound track is all too often the whitewashed version of, 'Hell, we've lost the bloody feed from Kapuskasing!'

In so far as such whitewashing – and many other more serious manifestations of it – occurs, television is diminished as a valid and reliable proxy agent for our sensory-cerebral perception of the world around us.

That's the overview.

No television outlet can really ignore its source of support in its dedication to the presentation of a realistic portrait of the human condition.

Unlike other media the stakes are too high for losers to persist with TV.

More detailed consequences follow. Costs vary according to the type of programming offered; budgets have not yet been allocated that allow for the best of everything; as a result, considerations of cost dictate, in part, the range of offerings made available. For every lavish special production there have to be several cheap fillers. For every piece of magnificent equipment, there have to be compensating scrimps and saves with baling wire and string. For every super-star there has to be a flock of lower-priced help.

This pressure to economize can take a variety of forms in practice – all of them reasonably demonstrable distortions of reality. Major expenditures can be scaled down through repetition of the program, for instance, with the result that the pattern of emphasis is shaken up. (Almost all network programs are repeated twice or more – the champion being 'I Love Lucy.') Major expenditures can also be offset through widespread distribution and syndication of the resulting programs, which are then offered out of their original time and context. (Imagine 'Dr Kildare' in Arabic in Saudi Arabia, for example.) Major expenditures can be balanced by cut-rate items, with the result that some people and topics will suffer from the curse of mediocrity and unbalanced presentation.

Further, the scope of televised activities can be manipulated. A study of news reporting, for example, established that almost four-fifths of international news on TV and other media presented in North America originated in a section of the globe christened

Internationaland

This is the world of major international capitals (London, UN-New York, Moscow, Paris, Geneva, Berlin, and Tokyo) in which enough in the way of specific events and significant reactions to outside happenings is available to keep a correspondent and camera crew busy all year round. With regular work and output, the cost per item in an Internationaland capital is well below the cost (and dif-

ficulty) of covering events in more remote areas. But, inescapably, such orchestration tends to over-emphasize Internationaland at the expense of the rest of the world. The accounting department might be happy, but our awareness of reality suffers.

Cumbersomeness is, in part, yet another consequence of the cost squeeze. Even though the technology necessary for greater mobility and flexibility is for the most part available as a by-product of the space program and other research, the price of this advanced technology is still prohibitive for mainstream television. As a result, the medium tends to be elephantlike. Attempts to move out of fixed studio locations often bog down in the masses of heavy, fragile, awkward equipment that have to be taken to the scene. Great lumbering vans have to waddle into place and, at best, are restricted in 'live' coverage to the area within line of sight of the station's receiving tower or a microwave relay system.

Inevitably, in such circumstances, the use of 'mobile' equipment and the general pattern of in-the-field coverage tend to become distorted. It is always much easier and more reliable for TV programming to settle for relatively predictable happenings – so more stress is given to formal conferences, scheduled speeches, and similarly organized activities in sports, the arts, and so forth. It is difficult, unreliable, and sometimes risky to prowl about following up hunches or rumours – so less stress is given to spontaneous happenings, to points of difficult access, to areas of present or latent hostility.

As all these influences work, the dimensions of reality suffer from shifts in emphasis. Watching TV newscasts, for example, one gets the impression that most of the people and activities in the world are to be found at press conferences, conventions, and the sites of speeches. Walking about any city, one's own eyes and ears tell a very different tale.

As an offset to this, of course, television often puts aside the elephantine equipment and relies on intermediary reality-watchers, just as radio and print do. But it still suffers from differential emphasis. The set pieces come complete with all the trimmings of live or taped illustration to take you where the action is or at least where it can be reached with the necessary equipment. The flexible reporter, on the other hand, can only be a talking head.

The third problem, selectivity, as we have already seen, is innate in the television medium. Costs dictate certain selectivity to balance the budget. Equipment dictates selectivity in the various ways various people and events are electronically perceived. The picture itself dictates selectivity in the limited capacity it has to handle numbers of people or details of scene.

As noted, such selectivity can, when honestly done to scale, facilitate our handling of the maelstrom of reality. But when such is not the case (alas, too often), our handling of reality is made more complicated.

The difficulty is primarily one that is encountered also in print, radio, and film. It is the difficulty implicit in selection *in advance of presentation* – that ■ **individual viewers can seldom know what they are missing.**

They have to make up their minds about the relationship of a television offering to reality on the basis of what they see and what they, at the most, can guess or suspect they don't see.

Immediately, the dice are loaded in favour of the TV version. On the screen will be the sounds and pictures of a selected version of reality. Artfully produced, technically excellent, such a version will tend to be engrossing, persuasive, entertaining, and almost tangible. To doubt it requires very considerable and sustained efforts of will and imagination. So to doubt it will be a relatively infrequent phenomenon.

Yet, on occasion, such doubt will be crucially important for our perception of reality and decisions based upon it. Remember Mr Nixon and Mr Trudeau. The negative and positive versions presented to us in these cases bore no serious relationship to the views, abilities, or even actual appearances of the individuals involved. Yet enough of us were apparently swayed by such selectivity – innocent as it probably was – to decide who was to form a government. It wasn't a case of voting on policies or actual people. It was a case of voting on the merits of an array of phosphors glowing on a picture tube – an array of inanimate, impersonal, insignificant, mindless phosphors.

This brings up the question of value-loading. We have noted already that print and radio suffer from predispositions towards value-loading because of their limitations in dealing with abstractions, their connections with the establishment, and their associations with frail human beings. Television as well is plagued with these problems. Abstractions pose difficulties wherever picture and sound fail to provide adequate means of expression. Establishment connections match up with the political and economic underpinnings of the medium. Frail humans – sometimes in remarkable numbers – are scattered everywhere in television, expressing their prejudices, preferences, and priorities.

In addition, TV has some predispositions towards value-loading that belong to it alone and are inherent in its physical nature. The stress in TV is on picture first, sound second, and print a bad third. Such a hierarchy of presentation automatically emphasizes some kinds of individuals and events at the expense of others.

Put bluntly, all things being equal, television will opt for the best picture. And what makes a good TV picture?

There are, first of all, purely technical considerations: Adequate contrast, sharpness, consistency of image from shot to shot, steadiness, freedom from interference.

Then there are content-audience considerations: movement of an interesting kind, uncluttered composition, interesting sizes and shapes, intelligibility, continuity of mood or idea.

Clearly, some people and some events will tend to meet these medium-determined standards more often and more easily than others. To that extent, some people and some events will be more effectively and probably more frequently portrayed. The advantages of impact and exposure will tend to build up one side of some aspects of our total reality at the expense of others.

For example, it can be argued that television is playing a very considerable role in the upgrading of what might be called ugly or, more accurately, unusual people. Those who persist and survive on the medium are not those blessed with the regular features, even teeth, and idealized bodies of the North American dream. Such perfection makes for visual monotony, as harem keepers knew long ago. Instead, the person who prevails will have, within certain bounds, very distinctive characteristics such as a Streisand nose, a Sullivan posture, a Grandma Clampett voice, Lorne Greene eyebrows, a Gleason shape, or the odd orchestration of oddities of Tiny Tim. And, no matter how hopeful and pleasant it is to see those wholly or partly denied perfection make good, such a state of affairs produces value-loaded interference with reality. The lines of such people, and of many events for that matter, tend to be overdrawn. Life itself is too timeless, tame, or undistinguished to be squeezed within the confines of the television medium. Television requires its own versions of life – larger or lesser than reality as the dictates of drama, perception, occasion, and technology specify.

Equally, content tends to be sculptured. Violence, for instance, makes magnificent pictures – lots of movement, shock value, emotional involvement, and arresting camera angles. Even without much conscious concern to distort reality, television tends to opt for pictures and programs portraying violence. Indeed, the classic themes of conflict tend to provide the operational models: suspense, hatred, jealousy, unrequited love, suspicion, orgiastic excess, panic, fear, and so on.

This, on one plane, is wholly defensible. As a medium at least aspiring to foster communication from humans to humans, television seeks to serve some human purposes. In seeking to serve human purposes, television is also prey to human predispositions. In so far as human predispositions include impatience, focusing on the main point, a general sense of wordless dread, and uncomfortable mortality, television will tend to exhibit and cater to such predispositions.

But at the same time the presentation of reality can and does suffer.

This in turn brings us to the question of outright artificiality. Here the problem isn't one of degree, as with value-loading. The problem is **bare-faced fabrication.**

One such fabrication is to be found in the medium's recurrent confusion between 'is' and 'ought.' As the equipment, production characteristics, and personnel of television are pressed from within by limits of capacity, funds, and time, and as the external pressures of competition and the urge to make contact mount, it is not terribly surprising that television feels a temptation to act and program about reality as it ought to be rather than as it is.

Take situation comedy. One of the frequent themes involves an average family and its amusing, lovable, lively life. That, so to speak, is the 'is' of the theme. Then the 'ought' starts creeping in. Limits of capacity, funds, and time conspire to recommend that, instead of real people in a real setting, the program use actors and stage sets. This way enough control is gained over the variables of performance, weather, scheduling, and availability, that it is actually possible to come up with a half-hour program every week. And the 'is' of the average family changes. The content of the average family's life is altered to introduce extra, and competitive, comedy, to shape the composition of the family, to include appealing or antagonistic characters, to allow for powerful commercial breaks, and so on. The scale of the average family's life is elevated to allow for greater variety, more incident, or faster pace.

The end is an unabashed fabrication. The average 'family' as it appears on the screen is unrepresentative in size and composition, about double the normal in income, and almost unbelievably mixed and manic in behaviour.

Now, this isn't a great surprise. The purveyors of such programming on television seldom suggest seriously that they are mirroring reality or engaging in profound social commentary. Most of them would cheerfully concede that they are concocting composite fabrications and, at the same time, would claim with some justice that this is neither a secret nor a conspiracy ... just good clean family entertainment.

But views on what is good and clean can differ; and some things can be overdone. Those are the central problems.

'Just good, clean family entertainment' is open to question on several grounds. First, it is acknowledged to be selected and artificial. Second, the nature of the medium is too compelling for such selection and artificiality not to be at least unconsciously convincing. Third, there is not enough alternate programming available to balance or offset such material.

Reality suffers.

This is no casual consideration. As selected and artificial versions of family life, youth, living standards, ideologies, and other ingredients of human existence are offered and emphasized (surrounded by the materialist bludgeons of more and more hard-sell commercials), human expectations cannot help but be affected. A slum dweller bombarded with the unattainable 'average' of 'I Love Lucy' will tend either to turn in rage on a society that appears to be cheating him of his birthright and self-respect or to lapse into unreachable despair. A foreigner viewing the mawkish materialism of American television series, peddled at fire-sale prices to his network, will tend to despise his own version of community values or become irrationally anti-American. Much of the time we can't check ourselves. And so the gaps between television's powerful and persuasive appearance of reality and actual realities will frequently be profound and damaging.

When the relatively new and growing phenomenon of colour is added, the potential for tinkering with reality becomes even greater. Preliminary studies indicate that colour television has a markedly different and greater impact than black and white. Colour induces much stronger emotional reactions and direct individual identification between the picture and the viewer. As a result, it can be argued that colour television brings us close to an illusion of reality, and one that is provided *for* us rather than *by* us, that is sufficiently persuasive and credible to outweigh reality itself.

In effect, colour television provides us with a new kind of alphabet, made up of these specific and interacting ingredients:

→ *movement,* which compels attention
→ *sound,* both natural and the spoken word
→ *time,* real and theatrical
→ *space,* also real and theatrical
→ *music,* something more than simple sound
→ *focus of attention,* with inessentials stripped away
→ *emotional ingredients* such as humour, hatred, and love
→ *technical leeway,* allowing for close-ups, dissolves, slow motion, and other enchantments
→ *illumination* in the entire range from brightness to darkness
→ *colour,* sometimes more impressive than that found in life itself.

Such an alphabet begins to approach the stage of offering most of the elements of total communication. An individual can be engaged almost completely with his attention caught and re-caught by motion, colour, tricks of presentation, and selected urgency, his emotions battered, tickled, and soothed, his mind bludgeoned or by-passed. All that is missing is three-dimensional contact in which the television offering can be wrapped right around the individual ... and work on that step forward is already under way with experiments in holographic or three-dimensional television.

Audience surveys indicate that about 50 million people in the United States (and presumably a comparable proportion of the population in Canada) spend *five or more hours a day* consuming television. The impact of such relatively total communication is impressive. Reality does not only suffer, it begins to disappear completely.

As a proxy agent, then, television poses some serious questions. In its scope, flexibility, variables, and capacity, the medium does an excellent job of duplicating our personal sensory-cerebral chains. It can act on our behalf in very close approximation to ourselves. But, because of its economic vulnerabilities, operational idiosyncrasies, and, most important of all, intrusion into each and every event it 'observes,' the medium cannot be regarded as a neutral mirror of the world.

Instead, television has to be regarded as a proxy activist rather than a proxy medium. Its perceptual contributions rate as positive gains only when the activism involved in the medium matches up with the kinds and degrees of activism that a viewer would engage in himself.

This isn't a put-down of television in general. It is only a set of reservations put forward in relation to television and reality.

Now, let us consider the step-father of television as a proxy agent: film, in all its weird and wonderful dimensions.

FILM

146   It is characteristic of the elusive unpredictability of film that it
should follow TV in any chronological review of proxy sense extensions, despite its longer history and its spattering of heydays well
before mass television.

The reasons lie mainly in present performance. TV now has become reasonably settled and predictable in its forms, impacts, and
relative adequacy. We *know* most of what we are getting from TV –
for better or worse. Until one or other of the looming technological changes breaks through to mass use (and we'll look at that in a
moment), TV is close enough to the morasses of formula programming and purely technical tinkering to be an almost traditional
medium.

But film, surprisingly, is in yet another of its spasms of change
and creativity. The varied aims underlying expressions as different
as MASH, *Catch-22, Love Story, I Am Curious (Yellow), 2001,
Bonnie and Clyde,* and the exploratory continuations of Expo 70
hint at shifting intent and changed impact bordering on revolution
within the medium. Add in assorted 'underground' films, and the
flavour of flux and flexibility becomes overpowering. As Anthony
Schillaci of Fordham University's National Film Study Program
concludes:

... The young have discovered that film is an environment which
you put on, demanding a different kind of structure, a different
mode of attention than any other art. Their hunger is for mind-
expanding experience and simultaneity, and their art is film.

Anthony Schillaci, 'The Now Movie, 1. Film as Environment,' *Saturday
Review,* Dec. 28, 1968, p. 8

To the extent, then, that popcorn sales have ceased to be the
primary preoccupation of filmmakers, any examination of the roles
of film in extending our senses by proxy becomes rather tentative
and speculative. We may be aware that things are happening – who

can miss them? – yet far from clear or conclusive about exactly
what is happening to what effect or with what consequences for
our senses.

So, with film, we will have to operate at two levels. From the
checkerboard of past performance, it is possible to draw some in-
ferences about the nature and effects of film that have been tested
out enough to rank as probabilities. Then, wandering through contemporary experiments which break the old rules and abandon the
old conventions, we can collect data on possibilities to temper or
even counter such probabilities. The result should provide an in-
terim assessment based on mixed fact and fancy.

Our main emphasis in this chapter will be on feature film. Both
news and documentary offerings have now become primarily the
preserve of television, together with cartoons and most educational
projects. To the extent that film still manages to retain its identity
as something more than a part of what the TV tube consumes, it
concentrates on features. (And even there, for that matter, we are
now seeing the rise of 'made-for-TV' features given their premiers
on various networks and channels.)

In its established and most familiar Hollywood forms, film can
be fairly clearly defined. It is the product of an antic array of individuals and artifacts that flows into movie houses and drive-ins to
offer two hours of tension, titillation, or escape, a backdrop for
courting or consummation, an oddly communal rite, and an array
of illusions. Eventually, it is sliced up, shortened, and squeezed out
of proportion for (ab)use on television.

Film is also a set of states of mind. It is the ballooning buffoon-
ery that has devalued our language and sense of individual commitment with the supersell of advertising claims for a blancmange of
content.

★ ☆ ★ ☆ ★ ☆ ★ ☆ ★

Doris Day as a *teenager* in a socially significant CINEMASCOPE SPECTACULAR

★ ★ ★ ★ ★ ★ ★ ★ ★

It is also psychodrama that allows all of us to be the good guys or bad guys we have always wanted to be (I *am* Doris Day as a teenage mother and look at all those bad guys *suffer for what they did*). Film is a sort of holiday and the womb of perpetual night and a chance for chuckling anonymity when you're ugly.

And, alas, film is also part of our array of inputs that adds up to the sense of reality that guides or misguides us from day to day.

In addition to, and somewhat apart from, impressionistic musings, we need to examine the phenomenon more carefully and specifically.

Well, what have we got?

In established and familiar forms, film is a

communications chain.

It links conceptualizers (bankers, writers, producers, directors, editors) via technicians (actors, cameramen, soundmen, lab workers, and so forth) through distributors (Columbia Pictures of Canada, for example) and exhibitors (Odeon or Famous Players, for instance) to audiences (you and me). As in most chains, each link is approximately equally important – at least in the sense that it can affect the content and even the form of the transmission and assign certain distinctive characteristics to it as well.

Conceptualizers are especially important; their impact on the audience is more direct and extensive than in any other medium. We observe the end results in rather special circumstances: a darkened hall with all-pervasive sound, emphasis on the film as the primary light (and attention) source, seats bolted down to direct us at the offering, deliberate muting or removal of rival attention-getters (even the candy counter is usually discreetly located outside the film shrine), vast enlargement of the 'life' we observe (such as the current fad for 60-foot cleavages), and careful orchestration of ingredients of air, temperature, and decor. Compared with the hodge-podge of print, the fleeting ephemerality of radio, the familial and comparatively microscopic TV tube, film in a cinema setting is overwhelming. As a result, the work of any and all the conceptualizers gets especially close and compelling attention.

Who are they?

The bankers are probably the most important. Ever since the 1920s when growth, excesses, and bad judgment produced enough fiscal errors to throw most of the film industry into the hands of outside backers, banks have tended to dominate the industry. They advance the huge sums needed to underwrite most contemporary feature films – about $150,000 minimum for a 'quickie,' around $700,000 for a reliable 'B' movie, and $2 million and up for a 'blockbuster.'

Being bankers, they try to protect their investments by arranging terms and precautions best suited to reducing risks and maximizing rewards. It doesn't quite reach the point, so often alleged, of requiring proof that the money isn't needed, but the care lavished by film bankers does go a long way. It includes, for example, the general industry practice of assigning cash values to various participants: such and such a star with so and so as a director and this cameraman and that set designer and these writers and those distribution outlets add up to a guarantee of so many hundred thousand dollars.

Equally, it tends to intrude into subject matter and treatment. Although film bankers usually are, to be fair, rather well informed about the medium's needs and possibilities, they also are well informed about the risks of dealing with some topics, the advantages in others, and most of all, the *past performances* of virtually all talent and topics.

This, willy-nilly, involves them in the process of conceptualizing. The delicate movement of their well-manicured hands to or from the cash box often decides whether a concept lives or dies. The size of the bundle they hand out has a bearing on the scale and style of production. While few but the most stagestruck actually make major suggestions, film bankers have a very large say indeed about the acceptability of ideas and themes.

Now, imagine yourself as an informed, experienced, and reasonably intelligent banker who specializes in lending money to filmmakers. On the one hand, you are aware of the messy, sweaty, irrational and chaotic real world – a great bundle of crises, challenges, inequities, and urgencies. Famines, plagues, political scandals, theologies, racial stresses, and sexual upheavals all clamour for attention and expression. At the very least, such themes and topics cannot be gainsaid as part of what is going on in the world.

But ... on the other hand ... you're a *banker,* dealing with *money.* Crisp, hard-earned, perishable *money.* Can you really venture to expose such a worthy substance to activities that will threaten it? Or lessen its magical earning power? Or upset public confidence? Or (gasp) run afoul of the law or the church? Think of your shareholders (widows and orphans)! Think of your Board of Directors! Think (gulp) of your job!

So o o ... **you compromise a little.**

Instead of facilitating the mirroring of the real world, you tend, quite naturally and reasonably, to design your own orders of priority. For a start, you place a premium on past performance simply because you know that a film about spies or cowboys or pop composers made a fat profit last time and has a good chance again, because you know that almost anything starring Liz Taylor or Burton or John Wayne works at the box office, because you know the odds in favour of a proven producer or studio.

Equally, you keep a wary eye out for serious troublemakers. Pickets, boycotts, censorship board rulings, condemned ratings, and politics in general are familiar sources of fiscal trouble for films. So, people or topics likely to seriously disturb significant organizations – such as the Legion of Decency, or the Theatres Branch of the Ontario Department of Tourism and Information, or Italian-Americans – are also likely to prompt warning signals. In extreme cases – such as the film *Salt of the Earth* – bank money will be refused outright because of the people and themes involved. (This was a film by a blacklisted producer on the sensitive theme of sweated labour.) More often, the traditional film industry will carefully restrict its material and talents so as to gain approval. Nudity, for instance, was a European commonplace for more than a decade before Hollywood bared a breast.

No one has yet examined film bankers very seriously as influences on the medium, but from varied comments and controversies, it is clear that – as with so much else in our materialist world – the holders of purse strings are a powerful force and, in turn, the direction of that force tends to be towards safety, proven performers, and muted muckraking. Even – Heaven help us – the late Walt Disney lived in some fear and trembling of such influence. As Richard Schickel recounts:

... Disney finally had to go to his principal backer, The Bank of America, and request an additional $250,000.
... Disney was forced to show an unfinished print of the film to one of the bank's vice presidents, Joseph Rosenberg, in order to secure the fresh backing.

Richard Schickel, *Walt Disney* (London: Weidenfeld and Nicolson, 1968), p. 214

(The film was *Snow White* and Disney, in this case, got the money. Had he not been making the investment in *Snow White,* Schickel points out, 1936 might have been Disney's most financially successful year to that point.)

Producers and directors – and to a lesser extent, writers – are more familiar than bankers as film conceptualizers. Each can put a distinctive stamp upon a film sufficient to affect content, emphasis, and impact. *The Caine Mutiny,* for example, emerged as a wholly different moral tale on film compared to either the original book or the stage play. Similarly, the re-make of the film classic *Ben Hur* (subject of a classic review, 'Loved Him, hated Hur'), was barely recognizable in relation to the 1926 original directed by the late Fred Niblo.

The reasons are fairly obvious. The processes of selection, pacing, location, and presentation in film modify reality – and all are personal decisions. In effect, the camera acts for *your* eyes, seeing and omitting as it wishes, but under the control of someone else – the producer-director-writer triumverate.

Paul Rotha, the noted filmmaker and historian, explained this succinctly:

A film is primarily a dynamic pattern or rhythm (achieved by the editing and cutting) imposed on nature (the material taken, preferably the reality). It is governed pictorially by the use of light and movement in the creation of visual images, and mentally by psychology in the creation of mental images. Music and synchronised sound, used in counterpoint and contrapuntally, heighten the emotions of the spectator aurally and subconsciously. This dynamic mental pictorialism is, I claim, the most powerful form of expression available today to a creative artist.

Paul Rotha and Richard Griffith, *The Film Till Now* (Feltham, Middlesex: Hamlyn Publishing Group, 1967), p. 336

(At this point, you may murmur, 'What about actors?' Indeed. There is little doubt that people playing parts in front of cameras can have some influence on the finished product. But, as the parades of replacements on problem films testify, it can be, and is here, argued that actors – like props – tend to be extensions of the conceptualizers' arts and, for our purposes, don't really affect films to any comparable extent. Mind you, there is an irreducible minimum, as Paul Almond's rather disastrous venture with amateur players in *Isabel* testified.)

Finally, there is the conceptualizing role played by film editors. Even more than book and other media editors – prissy nit-pickers and negativizers all – film editors have an important and extensive part to play in creating a finished product. They take the chaotic raw product and turn it into cinematic communication. With talent they can rescue poorly directed material, render skilful sequences poetic, and throughout provide the pacing, sense of continuity, and drama essential to excellence.

Really good editing, of course, tends to be unnoticeable because the aim is to create a film experience that catches the viewer up and sweeps him along on the wave of content. But, some time, try sitting back at a movie to watch what an editor has done. Keep an eye out for the sequences of shots he has selected, the rhythm that his selections seek to create, and the ways they vary with the mood of the material. Then you'll have an idea of the artistry that has been applied.

After this very general survey of conceptualizing in film, what can we conclude about its effect on the medium as an extension of our sense of reality?

The overriding impression, in all honesty, is one of

helplessness.

In taking film as a portrayal – even symbolically – of portions of reality, we are obviously at the mercy of the conceptualizers. They decide *entirely in advance* what we will see, which portions will be stressed or ignored, which emotional overtones will be introduced and, to a significant degree, what our reactions will be. With film, we have little choice but to surrender to conceptualizers or walk out. Certainly, in the traditional use of film at least, anyone else can have little influence on the product. This is in sharp contrast with 'live' presentations on radio and TV and with the ready availability of alternative versions in print.

Of course, such all-powerfulness can occasionally serve us very well. When an aspect of reality is truly portrayed, the selectivity and talent of the conceptualizers reinforce our own weak senses. We get a glimpse of the concentrated, multi-layered substance of a person or situation in a manner unlikely if not impossible on our own. Parts of the film *Blowup*, for example, illustrated aspects of the amorality of much of our contemporary society in ways that personal experience seldom can. In roughly 70 minutes, we were exposed to something close to a university course on ethics – and probably paid much more attention to boot. So too with MASH and *Catch-22*.

But the question really is, 'How often and how consistently do the conceptualizers seek to relate to reality?' Given the human frailty, the egos, the greed, the subjectivity, and the hothouse atmosphere of the traditional film industry, it is not too unreasonable to suggest that Hollywood's reality is more Martian than mundane.

In turn, technicians tend to compound the difficulties of the situation. Every time there is an actor who plays himself rather than his assigned role, a cameraman too lazy to find creative alternative shots, unions and managements too rigid to provide leeway in budgets or working conditions, inefficient processors and manufacturers, the distance from desired reality increases. The traditional film industry is famous for the excellence of its technicians – deservedly so – but it is at present also the preserve of old-timers (because it is one of the most tightly controlled sets of occupations in the world and one of the toughest to break into) and of values rather divorced from Main Street.

Distributors are something of a patchwork quilt in the traditional film industry. By commission (enforcing the acceptance by theatre-owners of lemons in return for award winners) and by omission (withdrawing films or refusing to handle them), they control some vital valves along the pipeline from producer to consumer. Although anti-trust rulings have generally divorced distributors from actual production companies, the power of this clan still remains substantial through their control of individual movie houses and the terms and timing of film releases. Most people in the film industry tend to pay close attention when distributors speak. Without them, the greatest films in the world would languish in storage vaults, marquees would be blank, and cash registers would cease to jingle.

Still, the interest of distributors in their wares is somewhat secondary. For most – there are some honourable exceptions – the films they dole out might as well be shoes or watermelons. They are simply means of making money. The distributor's interest is primarily in films that produce box-office lineups, not in films that necessarily communicate, relate to reality, or serve significant social purposes.

And so, ironically, at both ends of the production line there is a tendency to focus on cash first and content second. If *Son of a Teenage Werewolf* is a bigger grabber than, say, *The War Game,* it will be the film that gets the bank advance, the star treatment, and the prime theatre bookings across the land. To the extent that communication occurs we end up in such circumstances more likely to nibble necks than ban H-bombs.

Now, money isn't really a bad thing in itself (despite what Harold says in his more poetic moments). Where cash consciousness tends to make film come a cropper is in its consequences of caution, as we have noted, and of anticipation.

You see, the film money-seekers *have* asked themselves where their beloved money is coming from. And, quite apart from the bland bankers, their vision reveals that film money comes, in the final analysis, from some very specific people.

The bubblegummers.

The segment of our society between the ages of roughly 14 and 25 years of age provides most of the cash that ultimately finances mainstream films. Sure, there are exceptions such as the geriatric triumph of *Sound of Music,* but day to day, year after year, the people that can be relied upon to consume film fodder are young, unmarried, semi-urban people in the 14-to-25 bracket. Others chip in, of course, but they don't represent the core group that must be satisfied to keep films afloat.

Because they know the key money comes from the bubblegummers, film makers and distributors in the mainstream industry do a very sensible thing, so far as they are concerned. They cater. With regularity and dedication that is awesome to behold, they think, feel and foster bubblegumming. Reality, for them, becomes the bubblegum world – its interests, fears, fads, and feats.

As a result, the basic film output tends to be that which the bubblegum market will support.

The film world tends to be a bubblegum world.

This, so far as proxy communication is concerned, is a mixed blessing. Some aspects of the bubblegum point of view are wholly positive. There is a refreshing candour, a willingness to view things differently, a quality of energy and creativity, courage unqualified by the conditioning of great age, constructive impatience, frequent humour and enthusiasm and, especially nowadays, a sense of communality. Such aspects can add up to humanity and humaneness that are an asset and credit to the human condition.

Much of the candour and irreverence found in *Catch-22* or *Easy Rider,* for example, was really only possible because the primary bubblegum audience was deemed to be sympathetic. *The Boys in the Band* was able to acknowledge homosexuality explicitly because of bubblegum permissiveness. And *Woodstock* or *Gimme Shelter* represented opposite sides of the coin of the fact (or fancy) of an alternate bubblegum culture.

At the same time, there are some drawbacks. For instance, several studies of the bubblegum generation indicate that the major preoccupations of a majority of its members revolve around sorting out individual and collective views and experiences on the topics of sex, liquor, and drugs. That is fine and understandable, so far as it goes. But such preoccupations are not shared to the same extent or with the same priority by members of other generations. (The Admiral's crowd, for example, is much bothered by the verdict of history, his granddaughter [age 4] is enchanted by finger painting, and his nephew [age 40] is really worried about inflation.)

All this is self-evident. Communication of any kind that caters primarily to a special age group, race, sex, creed, or other ghetto in human life is bound to be partly unsuited to humans as a whole. Some aspects will inevitably be over-emphasized, others will be ignored.

The more cynical of movie makers are disturbingly candid in acknowledging that they program for 13-year-old mentalities. And they assume that the rigours of reality are rather more, in total, than such a mind can encompass. This also helps explain the me-tooism of feature film. Without evidence of interest in a given topic having been demonstrated in other media or forms of expression – books, plays, pop festivals, and so forth – the film moguls seldom dare to churn out even their garbage, let alone their award-winners.

That, then, is the broad canvas of traditional film. On the plus side, we have a medium capable of non-linear presentation, flexible and re-viewable and directly engaging to our senses. In potential at least, film adds up to a very powerful enhancement of our perception of reality.

On the minus side, however, traditional film is money-minded, conservative, formula-ridden, amoral, banal, and timid. Much of its offering is more an insult than an adjunct to our perception of reality. As Ezra Goodman, a critic, concludes:

Hollywood, with its insularity, ignorance, arrogance and avarice, with its colossal vulgarity and bad taste, is bad not only for the rest of America and the world but for Hollywood itself. It needs a breath of fresh air from the outside. It needs a cosmopolitan measuring rod that has more scope than its own rube rule of thumb. It needs to let the world in, to be de-Hollywoodized.

Ezra Goodman, *The Fifty-Year Decline and Fall of Hollywood* (New York: Simon and Schuster, 1961), p. 439

Fortunately, the traditional film of Hollywood is only part of the film spectrum. In and around it are other equally important methods and areas of endeavour that do add additional inputs if we use them.

One way to consider some of the main alternatives is to draw up a kind of balance sheet indicating alternatives to the traditional Hollywood model and equally the prices or complications that accompany them. Here's a sampling:

Alternative film sources

i/ **Foreign films**

For our purposes, foreign films do not include the glossy international productions actually hatched from Hollywood or (especially in England and Italy) copying Hollywood methods. We're concerned with truly 'foreign' films that are made, not only outside

California, but according to different rules, for somewhat different purposes, and in tune with different conceptions of the human condition. Ingmar Bergman's *Wild Strawberries,* Vittorio De Sica's *Bicycle Thieves,* and Satyajit Ray's *The Unvanquished* typify such alternatives, complete with beauty spots and blemishes.

On the positive side, foreign films of this kind tend to be less expensive (and so less obsessed with the box office) than the traditional variety, more explicit in reflecting realities, more experimental and critical, frequently more radical in theme, and even willing to deal with sophisticated abstractions such as faith, beauty, or insanity. In the '50s they were much fussed-about for pioneering nudity and four-letter words, but foreign films also gave us such benefits as unhappy endings, curbing of the 'star' system, the unabashed use of symbolism, accurate social comment on such unportrayables as poverty, and poetic and creative toying with mixtures of colour and black and white.

Partly because they could afford risks unthinkable for Hollywood and partly because they grew from roots of their own, foreign filmmakers have managed to offer true alternatives to Hollywood. They haven't always been successful or even good, but they have been different. To the extent that they have widened choices available to us, they have made film as a whole a medium better able to reflect reality.

But there have been flaws, too. Most foreign films suffer from horrendous distribution problems, for a start. Frequently cut off from the major Hollywood-oriented channels, they too often end up lurking in the obscurity of 'art' houses or the echoing isolation of the tail end of a triple feature. So, for would-be viewers, foreign films are rather hard to see except in major metropolitan centres.

When you do get there, there are pitfalls of unabashed propaganda (as bad as and sometimes worse than Hollywood's), mediocrity (most critics agree, for example, that only two or three of the roughly 300 feature films made in India each year are worth seeing), technical faults (Hollywood technicians are acknowledged to be the world's best by far), and obscurity that subtitles can't resolve.

Foreign films, in sum, are like a condiment. The ordinary film blancmange is enlivened by a regular sprinkling, but you can't really live on them as a sole diet.

ii/**Sponsored films**

Governments and private organizations both indulge in filmmaking. The results can, on occasion, be very useful indeed.

The National Film Board of Canada provides an instructive example of the best and worst that can be expected from government-sponsored film. Established as a Crown corporation, responsible to Parliament only for its annual budget and report, the NFB has many of the facilities available to Hollywood producers with few of the fatuities. As unsympathetic Parliamentarians and commercial rivals repeatedly stress, the organization doesn't always have to make a profit and so can play around with cinematic ventures both weird and wonderful. It doesn't have to meet too many fixed deadlines either, and so can concentrate on quality and innovation. Distribution comes almost as an afterthought, with the result that pressures from ignorant or cynical theatre operators tend to be diminished. And, to a degree, the bureaucratic buffers around and within the organization allow for enough confusion and obscurity to protect talented and sensitive artists (as well as a few incompetents) from competitive scrutiny.

The results speak for themselves. Norman McLaren's experimental films such as *Neighbours, Fiddle-Dee-Dee,* and *A Chairy Tale* have won awards by the hatful and enlarged the range of cinematic experience available to our senses. Feature films such as *The Drylanders* have provided glimpses of Canadian history that few books or archives can match. Open-ended, issue-provoking offerings such as *Pow-wow at Duck Lake* and *Encounter With Sol Alinsky* have facilitated constructive social criticism.

Similarly, private operators such as Christopher Chapman (who did the innovative *Ontario: A Place to Stand* for the Ontario Government), Bert Haanstra from the Netherlands (commissioned by Shell to make *The Rival World* and other oil-related films) and Crawley Films in Canada (makers of another oil-sponsored film, *The Loon's Necklace,* which won more than 25 competitive awards) reap some of the advantages in leeway that come from advance non-profit support. Though necessarily leaner than government-supported outfits, they often make up for this with efficiency and enthusiasm. And, provided the sponsor's axe is not too publicly or misleadingly ground in the films themselves, such private efforts too can be extremely creative and effective. Chapman's split-screen effects had a great follow-up effect on TV commercials, for instance.

The pitfall in all sponsored film, of course, lies in the purposes of the sponsors. Without the leavening influence of direct accountability to some kind of marketplace, sponsored films can be and often are exercises in the vilest propaganda. Governments tend to enjoy perpetuating themselves and their views in much the same way as do corporations, religious organizations, and assorted other film backers. With the skills and sophistication of modern filmmaking, such efforts can be enormously effective while still entertaining and seemingly innocuous. But there is a basic difference of scale in these films: no sponsor unconcerned with box office revenue can seriously contemplate a budget anywhere close to that of a major Hollywood operator. As a result, the makers of sponsored films have to cut corners to the point where their works suffer. Distribution is also a chronic problem for operators without established ties with commercial distribution houses.

iii/'Underground' films

This grab bag encompasses everything from slightly more than home movies to full-length feature productions such as *The Brig*.

With the advent of relatively cheap and highly portable equipment almost anyone can set out to make a movie these days and, possibly because of the visual emphasis and training of television, a great many people do.

The boon in this activity lies in the fact that few of this new wave of movie makers are aware of, let alone constrained by, the assumed limitations of the medium. Romping with creative intensity towards their goals, 'underground' filmmakers have trampled over all of the many taboos about content, technique, and the mixing of the medium with other forms of expression. From the ruins, a few creative flowers have emerged (as well as a lot of outright weeds). Here are just two examples. The short *Soul Freeze* by Bob Cowan (overtly dealing with the erotic fantasies of a priest while symbolically plumbing the desperate dimensions of the whole human condition) would probably never have been possible under regular auspices. Not only is its bluntly explicit content an innovation and step closer to one aspect of human reality, but also its techniques show impressive inventiveness. Similarly, *Cornucopia* by Lenny Lipton (a wild, colour overlay of multiple TV images to a mind-bending soundtrack) casually broke cinematic customs in the cause of capturing the essence of what TV and today's world are all about, and all in about four minutes!

Summed up, 'underground' films offer fresh inputs and repeated rule-testing of great use for film in general and its potential as a link with reality. Taken by themselves, they are to be expected to be patchy, raw, amateurish, under-financed, cruel, often boring, frequently unintelligible and inaccurate. (But as a means of counterbalancing John Wayne ... wow!)

iv/**Present and looming experiments**

Around the edges of the film medium there is an array of men and machines that can make mad-scientist tales pale by comparison. As current experience in psychiatry, physiology, linguistics, cybernetics, and even pharmacology grows, it is becoming apparent that almost all our uses and abuses of film to date rank as little more than tentative beginnings.

We'll examine some such projects in greater detail in our speculative section on the future. Suffice it to say now that computerized film, the conveyance of cinematic experiences directly to the brain by electrodes, truly three-dimensional film (holography), and seriously practical versions of smellies and feelies (an abortive attempt at Smell-O-Vision was actually introduced in 1929) are but a few of the relatively probable innovations for the near future. In addition, work is already well advanced in multi-screen, multi-image, and multi-sound films designed to engage our senses and move us into unprecedented contact with grim and glorious reality. The three-storey screen for the Japanese pavilion at Expo 70 is but one of many such drawing-board realities.

The big problem, of course, lies in the effectiveness implied in many such forecasts. As film becomes more and more forceful and all-pervading in its impact, its consequences become increasingly serious. Only a few of our minds were misled by *They Shoot Horses Don't They?* or *Midnight Cowboy*. Most of us knew that we were suspending disbelief, or at least trying to. Most of the time, the clear-cut distance and guardrails of artificiality between the screen offering and ourselves are quite sufficient to sustain healthy disbelief. But whenever any part of *They Shoot Horses Don't They?* or *Midnight Cowboy* engulfs us by slipping past mind-screens in the guise of 'entertainment' and then sets up expectations, conditioned reactions, emotional triggerings, or other reality reactions, we are faced with a serious situation. Some social scientists have argued, for example, that the Hollywood vision of 'normal' life presented in the '30s and '40s was a major factor in the Revolution of Rising Expectations that has wracked many developing nations since 1945. Fact and fantasy tended to become blended together with ultimate consequences of staggering proportions.

We'll dwell gloomily on all this at greater length later. Meantime,

it would seem clear that film as a proxy agent can be said to be somewhat flawed – in common with print, radio, and television.

So much, then, for the mass media as proxy agents. Like ourselves, they add up to a mixture of plusses and minuses, facilitating our ability to handle more variables in some instances, interfering with it in others. Obviously they aren't simply the agents of reality.

Where else can we turn? What else can we do?

Plenty. In particular, we can turn to a wide-ranging grab-bag of panaceas, probes, side-effects, and agitations lumped together here under the arbitrary title of The Subliminal Media. Let's go.

SUBLIMINAL MEDIA

10

The temptation to accept the mass media as the omnipresent and omnipotent agents of most human perception of reality is large. It is stressed by the media themselves ... a constant, chattering backdrop to most of our daily lives.

The temptation to assume that the rest of our input of reality is based upon direct, subjective use of our own frail senses at first hand is large too.

But there is much, much more to communication than that. Other proxy agents can be found to round out and enrich the services of the mass media. There are also direct means of communication which can improve upon the performance of our sensory-cerebral systems or act as useful alternatives to portions of them.

These various agents and means are not necessarily as central or as efficient as those we have examined. Yet they demand and deserve attention in so far as they hold promise of assisting us to perceive more of the reality of an infinite number of variables infinitely expressed. So, we press on.

Here, these agents and means are lumped together under the broad heading of 'subliminal influences.' They are so christened because many of them tend to be relatively unnoticed in both their day-to-day use and their conscious impact. They frequently fall well below the thresholds of our normal critical evaluation of input, ranging freely like footpads in the sleeping houses of our conscious attention. They also have a wavering, subliminal quality because they tend to be very unpredictable in their forms, incidence, and preferred manners of expression.

The relationship of such subliminal influences to the mass media and our own senses is roughly like that of spices to a stew. The mass media and our own senses provide the meat and vegetables (though not necessarily in that order). The subliminal influences make the flavours of media and senses more intelligible and sometimes add dashes of flavour of their own. We can't rely on them alone, but we need them, in some combination and concentration, to enliven the basic recipe.

An example is the 'Muzak phenomenon.' All about most of us, most of the time, there are background whisperings and suggestions tacked to music. Records, Muzak itself, live performances, intrusions into the expressions of mainstream media ... all sorts of organized and unorganized musical expressions combine to create a background noise about us that is rich in description, suggestion, and influence. The situation can be very disturbing, as indicated in *The Journal of Pop Culture* (Vol. III, No. 2, pp. 216-217):

... Professor Charles Seeger frequently tells the tale of two Spillane-like officers walking into the Archive of Folksong in the Library of Congress demanding to see the person in charge of writing revolutionary songs. Similarly, Congressional committees and private vigilante groups, such as the Police and Firemen's Research Association of Los Angeles, have pointed to folk music as a tool to subvert the minds of American youth.

The switch of music – popular music especially – from blancmange to a vehicle for expressing views of what is going on represents the emergence of a kind of subliminal medium: a medium in the sense that communications are made available to us, subliminal in that they ride upon the primary and impressive sounds and rhythms of the music itself. And, partly because this medium has that elusive subliminal quality, revolutionary suggestions such as the exhortation of the Beatles a few years ago to

ᘒ Go where you want to go ᘒ do what you want to do ᘒ

bother 'Spillane-like officers' because they i/*know* that something is going on but ii/can't quite pin down their unease in clear-cut terms (sometimes because they just can't figure out what is being said amid the wails).

Now, let's try to view all this in some sort of systematic way. Acknowledging that there are inputs and expressions about us that are not primarily the activities of the mass media and are frequently subliminal in their operation, how do they relate to our perception of that infinite number of variables infinitely expressed that comprises 'reality'?

Remember, we're not considering regular media – though some overlap is probably inescapable. Our attention now is focused upon alternatives, adjuncts, and, to a certain extent, opponents of mainstream communication. Put specifically, we are concerned with attempts to communicate by means of various kinds of *performance* (speeches, concerts, plays, recordings, parades, sit-ins, seances, dances, and so forth), *products* (leaflets, posters, the output of underground presses, games, devices, and so forth) and *processes* (the

mails, gossip chains, boycotts, clubs, and so forth). To the extent that any of these affect our ability to perceive reality, they are significant.

The number and the variety of expressions are obviously enormous. Thus any consideration of the subliminal media calls for simplification in order to bring them within the range of our understanding and evaluation.

By generalizing at the expense of absolute accuracy, we can search out the probabilities inherent in each general class of subliminal communication and try to decide whether they help or hinder our grasp of reality.

We can chart the subliminal media by function:

Proxy Role	Representative Agents
i/Provision of additional or alternative data	Minority and/or specialist publications, curricula, teach-ins, speakers, circuits, 'underground' outlets, etc.
ii/Provision of additional or alternative values	Those above plus 'conditioning' agents such as churches, entertainment, games, etc.
iii/Anti-conditioning and/or liberating	Those above plus forms of juxtaposition.
iv/Early warning systems	Those above plus simulation, the new witchcraft, accident, chemicals, etc.
v/Contact	Those above plus assorted ventures into psychodynamics.

This gives us a framework at least. Clearly, there is an overlap, not only with the mass media, but also among the various proxy roles played by these further media themselves. If we examine the roles in greater detail, we can get a glimpse of the differences involved.

i/**Provision of additional or alternative data**

Mainstream media in North America, naturally enough, don't and can't inform everyone about everything all of the time. They are restrained by limitations on their available time and/or space and their available funds. They suffer from gloomy illusions about the capacities and interests of so-called mass audiences. They are creatures conditioned by habit, curbed by their own ignorance, and subject to the limits of their own human whims and fancies.

At the same time, the poor, solitary individual isn't too well equipped to make up for their oversights and omissions. The Admiral may suspect that important details are lacking in the day-to-day media documentation of the Vietnam war, for example. But, short of hopping across the Pacific and attempting to check on the North and the South simultaneously, there isn't much that he personally can do about it.

The demand for additional or alternative data thus becomes apparent. We recognize the need to enrich the available mainstream supply of information, and the parallel need to get more and better tip-offs on the extent of hidden information.

Enrichment is often provided by specialists and 'inside dopesters.' These are the individuals and organizations who, by virtue of concentrated attention, abundance of time or money, compulsion of belief, or notable idiosyncracy, tend to go further than the established media. The Washington writer, I. F. Stone, for example, became exasperated with the incompleteness and half truths of reporting in the mass media on the Pentagon. He took some extra time, applied a great deal of talent, and came up with *I. F. Stone's Weekly* to serve as a printed periodical supplement to regular mass media.

There now are literally hundreds of such offerings, of varying quality and completeness. By newsletters, telephone services, telegrams, personal consultation, and, sometimes, pronouncements via the media, specialists of all kinds offer floods of facts on most topics of human concern. When they're good, they serve very useful proxy purposes.

Another source of additional and alternative data – frequently overlooked – is to be found in most communities in the great drone of the speakers' circuit. Literally thousands of expert or engaging individuals make themselves available each day for seminars, lectures, banquets, lodge meetings, conferences, and conventions concerned with some aspects of oversight in our portraits of reality. With versions of the 'I was there' theme, or flourishes of the 'I am a scholar' game, or dashes of the 'this is what we really did' revelation, such speakers hawk talk, slides, films, artifacts, and assorted pyrotechnics in the cause of convincing audiences that their perceptual tapestries are being enriched. The numbers involved (one Canadian city of medium size is estimated to average 1,200 mealtime speakers every month) alone make the speakers' circuit one of our more pervasive and least noted manifestations of subliminal communication. One suspects that many of the surprises that crop up in elections, polls, and other gauges of popular attitudes could be lessened if more attention were paid to the themes and topics being stressed on the speakers' circuit at the time.

Like the specialists and 'inside dopesters,' the players in the speakers' circuit game have become rather formally organized. From simple beginnings, such activities have grown to the point where there now are bureaux offering selected talents and annual conventions to provide for speakers' auditions. Here is an illuminating report:

Platform group previews top lecturers, entertainers

A unique method of bringing talent to the buyer was viewed at the International Platform Assn. (IPA) convention held annually at the Sheraton Park Hotel in Washington, D.C. This year some 1,400 attended July 28-31.

IPA, which boasts about 11,500 members, according to Dan Tyler Moore, director general and board chairman, draws its membership basically from four groups:

• **Talent,** the largest part of which are lecturers but includes also a large number of entertainers;

• **Bureau managers** and booking agents which include school assembly agents and "celebrity and club" bookers;

• **Club program chairmen** from women's, Lions, Rotary, and others who attend the convention to "look for bargains" and good programs;

• **"Public members"** who Moore says are very important because "they demonstrate at the convention in Washington, the same response as the performer would get in the local clubs across the nation."

Each day of the convention, entertainers and lecturers perform 15 minutes of their best material at the previews, an audition of sorts, attended by the membership. After these the best entertainers are asked to perform at the "Rendezvous Night Club" set up by the IPA's Paula Bishop in one of the hotel's ballrooms each evening.

"These programs serve to introduce talent to agents, management and program chairmen," Miss Bishop said. "We feel that it's profitable for all those concerned."

This year, for the first time, free space was provided for exhibitors on an experimental, first come, first served basis. Exhibitors taking advantage of the opportunity included Antrim Bureau, Programs International System, American and TWA airlines and a number of member talent personalities.

(Note too that the report of this convention was itself carried by a specialist publication, *Amusement Business.* Very few mass media outlets had the interest or space for the information.)

A further important – and often overlooked – source of additional and alternative data is provided by teaching curricula. Especially in state schools, where content is somewhat standardized and attendance is legally demanded of most citizens up to a certain age, the curriculum is, in fact, a central influence for the funnelling of information into eager and not-so-eager human minds. As such, it is an adjunct to both the media and (remember them?) the family as sources of information.

Curricula tend to be subliminal for several reasons. The aims and designs of the curricula formulaters are seldom fully revealed. The formulaters themselves are usually educational gnomes far removed from routine public scrutiny. And, probably most important of all, the consumers of curricula are mostly young people caught at an age and in circumstances where they are highly susceptible to both direct and indirect suggestions.

The impact of curricula is reinforced in a variety of ways. Audience of at least a nominal kind is guaranteed by the fact that, by law, almost everyone in our society is compelled to accept exposure. Challenges that might modify impact are relatively muted as well. Few people who have graduated beyond the curricula bother to question, examine, or evaluate what is included so long as the general babysitting and keeping-up-with-the-Joneses functions of education appear to be served.

Many other outlets providing enrichment and tip-offs are to be found scattered throughout our communities. Pilots and ham radio operators, for example, may be rich sources of data on contemporary happenings. (A goodly portion of African news comes from such individuals simply because they can cover the great distances involved.) Some pressure groups also are significant sources of data. Take, for example, the genuine reservations cited by some anti-fluoridationists in defiance of the virtually unanimous enthus-

162   iasm of the mass media. This broadsheet was distributed in Edmonton, Alberta, as a counter to the alleged refusal by the city's media to carry alternative information about fluoridation:

EDMONTON REPORTER

EDMONTON, ALBERTA, THURSDAY, JULY 27, 1967

EDITORIAL

This is the first — and last — edition of this newspaper. It has gone to press, at great personal cost to the publisher, as the only means of achieving true freedom of expression through the printed word in Edmonton . . . It is a move of desperation intent on proclaiming to Edmonton's citizens that we are at the mercy of a ruthless and callous journalistic monopoly — one which, while pretending to offer on its pages equal space for the dissenting voice, actually exercises dictatorial reign over what information appears in its publication.

The public has traditionally accepted the printed word of the press as gospel. "I saw it in the paper" is the oft-heard statement which illustrates the popular view that "if it's in the paper, it must be true — it must be fact". This awsome power of the press is a matter of great concern to the public, and to the responsible publisher, even in cities where there are two or more daily newspapers. But where this power is in the hands of ONE newspaper, where that newspaper openly takes a strong and vocal position in support of a given cause and refuses space to the opponent of that cause, public opinion can be manipulated according to the paper's own partisan whims — such a paper can, effectively and with impunity, ridicule, exclude, immobilize and silence anyone who opposes its views.

I charge the Edmonton Journal with being such a newspaper. I charge that in the recent fluoridation campaign The Journal refused to provide space to the opponents of its position, as a public service, despite repeated allegations that it offers equal space to the dissenter.

Reproduced on page 4 of this publication is an article turned down by The Journal three weeks ago, as an offering for the 'Journal For Dissent'. I charge that it was rejected because The Edmonton Journal doesn't really HAVE a Journal for dissent.

I accuse The Journal of creating this clever device to disarm its critics, by appearing to provide a forum, while in reality presenting only the controlled, censored, edited, sterilized copy it chooses to print — copy which may originally have been written by its critics, but which ultimately appears in a form which leaves The Journal's editorial position intact.

I claim the article reproduced in this publication was turned down because of the serious threat it posed to The Journal's deep commitment in favor of fluoridation. I claim it was turned down because The Journal can produce NO ACCEPTABLE ANSWERS TO THE QUESTION IT ASKS.

The Journal's greatest sin is not that it presents a biased, one-sided point of view; nor is it that it doesn't provide space for the critic of its editorial position. THE JOURNAL'S GREAT SIN IS THAT IT REPRESENTS ITSELF AS BEING SOMETHING IT IS NOT. The crass and blatant subterfuge of this out-and-out misrepresentation is insulting to the intelligence of its readers and degrading to the publishing industry as a whole.

TOO HOT
FOR THE
Edmonton Journal
TO PRINT

Bastion of 'Freedom of Expression' has clay feet

"An untrammelled flow of information on all questions is critical to the health of democratic order, and as a sure check on governmental folly and private malpractice" says The Edmonton Journal.

"An untrammelled expression of opinion", it goes on, "is the means of a democracy's refreshment and renewal . . . restrictions ultimately rob all of us of the insights of others, whether these insights are new truths or 'useful errors'."

Prior censorship, says The Journal, "is by definition an arbitrary process and therefore repugnant . . . . Covert censorship is equally repugnant"

At the very moment The Journal was championing freedom of expression in the manner quoted above, it was itself busy 'trammelling', restricting, censoring and obstructing freedom of expression. At that very moment the article reproduced here on page 4, was rejected by the editor of the 'Journal for Dissent'.

Why Was It Rejected?

In the days of the fluoridation campaign The Journal took a strong and vocal part in supporting the issue. It was, if not instrumental, certainly influential in the outcome of the last plebescite. Consequently it has an obligation to its readers to demonstrate the veracity of its utterances. The rejected article challenged The Journal to do just that — to 'put up or shut up'. It would seem The Journal was not equal to the challenge.

THE ARTICLE THE JOURNAL REFUSED TO PRINT

To: The Editor of the Edmonton Journal.

Mr. Editor: Your cause has already been won, yet you find the fluoride issue so important even today, that you invite a renewal of the controversy through your editorial column. I, too, regard the issue as one of tremendous importance, and so, cannot allow your editorial position to stand unchallenged. Your position paper on fluoridation vividly demonstrates the Journal's penchant for stating OPINION editorially, as though it were stating fact. I charge that your position is a completely one-sided, unexamined assessment — one that doesn't acknowledge the existence of an 'other side', when you make the rather peculiar claim that "evidence has produced no sign of any kind that anybody has ever been harmed in any way by drinking artificially fluoridated water in the prescribed concentration".

Where Have You Looked?

Your 'facts' are not facts. At best they are merely statements denying the existence of contrary evidence. If there is indeed 'no sign of any kind', then anyone who claims such evidence exists must be either uninformed, stupid, or some kind of nut. The proponents of fluoridation can hardly be expected to be the ones to produce derogatory evidence; is it possible that you have been looking in the wrong places for the 'sign'? One can only hope that in spite of appearances, The Journal's editorial policy is based on SOME degree of intellectual perception — on some idea of the Scientific Method as a means of arriving at CONSIDERED conclusions.

And if this is the case, you will want to know about and scrutinize all the evidence there is that is based on intellectual and Scientific Investigation particularly evidence coming from within the medical and dental professions themselves. The fact that this kind of evidence has aroused a strong and rapidly growing force of opposition among doctors, dentists and scientists indicates that there is something to the 'other fellow's' notion. No one — not even the most avid pro-fluoridationist has been able to attribute any base or ulterior motive to the opponent. The source, sincerity and strength of such opposition can no longer be ignored or lightly brushed aside. You owe it to yourself and to the reading public over whom you wield such disproportionate influence, to examine with deliberate and unbiased fervor, everything these professional men have to say.

Candy and Tooth Decay

On the question of fluoride 'doing good': I have no quarrel with the Journal's claim that it is 'beneficial to the development of children's teeth' (when intake is below the toxic level). But there is nothing exceptional or miraculous about this characteristic of fluoride. The same end can be achieved as effectively and much more safely through a well balanced diet. Fluorides merely provide one way of preventing dental caries: withholding sweets from children is equally effective. Perhaps laws forbidding the sale or feeding of candy to children would be more appropriate than to force-feed an entire population with a toxic chemical on the pretext that it is a vital and fundamental 'health measure'.

Medical Evidence Does Exist

With regard to The Journal's second argument, disclaiming the existence of evidence of harmful effects: the medical and dental sources previously referred to provide singularly well-documented evidence, as briefly illustrated in the conclusions and statements that follow:

THE AMERICAN DENTAL ASSOCIATION. Vol. 31, Page 1363

"We do know that the use of drinking water containing as little as 1.2 to 3.0 parts per million of fluorine will cause such developmental disturbances in bone as osteosclerosis, spondylosis and osteopetrosis, as well as goitre".

THE JOURNAL OF THE AMERICAN MEDICAL ASSOCIATION Vol. 123, Page 150

"Fluorides are general protoplasmic poisons, probably because of their capacity to modify the metabolism of cells by changing the permeability of the cell membrane and by inhibiting certain enzyme systems — The sources of fluorine intoxication are drinking water containing 1 part per million or more of fluorine".

JONATHAN FORMAN, M.D., former editor of OHIO STATE MEDICAL JOURNAL

"It is now known that such vital organs as the kidneys, thyroid, aorta, liver, lungs and others can be sites of an unusually high fluoride buildup — Further, it accumulates in certain organs in an unpredictable way. Some individuals may store up to 100 times more fluoride in certain tissues than others".

TESTIMONY ON FLUORIDATION BEFORE COUNCILS OF THE AMERICAN MEDICAL ASSOCIATION. Journal of Applied Nutrition. Vol. 12, No. 1, 1959

"Dr. Ford (water commissioner of New York City) has found variations as high as five-fold in different parts of the same distribution (P. 26) — fluoride when given by mouth for the purpose of preventing dental caries is a drug which requires the same responsible attention to safety and suitability of dosage as any potent drug — the use of the public water supply as a vehicle for the administration of any such drug is an unscientific and irresponsible procedure (P. 29)".

THE MEDICAL COMMITTEE ON EVALUATION OF FLUORIDATION. 'A Statement on the Fluoridation of Public Water Supplies'.

"This statement was issued originally on February 20, 1957 under the sponsorship of over five hundred physicians, dentists and scientists. Following a limited circulation, the sponsorship increased to over 1500 and provided information that thousands of such professional men are in accord with the analysis of fluoridation problems presented herein . . ."

Can these thousands of doctors, dentists and scientists be dismissed as cranks and rabble-rousers? It must have taken a tremendous amount of courage and personal conviction to stand up against what has become overwhelming pressure within one's own profession, particularly when to do so constitutes a threat to that profession's aura of omniscience. Time after time since the turn of the century, medical opinion has proven to be wrong. The thalidomide tragedy is one incontrovertible example of medical error. Medical opinion is just that — opinion. Can it be anything more than opinion when it comes to assessing the effects of placing a toxic chemical such as sodium fluoride in the water supply? Is it possible that this is one case in which medical (and editorial) opinion becomes absolute fact, absolute truth, in spite of a host of contra-indications?

Of What Consequence Is "Weight of Evidence"?

Five hundred thousand people took thalidomide with no evidence of harmful results. Five hundred thousand pieces of evidence in favor! — Then one woman had a 'thalidomide baby': no further evidence against thalidomide was needed. There may be a hundred thousand pieces of evidence supporting fluoridation, yet it takes only one valid claim in opposition for all of the 'pro' evidence to break down. That is why the proponent seeks so frantically to shoot down every claim which threatens his position. He knows that if you can accept ONE such claim as valid, you can no longer support his cause.

Compulsion and The 'General Good'

The most fundamental of the questions involved in this issue is the one raised in The Journal's final observation, in which you have endeavored to show a relationship between 'compulsion' and the general good. How do you define 'general good', and how does it apply to the fluoridation issue? Dental caries (tooth decay) is a serious problem, it is true. But how important is it as a social problem, compared to other problems in which the 'general good' is involved? For example take the population explosion. Here is a case in which using water as a vehicle for contraceptive drugs is by far the most practical and effective method of correcting a most serious and UNIVERSAL social problem, which profoundly affects the 'general good'. A woman drinking water so treated merely takes a pill to neutralize the contraceptive in order to become pregnant. Yet in spite of the obvious superiority of this method — in spite of the importance of this question to society as a whole, other means have been found or are being developed to provide more acceptable alternatives for those who want it, even though the alternatives may not be nearly as effective.

It happens that with fluoridation, there is a practical alternative. A proven and acceptable means of providing fluoride for those who want it is available and in use, Dr. Castaldi, Dr. MacRae and Dr. Ball notwithstanding. Switzerland, where legislation prohibits the use of the water supply for such purposes, has provided fluorides in milk successfully for many years. There you can buy plain milk, homogenized milk, or fluoridated milk with equal ease and give the prescribed dosage directly to those whom it is supposed to benefit, without involving anyone else.

The method is precise, economical, easy to control and proven effective: it is a method which has been prescribed for more than eight years by a number of Edmonton dentists. Administration by mothers to their children for periods up to 8 years has demonstrated its effectiveness. It is curious to note that while prescribing it privately for their own patients, no promoter of fluoridation has ever informed us of this means of providing fluoride for all those who want it. It would seem that instead, during more than eight years of campaigning, a 'negative electorate' was used as the excuse for doing nothing.

IN THE CASE OF FLUORIDES, THERE IS NO JUSTIFICATION WHATEVER FOR THE USE OF COMPULSION, based on what you refer to as the 'general good'. What a frightening precedent we have established, if this IS a case which calls for depriving a significant segment of the population of a fundamental freedom. — Oh, we can speak glibly and magnamously about 'removing fluoride salts by an inexpensive process' (I know of no such proven process), but such after-the-fact arguments do nothing to assuage or resurrect the principle involved — the right to freedom of choice has still been pre-empted. Provincial statute has made fluoridation legal: this does not mean that it is right. Laws that infringe on personal rights and liberties have been made — and rescinded — in the past. None could violate the right to freedom of choice more fundamentally than does legislation permitting the use of water for mass-medication, or as a vehicle for ANYTHING.

What Is The Journal's Answer?

In any case, we now find ourselves confronted with the inevitable. Soon the water pouring from Edmonton taps will be fluoridated. As a consequence of The Journal's current statement on the issue, those of us who do not want this chemical in our drinking water must look to you, Mr. Editor, to provide us with some very specific answers in support of your position:

Firstly, we will want to know the exact name, source of supply and price of the 'inexpensive process' for removing fluoride. We will want an assurance as to effectiveness and longevity.

Secondly, we will want to know who is going to pay for this device, in the case of those who can't afford the expense.

Thirdly, if we must relinquish our rights as far as mass prescription of fluorides is concerned, what assurance can you give us that this is the only concession we will be called on to make against our will? One recalls a voice, some thirty years ago, declaring while marching into the Sudetenland: "I have no further territorial claims to make." Did our willingness to appease and compromise a principle not take us to the brink of enslavement at Munich in 1938?

To quote Dr. R. V. Sampson of the University of Bristol, "The measure is incompatible with human freedom . . . No amount of ransacking constitutional law books, invocations of legal authorities, appeals to the principle of parliamentary sovereignty, touches the principle immediately evident to all unprejudiced men: that the forcing of any ingredient into the body of another is a most fundamental violation of his right to personal liberty — to treat individuals as though they were an undifferentiated mass is an insult to human dignity, as well as a grave violation of human freedom".

Fluoridation of the water supply is a GROSSLY UNWARRANTED incursion into the individual's right to personal freedom.

I will not have it in my family's drinking water. Can you, Mr. Editor, justify FORCING it on us?

We also gain much information from people acting in less formal or organized fashion. By virtue of location or vocation, some people become clearinghouses for information that often can't be found in the mainstream media. Club hostesses, whores, some criminals (especially dealers in stolen goods), community gossips, and, of course, the legendary city taxi driver possess additional and alternative data that is not only interesting but often of significance. (This aging writer still remembers with some zest, for example, a description of the politics of the Lebanon of remarkable accuracy, complexity, and detail that was furnished by three off-duty occupants of a third-class brothel in Beirut. As the Byzantine tales progressed, accompanied by spoon-dissolving Turkish coffee and the occasional casual solicitation, the official version of state affairs – based on the suggestion at that time that good Lebanese Christians were being victimized by bad Lebanese Muslims – dwindled into relative insignificance.)

To sum up, there appear to be quite a few adjuncts to the media and our own senses that can be tapped for data. Now, what about values?

ii/**Provision of additional or alternative values**

As we have noted, the mainstream mass media have made extensive commitments of money, equipment, time, and emotion to their regular activities. They cannot step too far out of line with their offerings. When and if they pose fundamental challenges to the entrenched laws and habits of the land – or, more importantly, to the value systems upon which the laws and habits are based – the mass media risk curtailment or even cancellation of the support upon which their survival depends.

Mainstream media cannot help but be somewhat muted. Over any period of time, they have to stay within the bounds of law – leery of libel, sedition, and obscenity. They must beware the major social taboos. The espousal of unpopular minority causes (such as capitalism in Czechoslovakia or communism in Texas) will have to be approached rather gingerly, and even a failure to attack them may be risky. Assorted conditions of work, such as broadcasting licences, government regulations, and the wear and tear of the comments and criticisms of friends in the community, cannot be ignored with impunity.

Yet interest in, and even demand for, expressions of additional or alternative values will probably persist. Particularly in areas of emotional involvement (sex, religion, and politics, in particular), there are likely to be interests and advocacies at odds with established values.

Let's indulge ourselves and take sex as our example. Relatively speaking, the mainstream view in North America today can be said to be hovering over a middle ground between totally permissive and totally restrictive value systems. This is not only confusing. It also provides some interesting illustrations of how subliminal expressions emerge to meet the demands of either extreme.

At the libertine end of the scale, you may find clubs, publications, organized orgies, exotic products, and language well outside the mainstream media range. They seek to express and exchange value-affirmations that few, if any, mass media outlets want or dare to handle.

Concern with the law and with community acceptance, for instance, has effectively muted the mass media so far as expressions such as these are concerned.

The Contemporary Swinger, vol 2, no 2, p. 24

Similarly, the so-called 'underground' press covers topics somewhat beyond mainstream taste or daring, such as a column for
homosexuals (a life style that, reasonably or unreasonably, the
mainstream is acutely uncomfortable with).

At an estimate, proponents of assorted libertine values in North
America are expressing themselves through more than 100 sex-club
journals, more than 600 'underground' publications, and a multi-
million-dollar market for photographs, bawdy books and magazines,
substances, films, and devices. It's kind of exhausting just to think
of all those busy people.

Meanwhile, we have our anti-libertines. Dedicated, imaginative,
evangelical, and profoundly concerned with alternative values – just
as the libertines are – they also seek to express and exchange their
wares in the face of the hesitance of the media.

In their case, it is not so much law as social practice that stands
in the way. On the grounds that relatively few members of the community support the anti-libertine extreme, that other topics are
more pressing or important, that possible libel might be involved,
and sometimes from outright disagreement, the mainstream media
tend to play down anti-libertine arguments and activities. Such intrusion into the mass media persists, of course (just as libido pops
up from time to time) but not to an extent or degree that satisfies
the apparent demand.

And so, subliminal expressions come forward. As with the libertines, these include clubs (Movement to Restore Decency for instance), publications, organized meetings by the hundreds (raising
an estimated $30 million a year, by the way), and rafts of buttons,
posters, bumper stickers, decals, and (oddly) flags.

An assortment of Decency rallies popped into prominence in the
spring of 1969 as a reaction against alleged sexual and drug excesses of rock and roll groups. With little trouble, on short notice,
and with the assistance of bodies such as the Fraternal Order of
Police, the organizers managed to assemble crowds of 16,000 to
40,000 teenagers in the cause of purity. Coincident with this up-
surge, the musical group deemed to be the last licentious straw –
The Doors – began to run into difficulties. As the pop music publication *Rolling Stone* (May 1969, p. 8) noted:

Ever since Jim Morrison (who's out on $5,000 bail) did what-
ever it was he did in Miami the Doors have found it difficult to get
work. At least a dozen groups have banned the group officially and
probably double that many more have turned thumbs down on the
band unofficially.

Sheer diversity and volume of information can be major factors
inhibiting the operation of the mass media, and thus calling forth
alternative means of expressing values. Take the case of religion –
or more accurately, religions. The mass media each week face a
daunting challenge to cover the value offerings of dozens of de-
nominations – each of them convinced for the most part that its
values alone are The Truth. The media settle for what they regard
as a manageable approach: they carry a few reports on the larger
groups and print advertisements (often at reduced rates) to advise
those interested where they can go for their value lessons.

"Blessed Is the Man That Endureth Temptation"

ANGLICAN

ST. COLUMBA'S
Mayfield at Lincoln, Waterloo
Rector: Rev. Rev. A. J. Hankin
Parish Priest — 576-1717
8:00 a.m.—Holy Eucharist
9:30 a.m.—Choral Eucharist

ALL SAINTS
Hickory at Hazel, Waterloo
Rector: The Rev. W. J. Janke
Phone 884-5040
8:00 a.m.—Holy Communion
9:30 a.m.—Family Service

CHURCH OF THE HOLY SAVIOUR
Water and Erb Sts., Kitchener
Rev. Denton Massey, O.B.E., B.A.

CHURCH OF ST. JOHN THE EVANGELIST
(ANGLICAN)
Water and Duke Sts. Kitchener
(Mother Church of the Anglican Communion in the K-W Area)

ST. ANDREWS MEMORIAL CHURCH
273 Mill St., Kitchener
Rev. Deane B. K. Junke,
Miss Helen Critchham, Organist

STIRLING AVE. MENNONITE
Stirling Ave., near West St. East
Rev. James R. Reusser, Pastor
Miss Helen Critchham, Organist

BETHEL CHAPEL
"Christians Gathered Unto the Name of the Lord Jesus Christ"
Bridgeport Road and Erb Street East, Waterloo

The United Church
of Canada

KITCHENER

CALVARY — PARK ST. NEAR COLLEGIATE

CHRIST THE KING — 167 Thaler

FOREST HILL — 121 Filsinger Rd.

HIGHLAND ROAD — Highland Rd. East, Near Shoemaker Ave.

OLIVET — 47 ONWARD AVE.

ST. JAMES' — ROSEMOUNT — Rosemount Plaza

ST. TIMOTHY'S — Leonard and Arnold Streets

TRINITY — 74 Frederick St.

ZION — WEBER ST. WEST at ONTARIO

EMMANUEL — LAUREL and DORSET STS.

FIRST — KING and WILLIAM

PARKMINSTER — 275 Erb St. E.

The Presbyterian Church in Canada
MEMBER OF THE FAMILY OF REFORMED CHURCHES

ST. ANDREW'S — CORNER OF QUEEN & WEBER STS.

CALVIN — FILSINGER AND VILLAGE ROADS

KNOX — 50 ERB ST. WEST, WATERLOO

The Fellowship of Evangelical Baptist Churches in Canada

Evangelical Lutheran Churches
Extend an Invitation to Worship

KITCHENER
ST. MATTHEW'S — BENTON ST.
GRACE — MARGARET & LOUISA STS.
ST. LUKE'S — 317 FRANKLIN AVENUE, NORTH
ST. PETER'S — 43 QUEEN ST. N.
ST. PAUL'S — BRIDGEPORT
ST. PHILIP'S — WOODHAVEN RD.

WATERLOO
REDEEMER
FAITH
MOUNT ZION

Focus on Youth
A Public Workshop on Counselling Youth and Their Families
at WATERLOO LUTHERAN UNIVERSITY

PENTECOSTAL ASSEMBLIES OF CANADA

DOON PENTECOSTAL TABERNACLE
1222 Manitou Drive
KITCHENER (Doon), ONTARIO
Morning Worship 11:00 a.m.

KITCHENER GOSPEL TEMPLE
9 CONWAY DR. AT RIVER ROAD (STANLEY PARK)
REV. R. L. DONNELLY (SASKATOON, SASK.)
11:00 A.M. "WHAT DOES IT MEAN TO BE FILLED?"
7:00 P.M. "WHAT DOES IT MEAN TO BELIEVE?"

Waterloo Pentecostal Tabernacle
395 KING ST. NORTH
"Where King and Weber Streets Meet"

Bulldozer Bishop Builds Schools

PRINCE GEORGE, B.C. (CP) — The Bulldozer Bishop has moved from building 2,500 schools to internal church operations.

THE BIBLE SPEAKS TO YOU

CHURCH OF CHRIST
Old Mill Road, Blair, Ontario

The Christian and Missionary Alliance Church

UNITARIAN

K-W PHILHARMONIC CHOIR presents "MAGNIFICATS"

Church of God
Rev. DONALD TALBOT, Pastor

The Salvation Army
130 Duke Street East, Kitchener

FIRST CHRISTIAN REFORMED CHURCH

The Menno Singers
and Orchestra
Director: Abner Martin
will present
Jewish Sacred Service
by Ernest Bloch
Thomas Pyle, Baritone
SIXTH CHANDOS ANTHEM
by G. F. Handel
at the
Rockway High School Auditorium
SATURDAY, MAY 10 – 8:30 p.m.

announcing
EMMANUEL CHRISTIAN CENTRE'S SOUL-WINNING SEMINAR
THE CHURCH WITH CAMP MEETING SINGING and CAMP MEETING PREACHING ALL YEAR ROUND!
at the JOHN MAHOOD SCHOOL, Elmira

Here's an indication of the scope of the challenge.

There are 83 ads on those two pages calling attention to various religious activities. This wasn't an especially unusual Sunday offering that was being advertised, and the audience being solicited wasn't particularly large – the total circulation of that issue was just over 53,000, or roughly 638 readers per ad. At least 20 other churches in the area didn't advertise in the paper that week.

Most of the subliminal means of promoting value additives or alternatives (religious, political, social, or what have you) are fairly commonplace. They parallel those employed by sexual pressure groups seeking to achieve communication (and conversion) by organization, agitation, and demonstration. Word-of-mouth, newsletters, conventions, rallies, arm-twisting, legal manoeuvring, occasional forays into blackmail, and even bribery all come to bear. They can best be charted by seeking out a friendly neighbourhood fanatic and asking him (or her) a leading question or two.

iii/**Anti-conditioning and/or liberating**

Habit emerged in Chapter 5 as an important factor fostering contact between people. Accurate and effective triggering of habit responses was suggested as a promising way of sharing meanings and, in turn, venturing to pool values and data.

At the same time, we noted that the conditioning underlying some habit response patterns can be out of whack. Responses to such trigger phrases as 'long hair' and 'hard hat' can mask the individual content rather than promote shared and enriched meaning.

As with humans generally, the media sometimes fall victim to such warpings. Reference to 'Red China' is commonplace in the mass media, for example, despite the fact that the phrase is highly misleading (the physical land space isn't red, mainland Chinese are not all 'reds,' and the pejorative connotation of ideological hostility or, for that matter, brotherhood doesn't stand up to close scrutiny).

Once again, a role for subliminal agents reveals itself. This time it's the challenge and opportunity to counter the conditioning that leads to dysfunctional habits – and possibly to foster the liberation implicit in replacing such habits with constructive ones.

As with other subliminal features of our communications landscape, these anti-conditioning and liberating manifestations will sometimes overlap into the realm of mass media. They will also frequently employ forms identified with other subliminal roles.

For instance, the promotion of challenges to existing habit patterns – such as campaigns to introduce new services or values (legal marijuana, curbs on pollution, equal employment laws) – will obviously rely in part on the mass media as a vehicle. They will also involve many of the clubs, publications, rallies, door-to-door campaigns, and other techniques.

Where do the main differences lie then?

Primarily, they lie in the blend of topic and technique. Anti-conditioning and/or liberation groups are primarily reactive in nature. They are concerned with some aspect of the existing landscape that needs to be changed or modified. They espouse issues such as women's liberation, law reform, ecological crisis, consumption or production habits, ideology, or arms control. And because existing habits tend to be entrenched and, to a degree, irrationally espoused, challenges to them require approaches and methods that demand revived attention and fresh evaluation.

Consider women's liberation as a case in point. As even the more generous of Harold's attitudes towards Sarah Minge testify, there are some aspects of the relationship that can quite reasonably be said to be open to change or modification. (Why, for example, should he have automatic employment advantages in wages, working hours, promotion, and seniority? Why should he assume that it's her responsibility to nibble the potentially dangerous pills so as to prevent conception? And so on ...)

The Kitchener-Waterloo Record, May 3, 1969

Yet, as the Admiral makes abundantly clear in his man-to-man chats with Harold (and his rows with his housekeeper), existing habits are profoundly well entrenched. Male-female relationship are the way they are ... because that's ... that's the way they've always been ... biblically sanctioned ... divinely ordained ... beyond question.

You have a topic involving some questionable habits that are, in part at least, irrationally clung to. What do you do?

As we've seen in practice, part of what you do will be mainstream. There will be media reports in abundance – stretching back through the centuries that this particular anti-conditioning attempt has been under way (remember Aristophanes' *Lysistrata* and all the fuss in the Athens *Daily Bugle*?) There will also be the requisite complement of chapters of the Society for Cutting Up Men (SCUM) and the National Organization for Women (NOW), assorted rallies and conventions, publications by the armful, and most of the other means used to supplement the media.

But that's not all.

You're trying to break through habit barriers, right? Dealing with the irrational and the automatic.

So, you set out to issue information, to act and challenge values in ways that shake up habit patterns. Call it juxtaposition: a few dozen babies deposited at City Hall to challenge the paper-shuffling habits that delay Day Care Centres; some garbage tins full of brassieres and girdles parked by the office water cooler to de-mystify the sex object habits; public ogling and whistling at a few construction workers in a turn-about to point up value assumptions about courtship; all sorts of major and minor vexations to flip habit patterns out of 'automatic' and start the red lights of reconsideration flashing.

To the extent that anti-conditioning and/or liberating agents serve to modify or even change habits of perception that are faulty, they make positive contributions to our attempts to perceive and express reality. There can be drawbacks, of course – ranging from psychic immobilization to the erosion of soundly-based habits – but most of the time the risk seems to be worthwhile.

iv/**Early Warning Systems**

Primarily because they are *mass* media, the main North American communications systems are at a particular disadvantage when it comes to discerning and describing aspects of innovation and discovery in our society. This is mainly because, reasonably enough, they have to operate with certain minimum thresholds of audience and seldom can venture below such thresholds if they are to remain intelligible, interesting, and solvent.

Consider inventions, for example. Every year in North America, thousands of patents are filed to register and protect a vast assortment of real and imagined, valid and invalid additions to our store of knowledge. Most of these in turn (about 99 out of every 100) never advance past the patent stage – mainly because they are unworkable, uneconomic, irrelevant, or insane. But every once in a while a patent is filed that leads to a product or process that has profound effects on our lives.

If every one of the patent applications were to be reported, there wouldn't be space for any other kinds of information in the mass media; there would also be howls of protest, cancelled subscriptions, dial turnings, and channel switchings on the part of consumers. We don't want to know about all the patents, simply because most of them are irrelevant and unintelligible.

On the other hand, any aspiration to perfect our grasp of reality requires that we take note of patent claims and be aware of their one-in-a-hundred significance.

Johnny Hart, *Back to B.C.*

This too is something we cannot do individually. Even our most impressively giant intellects are not yet capable of mastering the dozens of disciplines and hundreds of specialties required to be able to view and assess all the kinds of innovation and inventions filed for patent. If you weren't expert at locomotion, for instance, would you have recognized that the wheel was something new and important when it was first proposed? Probably not.

Again, alternative and subliminal media functions are called for. Scanning below the threshold of the mainstream media, we want individuals and organizations keeping an eye out for discoveries and innovations so that, when these are relevant – however rarely – we will be advised before it is too late and in time to benefit.

Our concern is with sensible anticipation – a concern of ever-growing importance as the rate and range of change in our society increase. We want to know about activities, devices, ideas, substances, and techniques *before* they emerge as full-blown mass phenomena.

Catering to such concern has become one of our greatest growth industries. Here's an inventory of the main means:

→ The fanciest – though not necessarily the most effective – methods of divining changes, innovations, and discoveries in our society and their possible consequences are now to be found in the hands of people like econometricians. Armed with computers programmed to simulate economies, industries, occupational groups, age groups, and so forth, they play around, in relatively subliminal privacy, with projections designed to indicate to us the consequences of present and varied behaviour. At the Department of Finance in Ottawa, for example, experts use their computer terminal to advise them on possible consequences of changes in the tax structure – able because of their equipment to work through permutations that previously would have taken years to canvass. (Mind you, there is always the lurking spectre of things like the Edsel motor car which proved to be a monumental flop in the market despite surveys and simulations that guaranteed that it would be an economic, psychiatric, and social winner.)

→ More resolute human experts now are beginning to come together to do their anticipating without the benefit of machines. They operate 'think tanks' such as the Hudson Institute run by Herman Kahn, where assorted individuals possessed of widely different skills and experience literally sit around and brainstorm their way into the future. Unfettered by the mechanistic limitations of technology, they sometimes manage to beat the machines with intuitive leaps and imaginative insights. One such group, for instance, came up with a design for a baby's bottle that marked the first really practical step forward in the field since the breast became partly obsolete.

→ Individuals and publications with the time, facilities, and mono-mania required to survey a specific field in great depth provide very effective early warning systems. The classic case has been the staff of Jane's *Fighting Ships* – a small group of imaginative experts which has perceived and warned of virtually every development in naval design and warfare during the last 50 years – usually well in advance of mainstream media. Similarly, specialist music publications and performers routinely manage a three-month to two-year jump ahead of their times in matters of taste, behaviour, and presentation.

→ Various digesting and abstracting services play a very important part in providing early warning in many fields. No one has time to keep up with current literature in most specialties these days and such services offer tip-offs on selected items that might otherwise be missed. Here's a current Canadian example:

CONCRETE BOATS ARE CATCHING ON IN US	US MAY USE AIRBORNE SENSORS TO DETECT ILLICIT DRUG LABS	JAPAN IS DEVELOPING 1500-MPH ROCKET TRAIN
SOCIAL ROLES OF MEN, WOMEN ARE BIOLOGICALLY DETERMINED	NEW MULTINATIONAL BANKING CONSORTIUM	BANKS IN SWEDEN MERGE DATA SERVICES
GROCERY CHAIN TESTING LABELING OF FOODS BY THEIR NUTRIENTS	NEW METHOD OF PRODUCING HOLOGRAMS BY SOUND	ORBITING TV SCANNER GIVES CONTINUOUS PICTURE OF EARTH
ARTIFICIAL BREEDING OF EELS MAY BE POSSIBLE	FRANCE TO AUTOMATIZE THEIR METRO SYSTEM	SEARCH FOR ALTERNATIVE TRANSPORT SYSTEMS IN JAPAN
TV AUDIENCE FOR MOON WALK IS CALLED DISAPPOINTING	CARMICHAEL URGES US BLACKS TO LOOK TO AFRICA	NEW APARTMENTS FOUND TO BE UNPOPULAR IN FRANCE
WORLD'S FASTEST COMPUTER, ILLIAC IV, NEARS COMPLETION	JOB/MAN MATCHING IN THE 70's	RAILWAY TUNNEL UNDER ENGLISH CHANNEL TO BE DELAYED AGAIN
TEST MARKETING IN UK PRODUCES POOR FORECASTS	9 FEB 71	ISOTOPES USED TO PRODUCE FORGE-PROOF CREDIT CARD
Analysis in London's *Financial Times* indicates the widely accepted practice of "test marketing" new products has limited value, at least in Britain. Test marketing consists of advertising products only in limited geographical regions before risking them on the national market. However, sales totals in test regions have not accurately predicted national sales. 4 FEB 71 FINANC.TIMES(LONDON) 15:1 24"+pic	CHANGES is published each weekday by Orba Information Limited, 418 Saint Sulpice, Montreal 125, Canada. (514) 844-8401; 844-9067. Toronto Office: Suite 719, 4000 Yonge Street. (416) 487-9067. The publisher is Robert Russel; the managing director, J.D. Lippens, and the editor, J.M. Glazner. Vol. 2, no. 87 copyright ORBA 1971	A Swedish firm has developed a credit card which it says is impossible to forge. The card, made by the firm AB ID-kort, has trace-element beta isotopes implanted in it. The isotopes are impossible to copy and can be checked by a desk-top Geiger measuring unit. The firm is seeking markets in the US, where credit card forging is a growing problem. 1-14 FEB 71 ELECTRONICS 121:2 13"

→ What might be called 'the new witchcraft' has also come to play an important role in the monitoring and presentation of indicators of innovation and discovery. The people involved do not rely solely on empirical evidence and thus can be neither proven nor disproven correct. Marshall McLuhan, for instance, has managed to mix portions of insight and obscurity sufficient to warn of consequences of the electronic age, the new tribal village, and related developments. On the basis of 'maybe he's right,' as writer Tom Wolfe observed, Dr McLuhan frequently persuades mass media operators and ourselves to test his theories and ... lo and behold ... sometimes he is right. Further up or down the scale (depending on whether he was right last time) we find authors such as Ken Kesey, Norman Brown, and Teilhard de Chardin and even the makers of horoscopes and almanacs, fortune tellers, and some operators of crystal balls and seances. Recent studies at several centres such as Duke University suggest that prescience and other vaguely supernatural qualities cannot be entirely ruled out.

→ Accident is a vital ingredient of alternative communications about innovation and discovery. For example, the current growth of the leisure industry in North America gained its initial impetus from a few isolated individuals and organizations who suffered the accidents of more free time (from layoffs, good union contracts, or sloth), appropriate location (usually in promising leisure areas), assorted talents (carpentry, etc.), and one or two causal connections. That is how it got started – almost by accident they laid out or built a resort, designed a leisure device, checked into more general trends. Then, almost by accident again, what they were doing became known and thus started the subliminal early warning of a coming trend. Most of that batch are rich and busy now too.

→ Once again, chemicals do play a part. As noted, LSD can – perils notwithstanding – promote problem-solving and anticipatory insights. The humble coffee bean produces qualities of wakefulness that can promote perception. Broadly speaking, many substances can facilitate contact between our perceiving senses and our conscious and unconscious minds to the extent of allowing causal connections that ordinarily don't occur or are suppressed.

→ The dogged persistence of the concept of the amateur in most societies also contributes to subliminal communication of prospects of change. There are two main reasons for this. First, amateurs seldom know all the established rules – and so they blunder on to innovation on their own. (Contemporary blues guitar techniques, for instance, came into being in defiance of what all the experts said was possible or permissible in playing the instrument.) Second, amateurs tend to meet and exchange experiences more readily than grudging professionals guarding a livelihood. Accordingly, the results of their experiments and innovations are usually disseminated very rapidly.

→ Finally, there is the largely non-verbal and formally incoherent field of intuition. As a consequence of the tone or tenor of the times, we repeatedly come upon waves of action or reaction through our society that suggest the onset or prospect of change. As frustrated behavioural scientists complain, the great difficulty in dealing with such lemming-like phenomena lies in finding out how, where, and for what reasons these largely spontaneous expressions and communications occur (for example, the Davy Crockett boom, the Frisbee craze, the Fort Lauderdale syndrome, to cite a few, all caught everyone, including the commercial participants, flat-footed). Summed up, such subliminal systems of communication seem to consist of people sensing themselves and, to some degree, looking around, and then, with little or no conscious evaluation, acting.

v/**Contact**

So far, the kinds of contact possible with other individuals and with the media, making use of the mass media, are limited indeed. With the media, the main difficulties lie in initiating and maintaining effective, extensive, and balanced exchanges. One can write in to the Editor or dial the hot-line number, but only occasionally and to limited effect. Regular and routine two-way flow between media and their users and among users themselves is still some distance away. The very disabilities that led to dependence on the mass media as proxy agents make it clear that, individually, we can do relatively little to take up the slack. Once more, we turn to alternative and subliminal agents.

The first four categories of subliminal proxy role that have been examined imply and contain much of the substance of contact. They depend upon some effective contact for dissemination.

There remains, however, an aspect of contact that might be called collectivity. This ties in with the aspirations of language considered in Chapter 5. No matter how successful we may become in formulating and receiving concepts by habit-triggering, we still need more and better ways to *universalize* communication.

Experience and experimentation have produced a remarkable number of alternative and proxy means of collectivizing contact. Not all are as well understood as they might be and some, possibly, are outright frauds; still, they deserve at least passing attention in our catalogue of means to handle variables. Let us glance therefore at psychodynamics, hypnosis, ESP, and group-mind theorizing.

Hypnosis and psychodynamics are important to us in so far as they can contribute to individual sensitivity and receptivity. The lumber cluttering our individual landscapes in the form of inhibitions, phobias, and irrational tensions can be tidied up or even, on occasion, cleared away to allow for a greater openness. Both the expression and reception of communications can benefit.

Mind you, this isn't the entirely unqualified blessing that enthusiasts proclaim. Tinkering with individual structures of repression of any kind is delicate and risky. Vital protections built up to foster at least shaky stability can be completely undone, physical and psychiatric problems that have already been successfully adjusted to can be escalated anew. It can be both foolish and cruel to encourage a one-legged person to take up tennis.

Yet, with such reservations, it is reasonably evident that hypnosis and psychodynamics can be helpful – particularly as media employed in challenging the substance of suppression in our society. We are often trained to restrain ourselves (acquire inhibitions) so that the peace, order, and good government (status quo) of the day may prevail. When change is necessary, we benefit from assistance in dissolving such inhibitions.

With hypnotic techniques, learned inhibitions can be modified or even eliminated entirely. Provided we really want, semi- or subconsciously, to escape a particular restraint, we can be assisted in persuading ourselves to abandon it. The visible methods of hypnotism of course are legion – as varied as pendulums, car windshield wipers, and acid rock – but they all relate basically to some method of focusing and concentrating our attention to accept a single suggestion which would ordinarily be ignored.

Subliminal manifestations of hypnosis, in turn, tend to be at one remove from our immediate environment. Instead of a white-coated clinician or a theatrical mesmerist, there may be a recurrent, rather monotonous piece of music (such as 'Sidewinder' by Lee Morgan) to lull us into receptivity while a gentle voice makes the pitch. The 'Do what you want to do' of the Beatles mentioned at the beginning of this chapter provides another good example. All the time dedicated students and workers are dutifully inhibiting themselves to follow orders, their record players or radios or Muzak are busy planting hypnotic suggestions.

Or our attention may be focused visually. For example, one major Canadian oil company ran a commercial to sell automobile batteries that featured a single dot in the centre of a TV picture. As people watched, their attention fixed upon the dot, they were told to think of that particular brand of battery the next time their car broke down. In the process, inhibitions against unthinking and carefree battery selection (part of the whole 'let the buyer beware' training) were challenged.

To carry our study one step further, environmental hypnosis is becoming a highly refined art. The thoughtful use of interrelated colours and shapes can influence mood and behaviour in all sorts of ways. Some people argue, for example, that the intricacy, vividness, and involvement of good psychedelic posters tends to concentrate attention and promote the reduction of inhibitions.

Group dynamics, in turn, is another burgeoning field in which the powerful and relatively subliminal weight of collective influence is brought to bear upon individuals to persuade them to modify or abandon their personal predilections (often inhibition-based) in favour of group standards. As Alexander and Selesnick note:

The advantage of group over individual psychotherapy, according to group therapists, is that the patient in individual treatment may consciously or unconsciously repress certain attitudes and experiences that a group may elicit as live and spontaneous reactions to group pressures.

F. G. Alexander and S. T. Selesnick, *The History of Psychiatry* (New York: Harper & Row, 1966), p. 335

Such procedures can, like hypnotic suggestions, work for or against suppression. If your group as a whole looks with horror on law-breaking, immorality, godlessness, or the flouting of property rights, few individuals are able to persevere against the tide. Equally, however, resolute good guys can be expected to falter in the face of the massed ranks of libertarians.

When one moves outside the careful confines of psychiatry and established therapy into the subliminal world of spontaneous groups, the impact of such anti-suppression influences can be considerably enhanced. No professional ethics remain to restrain enthusiasts; scepticism and rationality are no longer called for; the fires of fanaticism burn brightly. Consider, for example, the subliminal group dynamic that persuaded a girl member of a motorcycle club that it was worth beating and kicking another girl so that she would submit to indecent assault by other club members. Regardless of her own views, for her it was that important to belong.

What we need to recognize is that i/a lot of persuasion utilizing hypnotic and psychodynamic techniques is going on in our society, ii/some of these efforts foster greater receptivity and sensitivity on the part of the individual, and, as a result, more effective communications, and iii/there are dangers that need to be kept in mind.

With ESP (extrasensory perception) and assorted theorizing about group minds, we move to rather shakier ground. Opinions are sharply divided as to whether, and, in turn, how, extrasensory exchanges may be possible among humans. Evidence for and against has been collected for centuries. Yet, if we are to concern ourselves with augmented human capacity for communications, we cannot dismiss current speculation as 'not proven.' If, to any degree, extrasensory contact among any humans is possible, we are possessed of a very important additional means of contact.

In its more florid versions, ESP involves mind-reading (often at great distances), reconstruction of the past (as with the challenged reincarnation of Bridey Murphy), and, once in a while, foretelling of the future. We can't do much more than take note of these manifestations since such gifts do not yet seem to be persuasive enough or pervasive enough for general benefit.

The less spectacular qualities of extrasensory perception that foster ability to 'read' people and situations can, however, be both important and widespread. They appear, in fact, to be a combination of actual perceptual skills (taking up ordinarily unnoticed cues) and qualities of intuition. At the very least, such abilities deserve further consideration and study.

Group-mind theories are most often built upon a projection of organic growth. Evolution, it is argued, led to the progressive multiplication and specialization of human cells to the human brain. Surely then, one dimension of evolution beyond the point of the present human can be postulated – many human brains linked and acting in concert as a kind of super-brain.

174   There are organizations and individuals working on such a challenge. One in England, for example, has progressed to the point where it is claimed that the quantity and quality of contact and exchange among the associated individual minds is much greater than can be accounted for by familiarity, mathematical probability, or wishful thinking. Perhaps so ...

Now, in outline at least, we have an idea of where we can turn to supplement or secure alternatives to the established mass media and, on occasion, to our own sensory-cerebral processes. The survey indicates that, at present, there is a great deal we can do, but it also suggests that we will encounter vexation and frustration in the search for reliability, verification, and greater capacity.

Let us conclude by seeking to evaluate our present prospects as a whole and make a few ventures into the world of the future.

MOVING INTO THE FUTURE

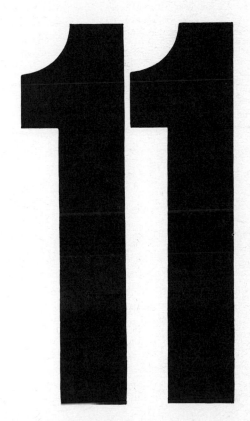

After this romp across the spectrum of communications, we should now be ready to attempt a hard-headed evaluation of the prospects of perceiving an infinite number of variables infinitely expressed. Then we can peer into the future to try to see what can be expected during the next ten years or so.

Well, where are we at?

Briefly, we're not very far ahead. Even with the massed array of our own senses, augmentations of our senses, and alternatives to our senses, our grasp of the world around us is till very tentative. The efforts of centuries have done little more than increase the amount, the volume, and the frequency of the equivalent of Stone Age grunts. Affairs may be somewhat more stylish, but behind the window dressing, the substance of what we are able to perceive, formulate, and express remains much the same.

In other words, we still don't really know much of what is going on. What little we do think we know is highly inaccurate, so far as we can tell.

Evidence?

Consider this basic report card:

i/We still don't know how the brain works ... or even how many brains we may actually possess.

ii/Our senses persist in insufficiency. When one of them is sharpened or focused through evolution, we end up with a tinkered balance that really offers little aggregate improvement. When any or all are augmented mechanically or chemically, we still face restrictions of mobility, sustained reliability, applicability, and economic feasibility.

iii/Alternatives to our senses – especially the media – are all flawed. Their incapacities, distortions, and intentions combine to war with reality on many occasions.

iv/New initiatives are precious few, for a start, and unproven or imperfect in their own ways as far as they go.

We get some of the feel of our limits when we meet specific cases. Here we are, for example, in the great global 20th century ... yet an Asian philosopher and a captain of Western industry remain as distant and unintelligible to each other as Earthlings and Martians; the Generation Gap evinces itself in grim statistics on runaways, incarcerations, and related manifestations of alienation; compartmentalization not only persists but grows – nourished by the frustration and despair of individuals unable to convey their perceptions and aspirations to one another; the number of separate languages in the world *increases* rather than the contrary.

Realistically, *and not glumly,* there are grounds for asserting that ours is more the century of massive incomprehension than the century of the common (and communicating) man.

What to do?

Well, there is much progress implicit in simply recognizing the situation. Every step we take towards dissolving the mists of illusory communication clears the way for honest examination and treatment of our failures. When 'Movies are better than ever,' or 'Daily Newspapers Surge Ahead,' or 'WEHT- TV Asks Why?' are sensibly qualified or discounted along with any undue faith in our own minds and senses, then it is easier to see true needs for remedial action.

Of course, this isn't easy. Habits and conditioning die hard. And there is always the very real possibility that we may merely swap cobwebs, brushing aside one batch to affix others. The zeal of the convert, for example, can lead to excesses or misconstructions comparable to prior sins. We need to try for a clean slate.

We need to step back from present attitudes and practices related to communication. We need to re-think – as much as possible without preconceived notions. And we need to do this at a variety of levels. Every once in a while, it is probably good for our soul to attend to the fundamental questions of what and why communications exist.

Yet, realistically, the efforts, rewards, and prospects associated with these questions are daunting. For variety, more tangible results, and ease, we can also try to answer such queries as:

why ears?
what better than ears?
what about no ears?
why print?
what better than print?
what about no print?

And so on...

Then, in addition to the occasional great 'Aha!' of fundamental discovery, we can seek to restore open-mindedness, foster the testing of alternatives, and learn to attach qualifications to the assumptions, techniques, or devices so queried. We can grow.

In addition, we can engage in exercises of 'otherthink.' We can try to place ourselves in the circumstances of the communicator, temporarily acquiring when possible, or at least recognizing, some of the attitudes and characteristics of that person, allowing for the influences of the setting, considering such variables as the time, type of medium, and available facilities. In addition to enriching our own lives with some vicarious imaginings, such exercises can provide constructive reminders of what flaws are likely to be involved in our perception – even to the point of improving our judgment and our understanding.

'Otherthink' applied specifically can be revealing. Let's go back to one of the examples examined in our media surveys, and see what happens. One item went as follows:

SCARBORO LOVELY NAMED MISS COOL
by Rhymer Blank

Halifax – Pert, buxom Sharon Starlet of Scarboro wiggled off with the 1971 "Miss Cool" crown today with a display of poise and skin that left 27 rivals wrinkled with envy.

The 19-year-old model drew a standing ovation in the final walk-through of the contest that displayed arts more than enough to make up for an earlier mediocre showing in the talent category.

Said Sharon "...

Now, let's 'otherthink' this item. For a moment, let us seek to become Rhymer Blank in Halifax at the Miss Cool contest. (You may recall that Rhymer Blank was described as 'general reporter, 41, significant for our purposes for his devout dedication to flesh and his sniggering mind.')

We end up like this:

(SCARBORO) LOVELY NAMED MISS COOL
by Rhymer Blank

(Halifax)— Pert, buxom Sharon Starlet of Scarboro wiggled off with the 1971 "Miss Cool" crown today with a display of poise and skin that left 27 rivals wrinkled with envy.

The 19-year-old model drew a standing ovation in the final walk-through of the contest that displayed arts more than enough to make up for an earlier mediocre showing in the talent category.

Said Sharon "...

'SCARBORO' ...
That'll boost local circulation.
So: A promotional stunt for textiles makes the paper because of a local angle

'Halifax' ... do I hate this city! Cold, damp, poor, dingy ... anything deserves a standing ovation here if it's even half-way passable.
So: Qualify the ovation.

'poise and skin' ...
she's got a bouncy back and frontside ... never got to look at her face ... or her teeth ...
So: Lovely breasts, bouncy bottom ... but did Rhymer or the other judges notice the rest?

'Talent category' ...
That's the part to keep the IODE quiet, the only talented one looked like my grandmother.
So: Discount 'talent' at beauty contests.

'Earlier mediocre showing' ...
She read 'The shooting of Dan McGrew' from cue cards! And stumbled!
So: Escalate the 'mediocre' to 'lousy.'

'Wrinkled with envy' ...
that will get a laugh at the telegraph desk, Old Rhymer and his vivid writing!
So: Maybe the appeal of the phrase outweighed the actual facts.

'Standing ovation' ...
The Mayor and his party, four drunken textile salesmen, and the media men stood up.
So: Qualify the 'standing.'

'Displayed arts' ...
Snigger, snigger, leer ...
So: Translate that to a sexy walk.

Here is a reasonably representative example of print communication. Now, put yourself in the shoes of the various people involved in its preparation and see what deductions and observations you would apply in 'otherthink.'

In this instance, 'otherthink' calls for role-playing in relation to i/the reporters in contact with Belfast, Londonderry, Lurgan, and Dungiven, ii/the editors of the news agencies concerned, probably in London, New York, and Toronto, and iii/the editors of the particular paper in which the report was printed. 'Otherthink' also calls for consideration of i/the circumstances of the communicators, ii/the attitudes and characteristics of the communicators, iii/the setting involved, iv/time variables, v/the medium for the communication, and vi/the facilities available for communication.

1,500 British soldiers move into Londonderry

BELFAST (CP—Reuters) — More than 1,500 British troops moved into riot-torn Londonderry yesterday to guard key installations and the Northern Ireland Government declared it is determined to end disorders that left scores injured and entire streets in chaos during the weekend.

A statement issued after an emergency Cabinet meeting said the Government will not be "held up to ransom" by the rioters.

It said the disorders were "irresponsible hooliganism which has been properly condemned by all decent citizens without regard to religious or political affiliations."

The Government announced it is sending to Londonderry 300 members of the special constabulary—controversial reserve police bitterly resented by the Roman Catholic minority in Northern Ireland. These police would be armed only with nightsticks.

An army spokesman said the troops will guard key installations and "tighten up security." Quelling of street riots would be left to the police.

The Roman Catholic quarter of Londonderry resembled a battlefield after the weekend of rioting, looting, burning and running street fights.

Police, who were forced to open fire above rioters' heads on Sunday, said 87 persons were hurt in the city, including 45 policemen, since Saturday. Two of the injured were wounded by bullets.

The cost in overturned vehicles, damaged stores and looting was estimated at hundreds of thousands of dollars.

A Londonderry police spokesman yesterday said: "There is debris everywhere. There were so many incidents last night it is almost impossible to list them."

Sporadic stone-throwing and looting in Londonderry during the day on Sunday turned into fullscale violence as darkness fell. It was the second night running that Londonderry was turned into a battleground.

The trouble began on Saturday after 100,000 militant Protestants of the Orange Order staged annual parades marking a battle in 1690 which ended Roman Catholic control in Northern Ireland.

July 12 is the anniversary of the final defeat of James II, the last Roman Catholic king of England, in the Battle of the Boyne River.

At one point during the fighting on Sunday night that raged through the predominantly Roman Catholic Bogside district of Londonderry, a squad of police found themselves trapped in a dead-end street by a stone-throwing mob. After several warnings, they fired into the air and made their escape.

A civil rights worker on Sunday night called the crowd "an unruly mob . . . not representative of any party, either civil rights or Roman Catholic or any other group."

In Lurgan, police locked themselves in their barracks as mobs roamed the streets burning two police vehicles and a Protestant hall.

At nearby Dungiven, a mob which trapped police in a hall made two unsuccessful attempts to burn them alive.

180 'Otherthink' is very personal. Since it serves subjective purposes – to enhance an individual's grasp of the validity and invalidity of a communication – 'otherthink' is of very limited use unless it is your own.

Therefore let us end discussion of this concept now. For your convenience, we bequeath a blank space for your possible 'otherthink' activities. Try it.

What else can we do?

We can, of course, **try harder.**

(What follows may seem somewhat lukewarm. We already do seem to be trying about as hard as anyone reasonably can ask ... but, like motherhood and apple pie, the exhortation is almost compulsory.)

One way of

trying harder

is to orchestrate. Instead of relying on GRUB-TV or radio station BLOB or the Daily Murk or any other single source of communications input, we can set out deliberately to cover a variety of bases in order to get as many perspectives as possible. Then we may be able to cancel out various biases, gain greater data input, and edge closer to the truths.

An investment of modest proportions might lead to a package such as:

Trying Harder Package

Primary:
The Daily Murk
GRUB-TV's 11 pm newscast
The BLOB 'World in Review' at 6 pm and 8 am

Supportive:
Time
Maclean's
Harper's or *Atlantic Monthly*
Atlas magazine
The World Today (Royal Institute of International Affairs)
The Georgia Straight or a similar 'underground' publication
The Modern Utopian
The Plain Truth (an 'anti communist' magazine)

Creative:
One movie a week
Letters to people and places asking what is going on
Cultivation of contact with two people who disagree with you
Hansard or *The Rolling Stone*

Yet another version of **trying harder** involves controls.

Quite apart from the negative forms of censorship, regulation, and prohibition discussed earlier, there are possibilities of control that are truly positive. Instead of playing at the 'Elephant? What Elephant?' game in which we pretend that aspects of reality are not present and pressing, we can shift the emphasis to efforts to acknowledge and facilitate expressions of reality.

Control then becomes a selection of objectives:
→ Censorship ... but only to tone down communications that are palpably unreal.
→ Regulation ... but only to facilitate access to the means of communication, to restrict (mechanically, economically, or administratively) the opportunities for anti-reality or counter-reality communications, to foster experimentation and exploration within confines that won't destroy us.
→ Prohibition ... but only in those rare and clear-cut circumstances where our frailty or the communication's enormity are such as to very seriously threaten the fact and delicate balances of human existence.

Few would challenge such proposals in general principle. When it comes to practice, the situation becomes rather difficult. *Who* is to decide? *How* are they to act? *What communications* should fall under their authority? Individually, we are faced with overwhelming evidence suggesting that we cannot rely solely on self-applied controls. Yet collectively, our experience with controls to date – no matter how well-intentioned   has been unsatisfactory at best.

Another way of **trying harder** is to suspend judgment.

This involves making a solemn vow never to believe any communication when you receive it. Instead, you toss off a noncommital, Is that so?' and wait. If and when, over time, supporting evidence accumulates, gradually lift the suspension.

For example, it has been relatively standard practice on the BBC to wait until at least two and preferably three news agencies report on an event before fully acknowledging that an event has occurred. Little harm has come of this and frequently wildly inaccurate or incomplete conclusions have been avoided – such as the false armistice reports towards the end of the first and second world wars that were carried by individual news agencies.

But, at best, any version of **trying harder** in today's context is really a stop-gap. What we *really* have to do is inform ourselves about new developments in communications – as they are today, and may be tomorrow. Here lie most of the really promising answers.

We can, if we try, envisage a concept of communications on the scale of a *system,* not as isolated techniques or devices.

We can start with the coaxial cable. This is the wire that comes into your house if you are a CATV subscriber. It differs from ordinary cables in the sense that it is made up of coaxial tubes – usually eight – rather than pairs of ordinary wire.

The coaxial cable is significant because of its capacity. As it is currently used, it is technically able to provide receivers with up to 30 channels of televisions (though 5 to 12 is the most common array offered) *plus* up to 1,000 other communications services utilizing the electromagnetic spectrum below, around the middle of, and above the TV frequencies. This means that, even now, there is a capacity for information input of vastly greater size than ever known before. In the reasonably near future, such capacity can be expected to include – via one coaxial cable – up to 70 TV channels plus the other communications services.

By itself, such capacity is already fostering changes in communications. In addition to the occasional vitality and general blancmange of the regular TV programming, the CATV operators are already offering their own services, such as:

→ time and weather reports
→ stock exchange quotations
→ FM radio over extended range
→ news channels (usually teletypes shown on camera)
→ sports channels
→ special 'educational' channels
→ all-film channels
→ background music channels
→ emergency warning systems
→ colour-bar generation for alignment of sets
→ locally produced programs: community television
→ computer access.

It is by no means far-fetched to suggest that the relatively unnoticed spread of CATV promises to transform contemporary communications. As specialist channels continue to grow, the number and variety of inputs increase. To the extent that such services continue to be directly subscriber-financed (at about $4 to $7 a month per connection), the mass-market orientation of broadcasting – and the resulting dependence on sponsors, commercials, and attendant cautions and propaganda – may diminish. From CATV alone, a vast increase of choice can be expected.

To this basic physical link, we can start adding attachments. Our concerns are with *time, form of communication, handling of volume,* and *retention.*

Time is probably the most irritating at the moment. As matters are in most places now, the individual has to adjust to the scheduling of communications offerings. Few but the very rich or very inventive are able to arrange matters so that they can see, hear, or read what they want precisely when they want to.

But, in being and on the way, we have the prospect of a complete reversal of this situation. Using time switches and audio and video tape recorders (plus intermediate gadgetry to deal with tuning, warm-ups, and other technical mysteries), it is quite possible to set daily or even weekly patterns of automatic monitoring by which the material you want will be recorded at the time of emission for playback at your convenience. As a result, for example, a beauty contest can be taped on your video tape recorder (VTR) while you watch the hockey game, and a talk on nuclear power can be stored away at the same time on audio tape. Then, elated or deflated by the hockey result, you can turn to your tapes for titillation or elevation.

At the moment, such additional capacity is fairly expensive at good quality levels. An outlay of at least $2,000 and more probably $5,000 is required to buy and install switches and recorders. Tapes for TV especially are also still fairly expensive. Even at that, the economics of mass production, discoveries of research, and probable readiness of most people to settle for less than super hi-fi all indicate that a continuing decline in costs can be expected. (After all, costs have already declined from about $25,000 for such home-quality installations only a few years ago.)

Now, consider form of communication. Let's say, for example, that TV isn't your prime contact skill or preference.

Two other media commend themselves.

First, there is facsimile. Equipment now has been perfected that is capable of providing in your living room a printout of type, pictures, and diagrams on re-usable plastic sheets at high speed. (The receiver can deliver a standard-size printout of the Bible in four minutes, for example.)

Think about this for a moment. With facsimile, two great advantages accrue: the advantage of an alternate and relatively lasting form of input, *and* the advantage of easy access to data relatively unsuited to TV presentation. With facsimile, for instance, it's practical to envision direct home contact with libraries, periodical sources, and news outlets virtually anywhere in the world. Via the cable link (and both facsimile itself and any demand-order system would utilize a frequency range apart from cherished TV), one could dial requests for i/information on available material on a topic, ii/indications of the preferred form of presentation, and iii/the material itself.

Costs? Here, surprisingly, the situation looks fairly promising. Actual facsimile receivers can be expected in the $300 range quite soon. (Current guesses are that at least one major communications conglomerate plans to launch facsimile as soon as the cost-plus-profit cycle of the first main colour TV wave is complete – in about three to five years.) Material for facsimile presentation will be costly so far as the first copy requested is concerned but – even with reasonably generous royalties or the equivalent – will plummet in price thereafter.

The second important future source of input is provided by the computer console. Such hardware doesn't require a vast office and a batch of men in white coats. In effect, you can assemble a keyboard, a data set, and a telephone line by renting the items at about $200, $30, and $15 a year respectively.

Then the form of your communication can acquire even greater variation. You'll work, primarily, with a high-speed typewriter printout, but with the added advantages of mathematical and other symbols, programs tailored to your own specifications, and a fantastic saving in time.

In addition, it now is quite feasible to anticipate use of your computer link in the handling and retention of great amounts of data.

Your system, to this point, is clearly threatening to engulf you – dozens of TV channels, thousands of alternative print, audio, and picture sources, plus the data bank capacity of the regional computer network into which you are plugged. Your communications potential is approaching virtually *all* television, radio, library, periodical, and raw data resources.

But who can handle it? Human limits on time, talent, interest, and training threaten to reduce this boon to

CHAOS.

If it ever developed, such a communications bombardment could have anyone curled back in foetal immobility in no time.

So, we multiply our selves ... *our individual selves.*

How? To start with, fairly crudely and tentatively, we set up progressively more sophisticated computer programs (with individual or group privacy barriers, one would hope and assume) of our own interests, needs, priorities, likes and dislikes. We specify – simply with ever more numerous yes-no answers – a map of ourselves which, in a sense, becomes a crude version of ourselves.

All that is necessary then is to put all inputs through such a program on their way to our home communications system. Then, un-

sleeping, constantly alert over the whole spectrum

the equipment can monitor all the potential input.

Then it can order, translate, evaluate, and arrange the input according to our individual priorities ... and, equally, in the languages best suited to our individual purposes.

So, you come home. You've got 25 minutes free. You approach your system and select
→ the most important 25 minutes of communication to you.
→ the most entertaining 25 minutes for you.
→ the newsiest, or most historically significant 25 minutes for you ... in fact whatever you want ... in your best language, form, or combination.
(Costs, at the moment, are prohibitive, but we can look ahead.)

At first, it is likely that this won't really do much to enhance communication as such. Some people will go berserk on nudes. Others will opt for an undiluted diet of sports, opera, or acidland. There'll also be the danger of vegetation: passively becoming sodden with input, with little in the way of action or output, tends to make a person more turnip than human.

But why not have faith? Human experience, in varying degrees and intensities of course, is implicit in *all* aspects of all events and all people. One can find the secrets of life by starting with burlesque, or Bach, or Bechuanaland. There's a good chance that many, if not all, will find themselves digging deeper and wondering more widely as the multi-media, near-global assets of their communications system continue to operate. There's also a good chance that, instead of diminishing, interpersonal contact will mushroom. (You find out, for instance, that dandelions foster euphoria – something of a unique discovery in your immediate world – and ... you want to tell someone, maybe share euphoria with them, even go into the formation of a vast dandelion marketing combine ... and before you know it everyone's rushing about, celebrating the end of desultory small talk, the progressive initiation of shared experiences, the individual delights of imparting discovery.) Turnip? More of an Einstein or Namath or Mao – or a bit of all three.

Besides, if we are to be a little bit realistic, there is every prospect that regulation – formal or informal – will appear. Just as, ever since Eve blew it in the Garden of Eden, human fears, impatience, distrust, and fanaticism have combined in the past to insist on rules for all aspects of life, it is certain that the progressive evolution of individual communications systems will be accompanied by the progressive application of rules and regulations. If they are of any value, they will serve to save us from ourselves.

Well, there in limited terms – auguries of sorts plus a host of stated and implied questions – you have it.

Put as simply as we can conceive of it, the situation is just this:

Fundamental changes in the volume, variety, means, and content of communications are under way. Fundamental issues are raised by them – touching on definitions of what we mean by 'human,' what we can tolerate, what we must reject. Fiercely competitive bids for priority of time, talent, and resources are associated with these changes.

Turmoil. More of the infinite number of variables infinitely expressed than we have ever dreamed of perceiving.

Sarah, Harold, and even the Admiral, are part of it.

So are you.

It's yours.

Why not get on with it?

SUGGESTED READINGS

Buzzi, G. *Advertising.* Minneapolis: University of Minnesota Press, 1968

*Casty, A. *Mass Media and Mass Man.* New York: Holt, Rinehart and Winston, 1968

*Chusid, J.G., and McDonald, J.J. *Correlative Neuroanatomy and Functional Neurology.* 14th ed. Los Altos, California: Lange Medical Publications, 1970

*Condon, J.C., Jr. *Semantics and Communication.* New York: The Macmillan Co., 1966

de Bono, Edward. *The Mechanism of Mind.* New York: Simon and Schuster, 1969

*De Ropp, R.S. *Drugs and the Mind.* New York: Grove Press, 1957

Drucker, P.F. *The Age of Discontinuity.* New York: Harper and Row, 1969

*Ebin, D. *The Drug Experience.* New York: Grove Press, 1961

*Fabun, D. *The Dynamics of Change.* Englewood Cliffs, New Jersey: Prentice-Hall, 1967

*Gordon, D.R. *Language, Logic and the Mass Media.* Toronto: Holt, Rinehart and Winston, 1966

Halacy, D.S., Jr. *Man and Memory.* New York: Harper and Row, 1970

*Halloran, J.D. *The Effects of Mass Communication, with Special Reference to Television.* London: Panther Books, 1970. Paperback title: *The Effects of Television*

*Halloran, J.D., Brown, R.L., and Chaney, D.C. *Television and Delinquency.* Leicester: Leicester University Press, 1970

Handler, P., ed. *Biology and the Future of Man.* New York: Oxford University Press, 1970

*Irving, J.A., ed. *Mass Media in Canada.* Toronto: The Ryerson Press, 1962

Kahn, Herman, and Wiener, Anthony J. *The Year 2000.* New York: The Macmillan Co., 1967

*Available in paperback

*Kesterton, W.H. *A History of Journalism in Canada.* Toronto: McClelland and Stewart, 1967

*Kracauer, S. *Theory of Film.* New York: Oxford University Press, 1960

Liebling, A.J. *The Press.* New York: Ballantine Books, 1961. (Out of print)

*Lyons, Louis M., ed. *Reporting the News: Selections from Nieman Reports.* Cambridge, Mass.: Harvard University Press, 1965. Available in paperback from Atheneum Publications, New York

*MacCann, R.D. *Film: A Montage of Theories.* New York: E. P. Dutton, 1966

*McLuhan, M. *The Gutenberg Galaxy.* Toronto: University of Toronto Press, 1962

*McLuhan, M. *Understanding Media.* Toronto: McGraw-Hill, 1964

*Osgood, C.E., Suci, G.J., and Tannenbaum, P.H. *The Measurement of Meaning.* Urbana: University of Illinois Press, 1957

*Packard, V. *The Hidden Persuaders.* London: Penguin Books, 1960

Peers, F.W. *The Politics of Canadian Broadcasting 1920-1951.* Toronto: University of Toronto Press, 1969

*Pei, M. *The Story of Language.* Philadelphia: J.B. Lippincott, 1965

Pepinsky, H.B., ed. *People and Information.* Toronto: Pergamon Press, 1970

*Qualter, T.H. *Propaganda and Psychological Warfare.* New York: Random House, 1965

*Rubin, B. *Political Television.* Belmont: Wadsworth Publishing Co., 1967

*Schramm, W., J. Lyle, and Parker, E.B. *Television in the Lives of Our Children.* Stanford: Stanford University Press, 1961

*Siebert, F.S., Peterson, Theodore, and Schramm, W. *Four Theories of the Press.* Urbana: University of Illinois Press, 1963

*Skornia, H.J. *Television and Society.* New York: McGraw-Hill, 1965

*Steinberg, C.S., ed. *Mass Media and Communication.* New York: Hastings House, 1966

Stephenson, William. *The Play Theory of Mass Communication.* Chicago: University of Chicago Press, 1967

*Theall, D.F. *The Medium is the Rear View Mirror.* Montreal: McGill-Queen's University Press, 1971

*Ullmann, S. *Words and Their Use.* New York: Hawthorn Books, 1966

INDEX

ACKNOWLEDGEMENTS

Medical illustrations, pp. 29, 33, 37, 39, 43 by Margot Mackay.

Page 52 photograph of microscopic indentation in an aluminium sheet, caused by corrosion, from M.A.Sc. thesis of Osamu Iwao. Reproduced by permission of Professor K. T. Aust.

Page 56 'Electronic Eyes for the Blind' reproduced by permission of *The Medical Post.*

Page 65 quotation from *Light Through Darkness* by Henri Michaux reprinted by permission of The Viking Press and The Bodley Head.

Page 85 lines from 'The Dangling Conversation' © 1966 Paul Simon. Used by permission of the publisher, Charing Cross Music, Inc.

Page 93 quotation from Rolling Stone © 1969 by Straight Arrow Publishers, Inc. All rights reserved. Reprinted by permission.

Page 104 Canadian Press report reprinted by permission.

Page 106 'An Arbitrary Guide to Soul' reprinted by permission from TIME, The Weekly Magazine; Copyright TIME Inc. 1968.

Page 107 quotation from *The War Game* by Peter Watkins reprinted by permission of André Deutsch Limited.

Page 108 'Censorship' reprinted by permission from TIME, The Weekly Magazine; Copyright TIME Inc. 1964. Advertisement reproduced by permission of SAS – Scandinavian Airlines.

Page 112 'Reporting: Listening with One Ear' reprinted by permission from TIME, The Weekly Magazine; Copyright TIME Inc. 1964.

Page 117 Associated Press report reprinted by permission.

Page 118 United Press International report reprinted by permission.

Page 124 excerpt from article by Herb Russcol in *The New York Times* © 1968 by The New York Times Company. Reprinted by permission.

Page 161 'Platform group previews top lecturers, entertainers' reprinted by permission of Billboard Publishing Co.

Page 166 Pages from *Kitchener-Waterloo Record* reproduced by permission.

Page 169 Cartoon reproduced by permission of Johnny Hart and Field Enterprises, Inc. *Back to B.C.* is published by Fawcett World Library, 1961.

Page 170 'Changes' reproduced by permission of Orba Information Limited.

Page 179 Canadian Press-Reuters report reprinted by permission.

This book was designed by Allan Fleming and William Rueter and printed by University of Toronto Press